THE SECRET MIRROR

THE SECRET MIRROR

Literary Form and History in
Tocqueville's *Recollections*

L. E. SHINER

Cornell University Press

ITHACA AND LONDON

First published 1988 by Cornell University Press.

International Standard Book Number 0-8014-2150-0
Library of Congress Catalog Card Number 88-3679
Printed in the United States of America
*Librarians: Library of Congress cataloging information
appears on the last page of the book.*

*The paper in this book is acid-free and meets the guidelines for
permanence and durability of the Committee on Production Guidelines
for Book Longevity of the Council on Library Resources.*

For Catherine

CONTENTS

viii

Contents

ACKNOWLEDGMENTS

I am deeply grateful to my colleagues J. Michael Lennon, Charles B. Strozier, and Bruce Holroyd, who read the entire manuscript as it developed. J. Michael Lennon has offered many valuable suggestions on later drafts. The project was begun while I was on a sabbatical leave from Sangamon State University in the spring of 1983. I am grateful to the university for its support and to the University of California at Santa Cruz for a visiting research appointment, especially to Hayden White, whose conversations have been an important stimulus to my work. In 1983 an NEH Summer Seminar at Princeton University with Alvin Kernan on literature and society contributed to several parts of the book, and I deeply appreciate Professor Kernan's generosity and encouragement. In the summer of 1986 I had the opportunity to participate in an NEH Seminar on French classical literature at Harvard University under the direction of Jules Brody. The resources of the Harvard libraries and the experience of a close philological reading of seventeenth-century texts offered an occasion to review and modify my translations and analyses of key passages in the *Souvenirs*. Monique Benesvie of Harvard provided crucial advice on the translation of several terms. I am also grateful to Marjorie Wynn and the Beinecke Library of Yale University for granting me access to the Tocqueville letters and manuscripts in their possession.

Given the nature of this project, it was important to see the original manuscript of the *Souvenirs*. The descendants of Tocqueville, M. le comte and Mme la comtesse d'Hérouville, not only allowed me to consult the manuscript but graciously received me and offered an informative tour of the château de Tocqueville where part of the *Souvenirs* was written. In Paris, André Jardin, the leading Tocqueville scholar and secretary of the Comité de travail of the Commission nationale pour l'édition des oeuvres d'Alexis de Tocqueville, gave generously of his time in consultation, providing many insights and points of confirmation beyond the invaluable material in his definitive biography of Tocqueville. While in Paris I also had the opportunity to discuss my project with Paul Ricoeur, whose inspiration as a teacher and scholar over the years is part of the deeper source of the ideas in this book.

Many others have provided encouragement and valuable suggestions on specific points: George Agich, Royce Jones, Hans Kellner, Dominick LaCapra, Richard Palmer, Eric Springsted, Richard T. Vann, and Daniel Wilson. Daniel and Carol Wilson provided a peaceful and supportive atmosphere for work one summer at Muhlenburg College.

Among those at Sangamon State University who have labored through innumerable drafts with patience and skill are Adalin Borman, Deborah McTaggart, Samme Schramm, and Tonia Wright. Elizabeth Pera and her student staff at Sangamon were helpful in many ways. I am especially grateful to Jacqueline Wright, who prepared the final drafts of the manuscript.

Portions of Chapter 3 appeared in *History and Theory* 25 (1986) and parts of Chapter 4 in *The Psychohistory Review* 14 (1985). I am grateful for permission to use them here.

Since finishing this manuscript I have read two works that, had I come across them earlier, would have enhanced my discussion of the relation of fiction and history in Chapter 6. Thomas G. Pavel's *Fictional Worlds* (Cambridge: Harvard University Press, 1986) contains a rich discussion of the relation of fiction and nonfiction which integrates recent philosophical work on fictional discourse with perspectives from literary theory. Barbara Foley's *Telling the Truth: The Theory and Practice of Documentary Fiction* (Ithaca: Cornell University Press, 1986) deals with the issue of the boundary between fiction and fact through a Marxist analysis of documentary fiction, including the historical novel.

My one regret as I finish this manuscript is that neither of my parents, who encouraged me in its completion, has lived to see its publication. The dual subject matter of the book reflects in microcosm some of the distinctive contributions each made to my life: the interest in history and biography of Ernest Antrim Shiner (1898–1985); the love of French language and literature of Nelda Downtain Shiner (1909–1987).

L. E. SHINER

Springfield, Illinois

CHRONOLOGY OF 1848

The left-hand column lists major events of 1848 which are narrated or discussed in the *Recollections;* the right-hand column lists those events omitted from the *Recollections* or mentioned only in passing (e.g., the crucial event of the shooting on the boulevard des Capucines is merely alluded to by Tocqueville, who did not witness it but only heard about it). Both columns, read together, provide a continuous chronology of the 1848 Revolution.

	Recollections (recounted in the *Recollections*)	*General History* (not discussed in the *Recollections*)
	Part 1	
	1846–1847	
	Character of political life under July Monarchy; portrait of bourgeoisie and Louis-Philippe.	Severe agricultural crisis, food prices increase 100–150%, wages drop 30%, high unemployment.
	1848	
Jan. 29	Tocqueville warns Chamber of Deputies of possible revolution.	
Feb. 12	Debate on Banquets in Chamber; Tocqueville discusses Banquets with various leaders.	
Feb. 22–23	Tocqueville in Chamber learns of National Guard defection and witnesses Guizot's announcement of his dismissal;	Troops shoot down demonstrators on boulevard des Capucines and people parade corpses through streets.

Chronology of 1848

	Recollections (recounted in the *Recollections*)	*General History* (not discussed in the *Recollections*)
	refuses to share his friend's enthusiasm.	
Feb. 24	Tocqueville in streets learns of events by hearsay; tumultuous session at Chamber where invading mob prevents vote on Regency of Duchess of Orleans; Republic proclaimed.	Louis-Philippe's abdication and flight after hearing of defection of National Guard units.

Part 2

1848

Feb. 24	Tocqueville returns home despondent about future (chap. 1).	Universal suffrage proclaimed by provisional government.
Feb. 25–26	Tocqueville walks streets, observes popular character of revolution (chap. 2).	"Right to work" proclaimed; death penalty for political crimes abolished.
Feb.–Mar.	Tocqueville visits former political associates, observes bourgeois reaction to revolution, decides to run for a seat in new Assembly (chap. 3).	Universal suffrage, freedom of press and assembly proclaimed; slavery abolished (Mar. 4); National Guard opened to all adult males (Mar. 8).
Mar. 14		Elite companies of National Guard dissolved.
Mar. 16		Demonstration by elite companies of National Guard (*bonnets-à-poil*).
Mar. 17		Counterdemonstration by republican elements.
Mar. 19–20		Revolution in Berlin and Vienna.
Mar.–Apr.		Popular protests in provinces (peasants claim forest rights, workers attack railroads, tax protests).
Apr.	Tocqueville campaigns in La Manche and easily wins on Apr. 23 (chap. 4).	
Apr. 25–May 4	Tocqueville finds Paris tense and describes factions in new Assembly that meets May 4 (chap. 5); describes relations with Lamartine (chap. 6).	
May		Crowds gather almost nightly on boulevards in working-class areas for next six weeks; revolt in Cracow.

Chronology of 1848

Recollections (recounted in the *Recollections*)	General History (not discussed in the *Recollections*)
May 15 — Tocqueville describes invasion of Assembly and arrest of radical leaders (chap. 7).	
May 21 — Tocqueville describes Festival of Concord and signs of coming civil war (chap. 8).	
May 22– June 19 — Tocqueville describes the work of the Constitutional Commission (chap. 11).	
June 23– 26 — Tocqueville describes the June fighting brought on by closing of National Workshops (chaps. 9 & 10).	Massacre of prisoners in some occupied areas as fighting ends.
July 28	Decrees restricting political clubs.
Aug. 9– 11	Decrees restricting freedom of the Press.
Sept.	Debate on the Constitution; Tocqueville speaks against "right to work" provision; partial elections.
Nov. 21	Constitution proclaimed.
Dec. 10	Louis-Napoleon Bonaparte elected President of the Republic.

1849

Jan. 29	National Assembly votes its own dissolution under conservative and Bonapartist pressure.
Apr. 30	French troops attack Roman Republic in defense of the exiled Pope.
May 14	Election of new Assembly with surprising strength shown by the "Montagnards."

Part 3

1849

May 25 — Tocqueville rushes back from Germany at news of elections; becomes part of moderate coalition cabinet designed to contain radicals in Assembly (chap. 1).	
June 3– 13 — Tocqueville describes character and aims of new Barrot cabi-	

Chronology of 1848

Recollections (recounted in the *Recollections*)	General History (not discussed in the *Recollections*)

	net, character of Louis-Napoleon; abortive insurrection of June 13 (chap. 2).	
June 13– Oct. 1	Tocqueville describes his own and cabinet's maneuvers to stay in power and keep a moderate republic going by cultivating Legitimists on one side and Louis-Napoleon on other; embraces policies further restricting press and assembly (chap. 3).	
June 3– Oct. 29	Tocqueville describes his conduct of foreign policy and its limited success vis-à-vis Switzerland, Prussia, Austria, Russia, until fall of cabinet (chap. 4)	Rome falls to French troops; Pope successfully resists French efforts to impose a moderately representative regime and secure limited amnesty for political dissenters.
	End of *Recollections* account.	

1849

Oct. 31		Louis-Napoleon reprimands Barrot cabinet of which Tocqueville is a member, and it resigns.

1850

Mar. 15		Falloux law granting Catholic Church rights in education.
May 31		Conservative Assembly majority passes new electoral law designed to eliminate lower classes from voting, disenfranchising about one-third of electorate.
June–July		Additional laws restricting press and assembly passed.
July	Tocqueville writes Part I of *Recollections* at Tocqueville.	
Nov.– Dec.	Tocqueville in Sorrento begins Part II of *Recollections*.	

1851

Jan.–Mar.	Tocqueville in Sorrento completes Part II of *Recollections*.	General Changarnier replaced as commander of Paris military division by an officer loyal to Louis-Napoleon.

Chronology of 1848

	Recollections (recounted in the *Recollections*)	*General History* (not discussed in the *Recollections*)
Mar.– Apr.		Petitions circulated in favor of revising constitution to allow Louis-Napoleon a second term; petitions circulated against electoral law.
July 19		National Assembly votes against commission report (written by Tocqueville) proposing constitutional revision, the effect of which would have allowed Louis-Napoleon to run for a second term.
Sept. 16	Tocqueville begins Part 3 of *Recollections* at Versailles during prorogation of Assembly.	
Oct.	Tocqueville stops writing Part III of the *Recollections* to return to Paris for the opening of the Assembly.	
Nov. 4		National Assembly opens.
Nov. 17		National Assembly votes against proposition that would allow it to call out troops to defend itself.
Dec. 2		Napoleon's coup d'état; National Assembly dissolved and many members arrested including Tocqueville.
Dec. 3–10		Resistance in Paris and provinces crushed; Tocqueville and others released.
Dec. 11		Tocqueville's letter to London *Times* condemning the coup and the repression that followed and appealing to English not to support it.
Dec. 21		Plebiscite in which Louis-Napoleon wins an overwhelming endorsement.

THE SECRET MIRROR

I

RHETORIC, READING, AND HISTORY

In the twentieth century many historians have recalled their profession to the "art" of history, but few have doubted that "science" comes first. One should write as well as possible, the advice goes, but the real work of history is critique, analysis, and the solution of problems. Inevitably, writing has come to be regarded as a mere form for a scientific content; art becomes adornment. Although "elegance" may be one of the properties that make some proofs in mathematics or some theories in physics preferred to others, history and the social sciences have generally resisted any blurring of the science/art boundary. Many literary theorists, however, are increasingly drawn to kinds of writing which have been on the border of the canon (autobiography) or traditionally outside it (history, political theory, social science), while others, inspired by semiotics, treat writing as simply one among many sign systems. The fields of literary theory and semiotics, therefore, have already developed an extensive body of reflection which is available to anyone who wants to explore the inner workings of historical writing. Among works by historians which treat writing in history more seriously, Hayden White's pioneering *Metahistory* and Dominick LaCapra's recent *History and Criticism* have been the most important general demonstrations that literary structure impinges on the substance of historical argument.[1]

1. Hayden White, *Metahistory: The Historical Imagination in Nineteenth-Century* (Baltimore, Md.: Johns Hopkins University Press, 1973); Dominick LaCapra, *History and Criticism* (Ithaca, N.Y.: Cornell University Press, 1985).

The Secret Mirror

The present analysis of Tocqueville's *Recollections* (*Souvenirs*) is intended to be a contribution to the study of this deeper relation between writing and history. By now the work of White, Ricoeur, Veyne, and others has shown the many parallels between fictional and historical narrative and the usefulness of literary theory for the analyses of such texts.[2] But if the poetics of history is to take its rightful place alongside the epistemology of history, it must show that literary and rhetorical analysis can illuminate nonnarrative as well as narrative aspects of historical discourse. Accordingly, I will examine not only narrative structure and plot but also genre, code, and voice, which are as applicable to analytical as to narrative histories. Focusing on these aspects of a single text will not only generate some unexpected readings of Tocqueville but also show that texts like the *Recollections* retain their interest for us in part because of the *way* "content" becomes "form." A current term for the phenomenon in which content and form are fused and transcended in the spontaneity of writing is "text." Instead of reading the *Recollections* as a documentary source or as a "work" in the career of Alexis de Tocqueville, I will focus on the *Recollections* as text. I want to see how it is made, how its parts function within a particular kind of whole, and how it achieves its effect on the reader.[3] Exploring the effects and limitations of the *Recollections* as a memoir, for example, uncovers the important discursive role of its component genres, the portrait and the *tableaux* (Chapter 2). An examination of the *Recollections'* narrative structure illuminates both the way in which the text condenses and expands

2. Paul Ricoeur, *Time and Narrative* (Chicago: University of Chicago Press, 1983); Paul Veyne, *Writing History* (Middletown, Conn.: Wesleyan University Press, 1984). Hayden White's study of nineteenth-century historians and philosophers of history included a chapter that discussed Tocqueville's work as a whole under a fourfold scheme that integrated analyses of plot, argument, ideological implication and tropic orientation (*Metahistory*, 191–229). In the present essay I focus on a single text which permits the use of a different scale and type of analytic techniques than was feasible in a study such as White's. His more recent position on the general problem of historical narrative may be found in *The Content of the Form: Narrative Discourse and Historical Representation* (Baltimore, Md.: Johns Hopkins University Press, 1987).

3. I subscribe to Barthes's contrast between the work as a "garment of substance" and the text as "a methodological field," but there is a tendency in his thinking to shift from a methodological view of text toward a substantive view when he begins to use characteristics of modernist or postmodern writings (play of signifiers, "unreadability") to distinguish "text" from "work." Roland Barthes, "From Work to Text," in *Image, Music, Text* (New York: Hill and Wang, 1977), 155–64.

represented historical time and the way in which its narrative order and shape assume the form of a dual level tragic-ironic plot (Chapter 3). A study of the *Recollections'* codes then lays out the system of binary moral-social operators which controls the discourse of the text and yet at crucial points subverts the unity of the code itself (Chapter 4).

Tocqueville's authorial intention, as known either from the text or other sources, is not irrelevant to these initial tasks, but it cannot be a deciding criterion since the forms of discourse, however one may try to control them, often say other than we intend. It may seem especially paradoxical to give authorial intention a secondary status in the case of a first-person narrative and analysis such as the *Recollections,* but the presence of the author in a text is a matter of some complexity. The unified self that we normally project "behind" the narrator and the actor in the *Recollections* and with whom we connect the author of the other works "by Tocqueville" is just that: a construct dependent on a particular set of conventions surrounding the concept of "author." Although I prefer Foucault's notion of "author function" to Barthes' inflammatory "death of the author," it should be noted that one stream of scientific historiography has always sought the "death of the author."[4] The author, according to this convention for writing history, is allowed to appear in the preface where he makes a bow to the desirability of objectivity but the impossibility of achieving it, confesses his particular "bias," and walks off the stage never to be heard from again. The text of the history itself, whether narrative or analytic, is then written in a voice so neutral that we could ask with Benveniste "who speaks here?" and reply "no one."[5] Instead of approaching the *Recollections* looking for the author's intention, I will look for the ways in which authorship functions, for the kinds of narrative and analytic voice at work. Indeed, "someone" speaks there. Not an author fully in control of his text, but a writer whose character is as much constructed by the text as the text is constructed by him. In this book I

---

4. Roland Barthes, "The Death of the Author," in *Image, Music, Text,* 142–148; Michel Foucault, "What Is an Author," in *Language, Counter-Memory, Practice* (Ithaca, N.Y.: Cornell University Press, 1977), 113–28. For a perceptive and witty analysis of Barthes' exaggerations, see William Gass's essay "The Death of the Author," in his *Habitations of the Word: Essays* (New York: Simon and Schuster, 1985), 265–88.

5. Émile Benveniste, *Problèmes de linguistique générale* (Paris: Gallimard, 1966), 241.

will not only explore the surprising number of voices into which Tocqueville's discourse divides itself but also compare voice in the *Recollections* to voice in Marx's and Flaubert's texts on the Revolution of 1848 and to Tocqueville's other voices in *The Old Regime and the Revolution*.

In addition to demonstrating the power of writing over the writer, a textual analysis of the *Recollections* can also provide a case study for addressing two larger issues. The first is the question of reference and relativism, which has been a point of particular vulnerability for the rhetorical analysis of historical texts. The older historical relativism focused on the historian's inability to escape ideological bias. The current proponents of a rhetorical approach to historical texts are often accused of relativism because their critics believe that an emphasis on rhetoric will make truth the captive of literary device. Although no resolution of this issue may be possible in the abstract, an examination of the actual relation of rhetoric and reference in a particular text offers a useful way of reframing the problem. In this connection I not only consider the *Recollections'* treatment of 1848 in the light of recent research, but compare its discursive strategy to that of two other classic treatments of the Revolution, Marx's analytical history, *The Class Struggles in France,* and Flaubert's historical novel *Sentimental Education* (Chapter 6). Second, the close study of a single text can offer something to historical practice. A final chapter shows how the specific techniques and results of my analysis of the *Recollections* can illuminate the general character of Tocqueville's discursive practice and offer a new perspective on both *Democracy in America* and *The Old Regime and the Revolution*. Specifically, I show how Tocqueville grappled with the tension between rhetoric and narrative throughout his career and was still unable to resolve it in the last year of his life as he worked on the second volume of his history of the French Revolution (Chapter 7).

Although it would be disingenuous to deny an element of contingency and serendipity in my choice of Tocqueville's *Souvenirs* of the 1848 Revolution as an exemplary case for the study of literary form in history, there are some good reasons for choosing this author, this event, and this book. One need not subscribe to the entire program of Derrida or Foucault in order to recognize the illuminative power of the marginal or excluded, and each reason for my choice of the *Recollections* concerns the question of marginality.

Consider first the case of Tocqueville himself, certainly a marginal figure in French political life of the period 1830–1848. An aristocrat by birth, upbringing, and loyalty (his great-grandfather, Malesherbes, was guillotined and his parents were awaiting the scaffold when Robespierre fell), he spent his life trying to come to terms with the forces of revolution and democracy. To experience one's marginality most acutely, however, one needs to have once been in the center, which Tocqueville indeed was, since he grew up during the Restoration, the son of a prefect and peer, destined by family connections and tradition for a high judicial or governmental post. But after the 1830 Revolution, as a young judge who owed his appointment to his father's influence with the Bourbon court, Tocqueville risked family censure by taking the required oath of allegiance to the "usurper" Louis-Philippe, and promptly left for America—partly to let things shake out in France but also to study an advanced case of the apparently unstoppable drive toward democracy. The result of this trip, *Democracy in America,* can be seen as an ingenious solution to a problem at once personal, social, and intellectual. Inviting his own class to take up the role of pedagogues to the new democracy, Tocqueville deftly covers his family's allegiance to the Bourbons, suggests a role for men of his class in the new bourgeois-dominated society, and by the penetration of his observations and analyses, achieves immediate public prominence and a platform for election to the Chamber of Deputies. Although finally elected to the Chamber and the author of important reports on slavery and colonization, he remained aloof from parties and alliances and lived out his decade (1839–1848) in the parliamentary world of the July Monarchy, by his own account, "rather apart."[6]

Second, why a work dealing with 1848, a revolution that must seem marginal by comparison with those of 1789 and 1917? Not only is it a failed revolution but almost all commentators, including Tocqueville and Marx, have seen it as imitative and derivative of 1789. And yet, as Marx and Tocqueville also note, 1848 was strikingly new because it marked the first class war over the structure of society rather than over

6. Tocqueville is marginal, not only as a political thinker and actor, but also as a writer. Although his work was recognized by men as varied in outlook as Stendhal and Sainte-Beuve, his prose seems to look back to French Classicism. C. A. Sainte-Beuve, *Causeries du Lundi,* 15 (Paris: Garnier, n.d.), 93–121. Stendhal's passing comment is in *Mémoires d'un touriste* (Paris: Le Divan, 1929), 90.

the form of government. Derivative, failed, marginal, 1848 neverthe-less becomes a turning point in the thought of both Tocqueville and Marx—the first going on to rethink the "original" revolution in *The Old Regime and the Revolution,* the second to rethink the "future" revolution in the *Eighteenth Brumaire* and *Capital.*

Finally, among the texts of Tocqueville which one might choose as a focal point for examining the question of style, why the *Recollections* rather than *Democracy in America* or *The Old Regime and the Revolution,* works intended by their author to be stylistically accomplished and generally recognized by the public for their literary qualities? As Tocqueville's sole historical narrative, the *Recollections,* by its render-ing of events witnessed only two years before, gives us an opportunity to see a writer grappling with the problem of representing historical reality. Tocqueville consciously set out to give a spontaneous non-literary account of 1848 because he believed such immediacy would guarantee truthful representation. Tocqueville's explicit nonliterary intention offers the reader an excellent occasion for exploring the un-conscious working of literary and rhetorical devices in a text that disclaims them. Moreover, the *Recollections* is not only an example of a historical representation of 1848, but is itself a primary document for the study of 1848 and of nineteenth-century intellectual history. This marginal position as both an instance and a source for historical writing makes the *Recollections* a good case from which to discuss the relation of rhetorical analysis to both the epistemological and practical dimensions of historiography. Too often traditional political or intel-lectual history has simply exploited documents like the *Recollections* for bits of evidence or subsumed them under the established themes of the author's "major" works. By treating the *Recollections* as text, I try to understand its constituent devices and inner unities and tensions before relating it to the better known Tocquevillian themes and ten-dencies. Then, I reverse the usual procedure and experiment with reading the "central" works in terms of this "marginal" one.

Since my concern is to show how a particular historical text works, and by that means contribute to a discussion within historiography and philosophy of history and only tangentially to a discussion in literary theory, I borrow whatever can be found in literary theory and semiotics that seems useful for my purposes. Two aspects of literary theory play a particularly important role in what follows: rhetorical and reader response criticism. There are many signs of a renewed interest in rhetoric, not only among literary theorists but across the spectrum of academic disciplines, and there now exists a significant body of work on the rhetoric of the sciences.[7] In these studies as in my own, the term "rhetoric" is used in both a wider and narrower sense. Its broader reference is to any of the formal devices explored in semiotics and literary theory such as code, trope, voice, point of view, narrative structure; its narrower reference points to the classical tradition and its codification of devices for communication and persuasion. Since Tocqueville was trained in classical rhetoric and even won a prize in rhetoric for his essays at the Lycée in Metz in 1822, attention to the traditional rhetorical devices of the *Recollections* would seem doubly appropriate.[8] Yet there is a sense in which classical rhetoric and narrative are *opposed* to each other, narrative following the contingency of diachronic development, rhetoric striving through disposition and invention for a synchronic integration that brings the reader to the point of assent. Tocqueville by his own admission had difficulty with traditional historical narrative and preferred the rhetorical essay. Observing how the tension between rhetoric and narrative works in the *Recollections* affords a deeper understanding of Tocqueville's discursive practice as a whole.

If rhetorical criticism is concerned with the way certain devices are used with the intention of persuading an audience of hearers or readers, reader response criticism could be seen as its reverse side, focusing on how audiences respond to a text's persuasive devices. Actually, there are almost as many concepts of "the reader" today as there are varieties of criticism: encoded reader, implied reader, informed reader,

7. Two important symptoms of this interest are the well-attended conference on "The Rhetoric of the Human Sciences" held at the University of Iowa in spring 1984 and the series of monographs of the same name being published by the University of Wisconsin Press. Donald N. McCloskey's *The Rhetoric of Economics* (Madison: University of Wisconsin Press, 1985) is of particular interest since many historians have turned to economic models as one way of embracing "science" and avoiding the "rhetoric" of traditional narrative history. See McClosky's chapter on Robert W. Fogel's landmark study of railroads and American economic growth (113–37).

8. There are numerous studies of classical rhetoric and its continuing influence on both writers and literary theorists. Among the works I have found particularly useful are A. Kibédi Varga, *Rhétorique et littérature* (Paris: Didier, 1970); Peter France, *Rhetoric and Truth in France: Descartes to Diderot* (Oxford: Clarendon Press, 1972); John Porter Houston, *The Traditions of French Prose Style* (Baton Rouge: Louisiana State University Press, 1981); Tzvetan Todorov, *Theories of the Symbol* (Ithaca, N.Y.: Cornell University Press, 1982).

model reader, subjective reader, super-reader.[9] Despite the panoply of terms, these approaches to reading can be roughly grouped into three types: the study of the *actual reader*'s experience of comprehension and construction; the study of the *encoded reader,* that is, the text's assumptions about what the reader already knows versus what must be supplied; the *interactive* approach in which the marks of the encoded reader are seen as a solicitation of actual readers to assume or reject a certain role. Although I will draw on each of these three approaches to reader analysis, I have not adopted a special terminology but assume that "the reader" of Tocqueville's *Recollections* is similar to the likely reader of this book, namely, someone aware of the general conventions of western literature and history and possessing a minimal knowledge of who Tocqueville was, and what the Revolution of 1848 was about. Naturally, I was at one time just such a reader and my report of "the reader's" experience will in part reflect my own early attempts at reading the *Recollections.* For purposes of the textual analysis that follows, this rough specification will do since all concepts of the reader should be seen as heuristic devices for helping us articulate the conventions and ideologies at work within and without the text.

Despite the methodological electicism of my study, two other prominent tendencies of current critical theory have had a general influence on my analyses, even though I do not adopt their specific reading programs or their vocabulary: Marxist criticism and deconstruction. Marxist criticism is too rich and varied to permit a complete canvas of affinities and differences with the approach I have taken. Two points, however, are worth emphasizing. First, the present study, though resolutely formal and structural, is not formalist in its intention. It is not meant to exhaust what there is to say about Tocqueville's text, not even with respect to its discourse. I conceive of the kind of formal

9. The best general survey and collection of texts is Susan R. Suleiman and Inge Crosman, eds., *The Reader in the Text* (Princeton: Princeton University Press, 1980). In one way or another almost every critical direction today has its "reader" aspect. Among innumerable works that deal with readers the following have been particularly helpful: Wayne Booth, *The Rhetoric of Fiction* (Chicago: University of Chicago Press, 1961); Umberto Eco, *The Role of the Reader* (Bloomington: Indiana University Press, 1979); Stanley Fish, *Is There a Text in This Class?* (Cambridge: Harvard University Press, 1980); Barbara Johnson, *The Critical Difference: Essays in the Contemporary Rhetoric of Reading* (Baltimore, Md.: Johns Hopkins University Press, 1980); Jonathan Culler, *On Deconstruction* (Ithaca, N.Y.: Cornell University Press, 1982).

study undertaken here as a necessary stage in a larger process of analysis and appropriation. Even the formal and structural techniques employed in what follows have required constant reference to contextual information concerning social and economic conditions in their historical development, even though that information is not made an explicit topic of analysis. Second, I do mention from time to time what has been called the ideology of form, the connection of formal elements, whether genres, plot forms, or aspects of voice, that are clearly connected to class interests or in other ways reflect ideological commitments. Thus, the memoir genre, especially the kind within which Tocqueville worked, belongs in his historical period to a certain kind of governing elite and reflects a hegemonic discourse shared by certain classes. The conditions of production, distribution, and reception of such works—including those like the *Recollections* which were sequestered for later publication—are also important topics for examination. The absence of such topics from the present study is not a denial of their relevance but a matter of choosing to focus on a more limited dimension of discursive production.

As for deconstruction, the reader will note a number of places where the present study parallels some activities considered deconstructive, for example, the concern with the marginal or with the ways in which Tocqueville's text is self-subverting, specifically, the way its binary code seems to reflect a desire to preserve difference as such, yet at the same time undermines many of the differences it institutes. Nevertheless, I have not referred to my analysis as a deconstruction or to the self-subversions in Tocqueville's text as "undecidables." This is partly out of respect for the larger philosophical aims of Derrida's program and partly because it would be a pointless exercise to show how deeply Tocqueville's discourse is caught in the web of logocentrism; he was not caught in it, he embraced it. He accepts the general postulates of the Enlightenment and his discourse operates out of a systematic binary moral and metaphysical code. Yet it should be remembered that any such code uncovered by textual analysis, though indeed the matrix of the author's thought, is qua code also the product of the analytical techniques employed to uncover it. The same is true of the genres and plot forms and the network of voices which I display as part of the discursive framework of Tocqueville's text. In several chapters, when I show the ways Tocqueville's discourse is self-subverting, therefore, I also in effect contest my own analysis. That, it seems to me, is the best use to be made of deconstruction; one should use it in one's own discourse as well as on the discourse of the other.

No matter how eclectic one's approach to methods and techniques, if they are to be used with any consistency they will inevitably be employed within the perspective of general philosophical assumptions and political commitments. My philosophical assumptions are pragmatist, and my political commitments are liberal. I look upon theories and methods in the sciences as more or less useful ways to achieve understanding and improve practice. I have come to this pragmatic perspective from a long involvement with phenomenology and hermeneutics, both of which also continue to inform aspects of my work. As for the political liberalism that influences my reading, I have no doubt that Tocqueville's deep commitment to liberty allowed me a level of sympathy with his writings which I needed in order to work so long and closely on the *Recollections*. But I was also kept interested by what repelled me in his thinking, by his distaste for and fear of equality and his discounting of the ways capitalism limits freedom in accordance with wealth and class. To elaborate further or justify these positions here would be out of proportion, but it has seemed fair to alert the reader—who will no doubt see plenty of evidence of these commitments as the study unfolds. This consideration leads me to a final comment about a specific political dimension of reading Tocqueville's *Recollections*.

One thing that originally attracted me to this text is that it was written in a period of reaction not unlike the one in which we now live. The myths, slogans, and hatreds of the reactionary right in the America of the 1980s bear an uncanny resemblance to those of France in the 1850s: the fear of "socialism," the contempt for the lowest classes, the scorn for civil liberties, the incantation of "family, religion, and property" combined with a shameless materialism and selfishness. The *Recollections'* attitude toward the reaction of its time is highly ambivalent, and it is instructive to see how a thinker deeply committed to political liberty but thoroughly conservative in his social and economic views handled not only the Revolution but also its reactionary aftermath. Even so, the present study does not attempt to spell out the direct political relevance of Tocqueville's ideas (as tempting as it might be to rescue him from the current neoconservative embrace both here and in France), but focuses instead on the question how the Revolution of 1848 and the reaction that followed become embodied in discourse.

A Note on the Text

The text used in this study is that of the critical edition of the *Souvenirs*. In parentheses I give the page numbers of the French critical edition first, followed by those of the American translation.[10] There is a special problem, however, with the "text" of the *Souvenirs* in the more traditional philological sense. Normally, an authoritative text is not a particular physical entity but an ideal entity, an order of words which can exist in many exemplars, a handwritten copy, a deluxe edition, or a paperbound reprint. But in the case of the *Souvenirs* there is no fair copy prepared by Tocqueville for publication. The manuscript was left among his papers still covered with variants, marginal comments, passages marked for omission, reminders to himself to abbreviate or expand. There is, therefore, only a single manuscript that can be considered "the" text, a stack of pages tied with a cord, and at this writing, lying on a shelf in a tower of the Chateau de Tocqueville.[11] It is written in Tocqueville's customary manner with the bulk of the continuous text on the right-hand half of the page, the left reserved for second thoughts, insertions, modifications. Lines are drawn beside or around many sections, probably indicating an intention to delete, and innumerable words and phrases are crossed out, some with a single line, others almost obliterated as if to express a more extreme banishment. The task of the editor is an arduous one

10. Alexis de Tocqueville, *Oeuvres complètes* (M), 12, *Souvenirs* (Paris: Gallimard, 1964). In addition to the marginal notes and variants, this text includes as appendixes a number of fragments and notes either directly related to the main body of the text or to matters discussed in the narrative. There is also a useful introduction by the editor of this volume, M. Luc Monnier. A good translation of the critical edition has been made by George Lawrence with an introduction by J. P. Mayer: Alexis de Tocqueville, *Recollections* (Garden City: Doubleday, 1970). I have made my own translations, however, since I often need to employ a more literal rendering. The full critical edition under the editorship of J. P. Mayer is *Oeuvres, papiers et correspondance d'Alexis de Tocqueville* (Paris: Gallimard, 1951–). It will be referred to throughout as *Oeuvres complètes* (M) to distinguish it from the *Oeuvres complètes d'Alexis de Tocqueville*, edited by Gustave de Beaumont, 2d ed. (Paris: Michel Levy, 1864–66), which appears in my notes as *Oeuvres complètes* (B). I frequently cite Tocqueville's letters, several volumes of which have appeared in the critical edition. An excellent translation of some of the more important letters is available: Roger Boesche, ed., *Alexis de Tocqueville: Selected Letters on Politics and Society* (Berkeley: University of California Press, 1985), hereafter cited as *Selected Letters*.

11. I am grateful to M. le comte et Mme la comtesse d'Hérouville for allowing me to consult the original manuscript at the château de Tocqueville in May 1985.

because there is no way to be certain in every case which wording Tocqueville might have chosen for a "final" version. Hence the editor of the critical edition, M. Luc Monnier, had to parse each manuscript page into "main text," "marginal notes," and "variants." For purposes of my close reading, the material marked "marginal" or "variants" in the critical edition will be treated as part of the text. Only in that way can I appropriate the advantage of having a text marked by numerous erasures and alternative wordings, which reflect second thoughts and stylistic improvements that allow the reader to observe how certain problems of representation were attacked even if they were not resolved. A less comforting consequence of uncertainty about the final form of the text is that its boundaries become fluid; it can no longer be treated as a hermetically sealed object, nor can the many decisions as to what constitutes the text be separated from the act of analysis and interpretation.[12]

12. From a hermeneutic point of view, the establishment of the text is itself subject to the hermeneutic circle and thus always a tentative matter. For a recent discussion of these difficulties see Louis Hay, "Le texte n'existe pas," *Poétique* 62 (1985): 147–58.

2

GENRE

The Secret Mirror

Most texts are framed by some prior reference or question. Even if we pull a volume off the shelf at random, we first encounter the frame of its title. Although the word *Recollections,* used to translate *Souvenirs,* has a more intimate resonance than the familiar *memoir,* it is a *genre* term, and the genre conventions it evokes continue to have their effect, however much out of style genre rules or genre analysis may be at any point in time.[1] Autobiography has become the subject of a small critical industry in recent decades, but the memoir as genre has been relatively neglected. One of the reasons for this neglect is that the memoir is often seen as the illegitimate offspring of tendentious historiography and self-serving autobiography. Lying on the border between autobiography and history, many memoirs can be assimilated to one or the other, allowing us to contrast "autobiographical memoirs" with "historical memoirs" (in French, there is a tradition of *mémoires pour servir l'histoire*).[2] To know that we are about to read a historical

1. Genre is beginning to return as a focus of literary analysis. See Adena Rosmarin, *The Power of Genre* (Minneapolis: University of Minnesota Press, 1985), 3–51. Among the general discussions of genre from which I have profited are Paul Hernadi, *Beyond Genre* (Ithaca, N.Y.: Cornell University Press, 1972), Heather Dubrow, *Genre* (London: Methuen, 1982), and Alastair Fowler, *Kinds of Literature: An Introduction to the Theory of Genres* (Cambridge, Mass.: Harvard University Press, 1982).

2. Georges May, *L'Autobiographie* (Paris: Presses Universitaires de France, 1979), offers the best discussion of the relation of autobiography and memoir as genres. He points out that in France the term *autobiographie* does not become current until the

memoir, like the *Recollections,* prepares us to expect an eyewitness report from a single narrative viewpoint, exhibiting a subjective attitude toward occurrences. In addition we will not be surprised to find reflective political commentary and "revelations" about other participants, and we tend to regard what authors of memoirs say about themselves as personal apologia. This much, then, we know *without opening the book.* Our readerly defenses relax a little; we are not about to struggle with a demanding text of science or philosophy or face the difficulties of poetry or the critical results of archival research. There is instead an implication of intimacy, a likelihood of episodic structure, the possibility of diverting anecdotes.[3]

And who is about to address us in this genre? What does an author's name tell us? Alexis de Tocqueville . . . "the author of *Democracy in America.*" For what is "Tocqueville" but a proper name functioning as a sign? Unless we are already acquainted with his life, his name simply stands for a certain *oeuvre* and an associated complex of ideas, "liberty versus equality," "decentralization," "tyranny of the majority." Do we need to know more in order to read? Here we already come up against one of the ways readers' responses to memoir and history differ from their responses to fiction. We can expect a work of fiction, as it unfolds, to create much of the knowledge needed to understand it. But responses to memoir or history are more likely to vary depending on

---

second half of the nineteenth century and that *mémoires* or *souvenirs* has continued to be used in France for what the English-speaking world normally calls autobiography. May sees the difference of *mémoire* and *autobiographie* as depending on whether a text focuses on "what one has witnessed and/or done" in the world as opposed to "what one has been," but points out that in the particular case it is difficult to classify many works (126–27).

3. Like all genre criteria, the set I have constructed constitutes an ideal type of the conventional expectations that initially orient the reader but are revised as reading proceeds. As Fredric Jameson argues, genre categories are "devised for a specific textual occasion and abandoned like so much scaffolding" once they have served their purpose. *The Political Unconscious: Narrative as a Socially Symbolic Act* (Ithaca, N.Y.: Cornell University Press, 1981), 145. The notion of generic features as a contract or *"pacte"* between writer and reader comes from Philippe Le Jeune, *Le Pacte autobiographique* (Paris: Éditions du Seuil, 1975). Bakhtin has underlined how tied to a certain social milieu or class a genre may be. See the discussion in Tzvetan Todorov, *Mikhail Bakhtin: The Dialogical Principle* (Minneapolis: University of Minnesota Press, 1984), 80–85. In the case of the memoir genre as known to Tocqueville, there was both a high literary tradition from the seventeenth century (Cardinal de Retz, Saint-Simon) as well as an outpouring from the Restoration of aristocratic memoirs of the Revolution.

the depth and extent of our prior knowledge, particularly with a text like the *Recollections,* where the writer assumes a general familiarity with the course of events and the leading figures of the day. For today's reader this problem is solved pragmatically by editors offering necessary background information or explanations through an editor's introduction and a chronology. An important variable in readers' initial responses to a text like the *Recollections* will be whether they pause to arm themselves with the editorial intertext that usually lies ambiguously between the title page and the text itself.

The body of the *Recollections,* then, appears to be set within a series of frames. First, the frame of the title, which encloses it within a cadre of genre expectations; then the frame of authorship, which places the text in a particular historical-political milieu. But these frames bring into operation others: the frame of the reader's prior knowledge, the information supplied by editorial prefaces, and the more general frame of the readers' values, prejudices, class, gender, and race. Finally, there are all those potential frames by virtue of which one can read "as"—as a man, as a woman, as a Romantic, a Marxist, a feminist, a psychoanalyst, a formalist, structuralist, deconstructionist. So many frames, in fact, it seems we might never get to the text itself. So we must begin willy-nilly, dragging all our frames with us, aware that the question of what is inside and what is outside, what is frame and what is text, will itself always be in question.[4]

Beginnings are often difficult, hazardous, sometimes impossible for writers, but they are no less so for readers. Writers have as many chances as they like or must have to begin; readers have only one, the one they are given. Hence the traditional privilege given beginnings (and endings) and the modernist experiments in generating texts that are all middle. One must exercise some patience, therefore, and look closely at the beginning of the *Recollections.* Although the two open-

4. Of course, some have suggested that there *is* no text in itself, that even the external boundaries of a text and its formal features appear only as such in the light of a framework authorized by one or another interpretive community; Stanley Fish, *Is There a Text in This Class?* (Cambridge, Mass.: Harvard University Press, 1980), 13–15. Whatever metacritical position one takes on the issue of textual frames, these textual features (title, author name, preface, editorial insertions) can be studied in terms of their discursive function. Gérard Genette does just that in his recent *Seuils* (Paris: Éditions du Seuil, 1987) where he treats these threshholds (*seuils*) under the concept of "paratext." Unfortunately, Genette's book arrived too late for me to take advantage of his specific conclusions in my analysis.

ing paragraphs can be read as a typical activation of the genre conventions for the memoir, invoking such commonplaces as honesty, secrecy, and veracity, and such devices as the portrait and the *tableau*, this same opening can be seen also as contesting certain of these conventions and devices.

> Momentarily removed from the theatre of public life and unable even to engage in any continuous study due to the precarious state of my health, I am reduced in the midst of this solitude, to consider myself for a moment, or rather to contemplate the contemporary events around me in which I was either an actor or a witness. The best use of my leisure appears to be to retrace these events, to depict the men I saw taking part in them, to seize and, if I can, to engrave in my memory the confused traits which make up the uncertain physiognomy of my time.
>
>   I have only taken this resolution along with another to which I will be no less faithful; these recollections will be a form of mental relaxation and not at all a work of literature. This writing will be a mirror* in which I will amuse myself by looking at my contemporaries and myself, and not a picture for public view. My best friends will have no knowledge of them since I want to retain the freedom to depict without flattery both them and myself. I want to disclose candidly the secret motives that made us act, both them and me as well as others, and, having understood them, tell them. In a word, I want the expression of my recollections to be sincere, and for that it is necessary that they remain entirely secret.**
> (29/3)

> *All paintings that one makes of friends in front of them or of oneself in front of the world, are faulty. The only true portraits are those which are not made to be shown. (marginal note) (295/3)

> **My only aim in composing them, is to give me a solitary pleasure, the pleasure of contemplating a true picture (*tableau*) of human affairs, to see man in the reality of his virtues and vices, in his nature, to understand him and to judge him. (marginal note) (295/4)

"These recollections (*souvenirs*) will be a work of mental relaxation and not at all a work of literature." Why this negative? Why must there be writing but not literature? Of course, the word *literature* still retained its larger connotation in 1850, easily embracing memoirs, history, philosophy, criticism and political theory as well as poetry and fiction. Here, to be a work of literature means to be a work of con-

struction, a work of style. A moment later the text gives us a further
clue to this nonliterarity by declaring that it is *not* to be "a picture
(*tableau*) for public view." Tocqueville's marginal note at this point
contrasts the inevitable falsity of such public paintings with the truthfulness of completely private portraits.[5] If one is to be sincere, composition must give way to simple reflection—as in a mirror.

It is characteristic of Tocqueville that he invokes the ancient device
of the mirror not simply in the name of realism but also in the cause of
morality. The author of *Democracy in America* knows that a work of
literature is in part a product of rhetoric, and rhetoric is concerned
above all with the audience.[6] If literariness means the use of rhetorical
constructions in full consciousness of one's audience, nonliterariness,
or spontaneous mirror-writing, will be possible only if no one is
looking over his shoulder: the mirror is to do its work in secret. Secrecy
and the mirror go hand in hand: the mirror substitutes for the distorting devices of literature; secrecy works to overcome the distorting
subtleties of the ego in memory.

This second paragraph, however, goes on to tell of still another kind
of secret and another mirror function: the "hidden motives" (*les
motifs secrets*) of people's actions in 1848 are to be uncovered and
told. Whereas the first operation of the mirror is to give an honest
reflection of what Tocqueville saw and thought, this second operation
will offer a "true picture (*tableau*) of human affairs." The marginal
note in which the latter phrase occurs might seem to contradict the
earlier rejection of a "picture (*tableau*) for public view." But in French
tableau not only means picture in the sense of a painting (*peinture*) but
can also mean a classification or table.[7] The *Recollections* will give its

5. The critical text has the word *peinture* here with the variant *tableau* in the notes.
In looking at the manuscript in the château de Tocqueville I found *tableau* in the text
with no crossing out or variant. Although this small error in the critical edition is not of
great consequence, the frequency with which the term *tableau* appears in the *Recollections* and its broader span of signification does give an added importance to the
presence of this term early in the text.
6. In *Democracy in America*, for example, Tocqueville carefully cultivated a perspective which balanced the criticism and the celebration of democracy, and he chided
Henry Reeve for making the English translation sound too unfavorable to the democratic experiment. Tocqueville, *Oeuvres complètes* (M), 6, 1, *Correspondance anglaise*,
48.
7. Fontanier's 1830 textbook on rhetoric, *Les Figures du discours*, lists the *tableau*
along with the *portrait* as one of several devices available to the writer of descriptions.
By *tableau* he means a scene described with such vivid detail and sense of mood that the

author the "solitary pleasure" of contemplating a moral *tableau* of French society which will reveal "man in the reality of his virtues and vices, in his nature." Thus, there is a double reflection at work in Tocqueville's use of the mirror. The first is the surface reflection that occurs in the mirror-text as imitation, the sort of mirror Stendhal sent down the road in *The Red and the Black*. The second is the use of the mirror to reveal a moral table, the universal in the particular, a *speculum* of virtues and vices.[8]

There is yet a third function of the reflective surface of writing: to make the self visible to itself. "This text will be a mirror in which I will amuse myself by looking at my contemporaries and myself." "I want to remain free to depict without flattery both them and myself." At first glance these statements seem only to express a typical aim of the memoir or autobiography. Yet there are explicit signs later in the text that Tocqueville is working against—as well as within—such a memoir tradition, as in a passage where he contrasts his own effort at honest self-depiction with the famous *Mémoires* of Cardinal de Retz (101/80). Thus, the *Recollections* is admitted to be framed by the conventions for the memoir genre, yet it is also trying to break out of the "literary" implications of those conventions in the direction of veridic history on the one hand and a truthful self-revelation on the other.[9]

---

reader or hearer will "see" it as if they are looking at a picture; Pierre Fontanier, *Les Figures du discours* (Paris: Flammarion, 1977), 431–33. *Tableau* clearly means a *table*, however, in the passage of the *Recollections* illustrating the way political regimes undo themselves by focusing on avoiding the mistakes of some preceding regime: "one could make an unusual *tableau* of all the errors which have been thus engendered, . . ." and the text then lists Charles I of England, Louis XVI, Charles X, and Louis-Philippe (85/64). The idea of a table (*tableau*) and its linguistic connection to a picture (*tableau*) or an exemplary dramatic moment (*tableau vivant*) is, of necessity, often lost in a colloquial rendering. Thus instead of "One could make an unusual table . . ." the English translation has "One could make a weird collection . . ." (64).

8. On the medieval use of mirror or *speculum* as a term for an encyclopedia, see Michel Beaujour, *Miroirs d'encre: Rhétorique de l'autoportrait* (Paris: Éditions du Seuil, 1980) and J. I. Wimsatt, *Allegory and Mirror: Tradition and Structure in Middle English Literature* (New York: Pegasus, 1970).

9. One cannot help thinking of that other "spontaneous" memoirist who also spoke of his work as a *"miroir de la vérité."* Saint-Simon, *Mémoires* 7 (Paris: Gallimard, 1961), 397. He also makes a claim in the preface to volume 1 for secrecy and the mirroring of moral conduct.

With respect to this third function of the mirror—the reflection of the self—the *Recollections* moves in the direction of what Michel Beaujour has called the "self-portrait" (Montaigne's *Essays*, Nietzsche's *Ecco Homo*) as opposed to the autobiography (Rousseau's *Confessions*, Chateaubriand's *Mémoires d'outre tombe*). A self-portrait is distinguished from autobiography among other things by the absence of a continuous narrative of the subject's life. The portrait of Tocqueville in 1848–1849 which emerges from the *Recollections* will be, like the portrait of Montaigne in the *Essays*, a portrait discovered by the reader in the shards of the text rather than in the totality of a chronological narrative.[10]

But is all this talk of secrecy and the mirror itself even honest? We can see from the marginal notes and variants to the *Recollections* that Tocqueville took considerable care with style and organization. There are also points where the reader is addressed directly as though needing help in understanding some contextual detail. Moreover, there are notes to himself which show he had his wife read the text in order to advise him of style, and at one point he reminds himself to "omit this perhaps, at least when reading aloud" (244/242). He also mentioned work on the *Recollections* in a letter to his relative and close friend Louis de Kergorlay and may have shown parts of it to another friend, the writer J. J. Ampère.[11] Yet we hardly need external evidence of the literariness of the text; we need to read only a few passages to see that the *Recollections*, though far more spontaneous than his other writ-

10. Michel Beaujour, *Miroirs d'encre,* 7–26. In the strict sense, Tocqueville's work does not fit Beaujour's category of the autoportrait, but if we were to interpret "autoportrait" as a type concept we can see that many texts possess characteristics of the memoir, the autobiography, and the autoportrait all at once.

11. In the letter to Kergorlay (December 15, 1850), Tocqueville calls the work "a narrative (*récit*) of what I saw in the Revolution of 1848 and since, events and men (*choses et hommes*)," *Oeuvres complètes* (M), 13, 2, *Correspondance d'Alexis de Tocqueville et de Louis de Kergorlay* (Paris: Gallimard, 1977), 229. Writing to Ampère, who was planning to spend a few weeks with him at Tocqueville where Part I of the *Souvenirs* was finished, Tocqueville says "I scribble a little every morning. I will show you, but *you alone*, this work when you come here, if between now and then, it will take a form worthy to be submitted to you." The letter is dated June 26, 1850 and Part I of the *Recollections* bears the inscription "Written in July 1850 at Tocqueville." *Oeuvres complètes* (M), 11, *Correspondance d'Alexis de Tocqueville et Pierre-Paul Royer-Collard: Correspondance d'Alexis de Tocqueville et Jean-Jacques Ampère* (Paris: Gallimard, 1970), 187.

ings, is hardly the random jottings of a man intending to pass the time, amuse himself, or make a record to refresh his memory later.

Why the secret mirror? Is he trying to deceive us? Is he deceiving himself? I find no reason to doubt the sincerity of his initial intention. If Tocqueville possessed any quality on which his contemporaries could agree—and which he himself in the *Recollections* regarded as characteristic to a fault—it was his instinctive honesty (30/4). The ruse of the mirror and secrecy is for himself. The instrument and the vow are essential to avoiding the kind of literary constructions he believed were doomed to lie. The secret mirror gives him the *freedom to write*. Spontaneous eloquence is a recurrent theme in the *Recollections,* and Tocqueville's discovery of his own ability to speak compellingly in a time of revolutionary danger is an important part of its story. The prescription of the mirror and secrecy, I believe, is meant to achieve in writing a spontaneity similar to what Tocqueville had finally achieved in speech. By deliberately avoiding the production of "literature," writing can let itself be carried away by the urgency of whatever presents itself in the secret mirror of memory. Correspondingly, the effect of this spontaneity on the reader is a sense of being addressed in the direct and familiar language of conversation or the letter rather than that of the treatise or essay. Hence, the opening paragraphs of the *Recollections* mark the writing that follows them with the sign of intimacy and veracity and belong in the tradition of the rhetoric of antirhetoric which runs from Plato to Rousseau and finally merges with modern consciousness.

After the meditative nuances of these first two paragraphs on literariness, secrecy and the mirror, Tocqueville turns to a straightforward and apparently banal statement of the limits within which he will work: "My intention is not to make these recollections (*souvenirs*) go back before the revolution of 1848, nor to take them [beyond] my departure from office, October 30, 1849. It is within these limits only that the events I want to depict have something of greatness, or that my position permitted me to see them clearly" (30/4). Here are the criteria that will generate the content and scope of the *Recollections:* personally witnessed events and matters that had something of greatness (*grandeur*) about them. The first criterion, though simply the restatement of a central convention for the memoir genre, also has an important effect on narrative structure since it guarantees an episodic texture, with numerous gaps and extreme variations in the scale of treatment of individual scenes. An equally significant effect of adhering strictly to the eyewitness criterion is that an eyewitness narrative requires devices similar to those of a novelist who focalizes the story through one character but must give readers information about things not witnessed by that character.

The second criterion, *greatness*, might seem equally mundane and conventional, amounting to nothing more than that ambiguous and worrisome historian's standard of "importance." It is understandable, therefore, that most commentators on the *Recollections* have overlooked what will become a crucial clue to what the narrative is "about." It does not appear to be a concept of political or social analysis—like liberty, equality, decentralization—but a term from a social or moral code. Greatness (*grandeur*) can signify not only magnitude but also magnanimity, the epithet of those who strive for the highest honors, perform the most courageous deeds, excel in statesmanship, science or art; a synonym for disinterest and generosity, for intrinsic nobility, honor, and virtue. Ironically, however, the further one reads in the text of the *Recollections,* the more one finds of pettiness, selfishness, vanity, myopia, stupidity, and greed. As a result the reader begins to suspect that *grandeur* operates less as a criterion of magnitude for the selection of events than as a standard of moral and psychological judgment, a measure of those "secret motives which made us act," and a canon for sketching "a true *tableau* of human affairs."

It is perhaps not accidental that one antithesis of greatness, pettiness (*petitesse*), emerges in the very next paragraph, a paragraph that also marks the first movement of the text into its narrative matter. "I lived, although rather apart, in the midst of the parliamentary world of the last years of the July Monarchy and yet, I would have difficulty recounting in a clear fashion the events of this period so near and yet remaining so confused in my memory. I lose the thread of my memories (*souvenirs*) in this labyrinth of petty incidents, petty ideas, petty passions, of personal views and contradictory projects, in which the men of that time exhausted their public lives" (30/4). There remains in his mind, he continues, only "the general physiognomy of that epoch." Consequently, Tocqueville opens his account of 1848 with several pages describing the general character of the bourgeois regime of

Louis-Philippe in the years before 1848. With this fourth paragraph the text moves toward the mode of recollection and the "secret mirror" is rendered operative.

Portraits

Although one begins to read a work like the *Recollections* in terms of general expectations for memoirs, one's sensitivity to genre also operates in response to the constituent forms encountered along the way. Even a unit as brief as a sentence can belong to a recognizable genre, for example, an aphorism or exclamation.[12] Thus, in addition to narrative and analysis, traditional histories or memoirs can contain many other genres such as set portraits, brief essays, political or moral aphorisms, and illustrative anecdotes. The portraits and characterizations in the *Recollections* have been justly admired: acerbic, penetrating, seldom flattering, they are surely one of the most entertaining and memorable aspects of the text on a first reading. On a second reading one might want to examine them for their accuracy or fairness, appraise their psychological insight, or compare them to those of Cardinal de Retz or Saint-Simon, both of whom Tocqueville had read. But a careful look at how the portraits and other component genres *function* in the *Recollections* shows them to be part of a rhetorical strategy whose general aim far exceeds their documentary, anecdotal, or psychological value.

As part of its characterization of the July Monarchy in the years immediately preceding the February Revolution, the text opens with a portrait of the bourgeoisie within whose "narrow limits" after 1830 "the entire government was locked up and crammed" (30/415). The bourgeois spirit was

active and industrious, often dishonest, generally orderly, sometimes rash out of vanity or egoism, timid by temperament, moderate in every-

12. What I am calling "constituent genres" is less a category than a description of a functional relationship and in that respect bears some resemblance to Fowler's "constructional types"; Alistair Fowler, *Kinds of Literature,* 127–28. In his willingness to see all conventionally structured forms as genres in the broadest sense Fowler is surprisingly close to the views of Bakhtin/Medvedev. M. M. Bakhtin/P. M. Medvedev, *The Formal Method in Literary Scholarship* (Cambridge, Mass.: Harvard University Press, 1985), 129–34.

thing but the taste for well-being (*goût du bien-être*), and mediocre; a spirit which joined with that of the people or of the aristocracy, could work wonders, but alone could only produce a government without virtue and without greatness (*grandeur*). Master of all, as no aristocracy ever was or perhaps will be, the middle class, which one must call the ruling class, became so entrenched in its power and its egoism that it took on the air of a private industry, each of its members thinking of public affairs only to the extent they could be turned to the profit of his private affairs and easily forgetting in their petty comfort (*petit bien-être*), the needs of the people." (31/5)

The portrait given here is, of course, a type, the portrait of a class rather than of an individual, closer to the *Characters* of La Bruyère than the usual individual portraits of memoirs.[13] Yet this portrayal of the bourgeoisie has a structure similar to the portraits of individuals in the *Recollections* and other memoirs and histories: adjectival accumulation, a focus on psychological traits closely allied to moral qualities, and the mention of a characteristic behavior or activity. But what is most striking about this portrait when encountered on a second reading is the way it instantiates the implicit moral opposition of *grandeur* and *petitesse* which the reader of the *Recollections* has just encountered in the opening paragraphs. The bourgeoisie is depicted as a class whose government is totally without greatness since its only concern is private profit and "petty well-being" (*petit bien-être*). The portrait functions not only to characterize a class that will be a principal actor in the story of 1848 but also to illustrate a general moral polarity.

The immediately following portrait of Louis-Philippe suggests that he perfectly reflected the virtues and vices of this class. Although "born of the most noble race of Europe," the king had the typical moral qualities of a bourgeois: orderly and moderate with "no burning passions; no ruinous weaknesses; no brilliant vices; a single royal virtue, courage." He also exhibited an extreme politeness "but without discrimination or greatness (*grandeur*), the politeness of a shopkeeper rather than a prince." "His mind was distinguished, but constricted and cramped by his soul's lack of breadth and elevation." But

13. La Bruyère, *Les Caractères* (Paris: Union Générale d'Éditions, 1980). La Bruyère was the youthful Tocqueville's favorite writer according to Kergorlay. *Oeuvres complètes* (M), 13, 2, 360.

for Tocqueville, most irritating of all in a king was his lack of convictions.

> Well-informed, subtle, pliant and tenacious; concerned only with the useful and filled with such a profound contempt for truth and so great a disbelief in virtue that it obscured his understanding . . . an unbeliever in matters of religion like the eighteenth century and a skeptic in politics like the nineteenth; without convictions himself; having no faith in those of others; loving power and dishonest courtiers as naturally as if he had been born on the throne; an ambition limited only by prudence, which could neither be satisfied nor carried away and always remained close to the ground. (32/6–7)

In addition to the standard portrait elements already mentioned, this portrayal of Louis-Philippe also reflects specific devices drawn from a tradition of the portrait which goes back through Cardinal de Retz to the seventeenth-century salon exercise of the *portrait précieux*. The consideration in turn of heart, soul, and mind, and the enumeration of a series of virtues and vices in rapid antithesis is reminiscent of the bravura style of the classical French memoirist portrait.[14] Yet there is more going on here than pointed characterization or a literary *divertissement* for the reader. Once we have begun to notice the recurrence of certain terms and themes in the *Recollections,* we cannot miss the significance of the reappearance of *"grandeur"* and its synonyms/antonyms. Here it is signaled by the forms of its *absence* from Louis-Philippe's character, for example, the king's "shopkeeper" politeness, his soul's "lack . . . of elevation," an ambition "close to the ground," a lack of concern for truth or virtue, of any religious or political convictions, or any interest in art or literature. Considered in terms of its discursive function, this portrait too is not only the characterization of a major historical figure but also a place holder in the table (*tableau*) of virtues and vices mentioned at the outset of the text.

---

14. On the specific devices of the portrait as a literary form I have especially profited from A. Kibédi Varga, "Synonyme et antithèse," *Poétique* 4 (1973): 307–12. On Cardinal de Retz and his transformation of the *portrait précieux* see André Bertière, *Le Cardinal de Retz mémorialiste* (Paris: Klincksieck, 1977), 469–78, R. E. Hill, "Figurae verborum in Retz's portraits," *Texas Studies in Literature and Language* 13 (1972): 555–79, and Derek A. Watt, *Cardinal de Retz: The Ambiguities of a Seventeenth-Century Mind* (Oxford: Oxford University Press, 1980). On Saint-Simon see Dirk Van der Cruysse, *Le portrait dans les "Mémoires" du duc de Saint-Simon* (Paris: Nizet, 1971).

The next set of portraits opens up further moral polarities and also reveals an additional discursive function of the portraits. These new portraits form part of the account of the Banquet Affair, which was the precipitating occasion for the February Revolution. Before coming to the portraits, however, the text leaves a place for the insertion of passages from Tocqueville's famous speech to the Assembly in January 1848 predicting an imminent social revolution from below over the issue of property.[15] A paragraph near the end of this speech could easily be overlooked as a merely rhetorical turn but contains another important clue for understanding the function of the portraits. Comparing the July Monarchy to the ancien régime, Tocqueville challenges his listeners to remember that the regime of Louis XVI was older, stronger, and more deeply rooted in tradition than that of Louis-Philippe, yet it fell because "the class which governed then had become, by its indifference, its selfishness, its vices, incapable and unworthy of governing" (39/14). The general project of a table of virtues and vices announced at the beginning of the text can now be understood more specifically as a table or portrait gallery of those "worthy" and "unworthy" to rule.

As the text unfolds its story of how the government and the political opposition in the course of the Banquet Affair drove each other beyond their intentions into a revolutionary situation, the account is lined with brief character sketches and set portraits which reveal the unworthiness of all the actors. Of the opposition leader, Odilon Barrot, who let himself be tempted into the affair by Thiers: he "mixes a touch of silliness with his weaknesses and his virtues" and "did his best to secure his ally's triumph at his own expense" (43/19). Of Thiers, who drew Barrot and the other moderate leaders into the Banquet Affair but did not risk actively taking part: "he was eager to have the results but not the responsibility of so dangerous an agitation" (43/19). The text's treatment of the opposing figures on the

15. Tocqueville did not get around to selecting which portions of that speech to quote in his text. His nephew, the Comte de Tocqueville, inserted the entire last section of the speech in the first published version of the *Recollections* in 1893. This creates an interesting textual question: should one omit the speech, quote it in place in its entirety, place it in an appendix, or, as his nephew did, select the most likely passages? Each of these procedures has its advantages but since the Comte chose obviously appropriate passages for the first edition, his selection has come to seem definitive and is included in the main body of not only popular versions but of the critical edition as well. See the editor's note at 40/15.

conservative side conveys with equal force the myopia and inadequacy of the middle-class regime. Duchâtel, Louis-Philippe's Minister
of Interior, despite "a very quick, very subtle mind, encased in a
massive body," showed in the affair of the banquets a "consummate
clumsiness," and on February 22 as the unrest grew, Tocqueville
noted that he "twitched his neck and shoulders in his habitual tic
much more frequently and violently than usual" (51/29). But Duchâtel's clumsiness was nothing compared to that of Hébert, the Minister of Justice, of whom we are given this portrait: "Imagine a narrow
little face squeezed and weasel-like compressed at the temples; fore-
head, nose and chin all pointed; cold, bright eyes and thin, drawn-in
lips; add to that a long quill usually held across the mouth which from
a distance looked like a cat's bristling whiskers, and you have the
portrait of a man more like a carnivorous animal than any I have
seen . . . he had a stiff, ill-articulated mind, with no tact to bend or
turn in time . . . his language was so exaggerated and provocative that
Barrot, beside himself and scarcely knowing what he did, cried in a
voice stifled with rage that Charles X's ministers . . . would never
have dared to speak like that" (48/25). A little later in the text, the
Chamber president, Sauzet, is described as a frightened man, used to
acting only on orders from above, who had "the assumed dignity of a
church sexton" and a "large fat body with little arms he flailed con-
vulsively like a drowning man" (67/45). The physical characteristics
mentioned in the portrayals of Duchâtel, Hébert and Sauzet function
less to reinforce the ascribed psychological traits than to reduce each
of these figures to a near-comic status. One can see a kind of declen-
sion in this series of portraits leading us deeper and deeper into the
satiric mode.

The major political leaders of 1848 fare no better, especially Lamartine (126/108) and Louis-Napoleon (212/204), though the figure in
the text to most fully exemplify the moral inadequacy of France's
political leaders does not receive a set portrait—Thiers. Tocqueville
intended to include a portrait of Thiers in a section covering the period
June 1848—June 1849 which he never wrote. Nevertheless, through
the way Thiers is described in his many appearances, the reader comes
to have an impression as vivid as that left by any of the set portraits.
Most of these passing references depict Theirs as the pure politician,
grasping at power for its own sake, adept at inducing others to take
risks he will not take. The text especially singles out examples of his

cowardice, as in the incident during the first days of the June civil war
when Thiers is described as excitedly convening Tocqueville, Barrot,
and Dufaure to propose moving the government outside Paris lest they
all be massacred. To make Thiers's cowardice stand out more vividly
the text describes his encounter with General Lamoricière, who just a
few pages before is depicted as always in the thick of battle, three
horses shot out from under him in a single day:

> M. Thiers came along and threw his arms around Lamoricière's neck,
> telling him he was a hero. I could not help smiling at the sight, for they
> did not love each other at all, but danger is like wine in making all men
> sentimental.
>
> I left Lamoricière in M. Thiers' arms and went back to the Assembly.
> (175/161)

A year later when the cabinet in which Tocqueville was foreign minister was preparing for a possible revolt by the Left, we are given this
account of the incident: "Thiers, deep in one armchair with his legs on
another, was rubbing his stomach (for he felt some signs of the prevail-
ing illness) and was saying with arrogant ill temper in his shrillest
falsetto voice that it was very odd that no one should think of declaring
Paris in a state of siege. I quietly replied that we had thought of it, but
that the moment had not come, because the Assembly was not yet
sitting" (217/209).
   Are there no worthy actors in this account of 1848? No men and
women of integrity and disinterest ready to put their talent and courage at the service of the nation? In the June Days a few men like
Lamoricière emerge, but once the battle is over, politicians of Thiers's
stripe return to dominate affairs with their petty maneuvering. Amid
all the egotists, opportunists, bumblers, and madmen, the text leaves
only Tocqueville and certain of his friends and political associates with
sufficient integrity to lead the country and maintain a republic "at least
for a while." In Part 3, when Tocqueville joins the Barrot cabinet of
July 1849, the text speaks as if men of worth and integrity had momentarily appeared on stage. Yet it also makes clear that even this remnant
is flawed. Barrot, a man of talent and "sincere concern for the public
good" was unfortunately still a man whose "ambition was intimately
intertwined with his integrity" (206/197) and Dufaure, Tocqueville's
other leading associate, showed a streak of stubbornness and republi-

can rigidity that cost the moderates crucial support from both conservatives and legitimists (226/222).

What of Tocqueville himself? There is no set portrait; one learns of him by what he does and says, and above all, by what he betrays of himself in the process of writing. In that sense the entire text is a self-portrait. Yet, given the function of the other portraits, it is not hard to guess what traits will emerge. Within the moral system of the text Tocqueville must be presented as the man "worthy" of his time who disinterestedly places the *grandeur* of the nation above petty political or economic gain. He specifically states that he not only viewed most of his contemporaries as "unworthy to lead," but found them "lacking that disinterestedness I find in myself despite my faults" (103/83). Thus, even Tocqueville's own self-portrait will be less a psychological characterization than a placeholder in the table of worthy and unworthy actors.

Tableaux

Although the *Recollections* continues to use *tableau* in the dual sense of table and picture, in order to understand the discursive function of the *Recollection's* most characteristic scenes, one needs to consider a third sense of the term *tableau,* related to the *tableau vivant* of the theatre.

Theatre as a metaphor for public life plays a central role in the rhetorical strategy of the *Recollections*.[16] *Théâtre* and *tableau* have been associated in a specific tradition from the time of Diderot, who developed the idea of the *drame,* a morality play midway between comedy and tragedy which does its work not by the *coup de théâtre* of some passionate reversal but by the moving spectacle of a series of moral *tableaux.* In Diderot's theory, according to Karlheinze Stierle,

16. Theatre as a metaphor for public life was already established by the seventeenth century and is heavily used by Retz. André Bertière, *Le Cardinal de Retz,* 464–67 and 555. According to Lionel Gossman the theatre and tableau metaphors were also a familiar device in much nineteenth-century historiography, the Romantics preferring "set pieces and colorful tableaux" whereas others, like Macaulay, sought to exemplify the whole of a life or occurrence in a single portrait. *Augustin Thierry and Liberal Historiography, History and Theory,* Beiheft 15 (1976), 64. Tocqueville's use of the theatre and tableau metaphors tends more to moral and political typification.

"the *tableau* in the theatre designates the unity of the pathetic culmination of a scene in which the *drame* seems to stand still. The unity of this
moment is in structural equivalence to the *fruchtbare Moment* of the
pathetic scene chosen by the *peinture morale*. . . . For Diderot the
tableau as culmination of the *drame* designates the moment when
under the conditions of pathos, the acting persons lose their individu-
alities to become representations of the unchanging order of human
nature."[17] Stierle invokes Diderot, however, in order to explicate still
another genre derived from the *tableau vivant,* the tradition of the
tableaux de Paris. These were popular books of the early nineteenth
century which depicted Parisian life through portraits of representative social and moral types. Their origin goes back to the end of the
eighteenth century when Mercier, inspired by the culminating *tableaux* of Diderot's plays, composed a work consisting of short texts
which described not only the monuments and curiosities of Paris but
also "the moral physiogonomy of this gigantic capital."[18] Versions of
the *tableaux de Paris* continued to be produced down to the Revolution of 1848 after which, according to Stierle, the genre changes from
moral *tableaux* into the typical modern guidebook for foreigners or
provincials. One need not assume a direct influence of the *tableaux de
Paris,* Diderot's *tableaux vivants* or Greuze's *peinture morale* on the
Recollections to see that many of its set scenes are less the "vivid
pictures" of traditional histories and memoirs than moments when the
actors and actions lose their identities and become representatives of a
system of moral/political values. Only certain of the smaller, more
discrete occurrences are explicitly called *tableaux* in the *Recollections,*
but even the larger, more complex scenes are often constructed from a
series of smaller *tableaux.*

I will begin with one of the briefer instances of a morally exemplary

17. Karlheinz Stierle, "Baudelaire and the Tradition of the *Tableau de Paris,*" *New
Literary History* 10 (1980): 346. An important recent work on the *tableau* in Diderot is
Jay Caplan, *Framed Narratives: Diderot's Genealogy of the Beholder* (Minneapolis:
University of Minnesota Press, 1985). On the moral *tableau* in French painting and its
relation to Diderot and Greuze see Michael Fried, *Absorption and Theatricality:
Painting and the Beholder in the Age of Diderot* (Berkeley: University of California
Press, 1980), chaps. 1 and 2. For a discussion of the sociopolitical implications of the
tableau see Peter Szondi, "*Tableau* and *Coup de théâtre*: On the Social Psychology of
Diderot's Bourgeois Tragedy," *New Literary History* 10 (1980): 324–43.

18. Stierle, "Baudelaire and the Tradition of the *Tableau de Paris,*" 345. The quotation is from Mercier's preface.

scene called a *tableau* by the text. Early in the days of the June fighting Tocqueville became acutely aware that the worker's revolt had infected every part of "that vast class" and had "penetrated into our houses, around us, above us, below us. . . . Even the places where we thought we were masters were creeping with domestic enemies" (157/142). So impressive was the fear generated by these domestic enemies that even as he wrote amid the tranquility of Sorrento in 1851, Tocqueville felt compelled to violate his eyewitness rule and recount a story told him, appropriately enough, by Adolphe Blanqui, the prominent liberal economist and brother of the famous revolutionary. Out of pity for a poor man of the countryside, Adolphe Blanqui had brought the man's son to Paris as a house servant. On the first day of the revolt, Blanqui heard the child say as he was cleaning away the dinner dishes, "Next Sunday it is we who will be eating the chicken wings." A little servant girl who was helping replied, "And it is we who will wear the lovely silk dresses." The children so frightened Blanqui that "it was only after the victory he dared take this ambitious youngster and the vainglorious little girl back to their hovels." The text refers to the incident as "the childish picture of this naive greed" (*le tableau enfantin de cette cupidité naïve*) (157/143).

An equally pointed *tableau* of greed is given earlier in the text though without the name. On the first day of the February revolt, Guizot suddenly appeared before the anxious Assembly and announced that the king had asked Molé to form a new cabinet (53/32). Cries of victory and satisfied vengeance rose from the opposition; cries of indignation and consternation, from the suddenly deposed majority. The latter milled about the floor in despair, shouting injuries at their own ministers since the fall of the Guizot ministry "comprised the entire fortune of this deputy, the daughter's dowry for that one, the son's career for this other one" (54/32). Tocqueville remained in his seat watching "this swaying crowd . . . I saw the surprise, the anger, the fear, the greed (*cupidité*) . . . I compared all these legislators apart from myself to a pack of dogs that one pulls off the prey, their mouths still half full" (54/32). Here, where the bourgeoisie's petty comforts are about to be taken away, the text offers a moral *tableau* of the violent greed that underlies the preoccupation with petty well-being (*petit bien-être*).

One of the more often cited passages from the *Recollections* derives its point and memorability from its form as a comparative *tableau*.

The text's account of the June civil war is divided into two chapters, the second opening with the description of a pair of exemplary encounters. Tocqueville returned to his house after midnight even though he had been warned that his porter had been overheard bragging he would kill him. The porter is described in the text as "a slightly daft, drunken, old soldier who spent what time he could spare from beating his wife, frequenting the taverns . . . one might say he was a socialist by birth or rather by temperament" (169/155). Tocqueville had taken the precaution of putting pistols in his pockets, and he made the porter walk in front of him as they went through the house, standing behind the porter while he opened each door until Tocqueville was finally inside his own room. "It wasn't until he saw me about to disappear that he made up his mind to take off his hat and bow. Did that man intend to kill me and, seeing me on guard with my hands in my pockets . . . change his mind? I did not believe so then or now . . . I have always thought that his poor wretch would have become dangerous only if the fight seemed to be going against us" (170/156). The tableau of the rebellious porter reluctantly doffing his hat to an armed Tocqueville is followed without break or transition by the picture of an encounter with a very different kind of servant: "At daybreak, I heard someone enter my room and I awoke with a start: it was my man-servant letting himself in with his key; this fine young man had left his bivouac (I had given him the National Guard uniform for which he had asked and a good rifle) to see if I had come home and needed his services. He was certainly no socialist, neither in theory or in temperament. He was not affected in the least degree by that most usual sickness of our times which is restlessness of spirit, and it would have been difficult to find in any day a man more satisfied with his station and less troubled by his lot" (171/157). The servant, Eugène, assures Tocqueville all is going well, takes off his National Guard uniform, polishes Tocqueville's boots, puts the uniform back on and politely asks permission to return to the battle: "It gave me a sense of repose in the midst of those days so agitated by savagery and hate to see the peaceful and contented face of that young man" (171/157). These extraordinary scenes have been quoted and commented on by various writers for their astonishingly candid revelation of Tocqueville's social outlook, but the form and placement of this dual tableau is equally striking. Although there is no reason to doubt that the events occurred as described, by opening the second chapter on the June civil war with this tableau, the text heightens the exemplary status given to its diptych of the greedy, vicious servant and the worthy, contented one.

The *tableaux* and the portraits in the *Recollections* perform similar functions. The portraits give us individual personalities or groups as character types within a moral system; the tableaux give us groups or individuals arrested in a typical moral gesture or action. Naturally, both these constituent genres also serve the more traditional narrative functions of characterization, setting, action, and commentary. Yet if we treat them only as the traditional components or ornaments of memoir and history, we miss their specific function as exemplars within a system of moral/political values. To the extent the text is made up of a series of portraits and tableaux which gives us moral types, we could consider the *Recollections* itself as an extension of the *tableaux de Paris* books, a *tableaux de la Révolution*.

Aphorisms, Anecdotes, and Modes

The memoir, next to the novel, is among the freest of genres in terms of the forms it can incorporate. In addition to portraits, scenes and tableaux, the *Recollections* contains numerous other constituent genres: aphorisms, anecdotes, commentary, analysis, the essay, and of course, stretching across and incorporating many of these others, narrative. Of these typical memoir forms, only anecdotes—those semiserious digressions for piquant incidents—are infrequent in the *Recollections*. Tocqueville was not a raconteur. But he *was* an aphorist, and we find in the *Recollections* many highly compressed social and political observations. We have already encountered some, for example, the incident where Thiers throws his arms around the neck of Lamoricière: "danger is like wine in making all men sentimental." In a passage on Louis-Philippe's error in relying on the National Guard rather than the Army to save him (since he and his advisers remembered how the Army had failed Charles X in 1830), Tocqueville comes up with a frequently quoted line: "In politics one often perishes for having had too good a memory" (59/37). Some of the *Recollection's* sayings are given a formulation so carefully wrought they seem to stand apart from their context, ready-made for citation: "In France there is only one thing we cannot make: a free government; and only one institution we cannot destroy: centralization" (182/170). The near absence of anecdotes combined with the frequency of aphorisms at once confirms the reader's memoir expectations and puts the text in the class of those historical memoirs which primarily pursue edification rather than apologia and diversion. When one adds the use of aphorisms to the exemplary function of the portrait and the *tableau*, it becomes clear that the *Recollections* belongs in the general tradition of the French *moralistes*.

Later on, in a chapter on voice, I will consider some other discursive functions of the aphorism along with the role of commentary in the text's pattern of discourse. At this point I want to call attention to a final generic phenomenon: mode. Although Frye and others have treated modes as categories of works on a par with genres, I follow Alistair Fowler's suggestion that mode be considered more an effect of discursive quality than generic structure.[19] In keeping with its adjectival use, for example, tragic or satiric mode, readers look to a variety of clues in identifying modes. Some concern matters to which Frye has already called our attention, such as the strength of the hero vis-à-vis the world; others concern tropes, figures, level of vocabulary, and selection of detail and incident. For example, I noted above how the *Recollections'* mention of a person's physical characteristics or gestures is often discursively less important as individual characterization than as reducing them to a comic status, thereby tilting these passages toward the satiric mode. A more generalized satiric impression results from the cumulative effect of the portraits and *tableaux* in showing almost everyone in the *Recollections* as unworthy of the task before them. At each turn in the crisis of 1848 the reader encounters new forms of weakness, venality, corruption, and ineptitude. One chapter in the *Recollections,* however, echoes a more specific and restricted literary mode, the pastoral. Although originally concerned with shepherds and the erotic, the pastoral mode has found an extension and transformation in a number of subgenres such as the "rustic" or country novel of the nineteenth century, for example, George Sand.[20] Without pushing the parallels too far, one can see in Tocqueville's account of his campaign for a seat in France's first popularly elected

19. Fowler, *Kinds of Literature*, 106–11.
20. On the nineteenth-century rustic novel in France see Paul Vernois, *Le Roman rustique de G. Sand à Ramuz* (Paris: Nizet, 1962).

Assembly (Part 2, Chapter 4) a pastoral narrative. The value of ending an analysis of generic forms in the *Recollections* with this pastoral chapter is twofold: as a *unit* of narrative, Chapter 4 of Part 2 uses in context the major generic devices I have so far considered in isolation (portrait, tableau, aphorism); as a *pastoral* narrative this chapter is the first part of a diptych contrasting country and city, province and Paris, and demonstrates that even some of the largest units of the text tend to fall into a binary moral framework.

Chapter 4, set in the predominantly rural department of La Manche, where the Chateau de Tocqueville is located, opens with a description of the countryside's reaction to the February Revolution: "Everyone who owned property drew together. . . . No more jealousies or pride of place between the peasant and the rich man, the noble and the bour-geois; but a mutual confidence, a reciprocal benevolence and regard. Property had become among all who enjoyed it a kind of brotherhood. The rich were elders, those less well off the younger; but all considered themselves brothers, having the same interest in defending a common heritage" (107/87). Bucolic as the scene is, the force holding people together is noted to be a merely external one: fear and resentment of the attack on property and of the new taxes emanating from Paris. The result was a determination to elect men to the new Constituent Assem-bly who would fight "Parisian demagoguery." Tocqueville feels in his element now. Although desiring election, his diffidence toward the new regime left him with a "tranquility and clarity of spirit, a respect for myself and a disdain for the follies of the time that I would scarcely have had to the same degree if I had passionately desired success" (108/88).

The text then offers images of Tocqueville, the serene and superior statesman, easily triumphing over the new candidates who wandered "from stage to stage" declaiming their republican faith in the language of 1792 (108/88–89). By contrast, Tocqueville's dignified circular, which juxtaposes the image of a republic of liberty with a republic of socialist propaganda, made him the man to beat in La Manche. Tocqueville is obviously pleased with himself as he remembers the ease with which he handled hostile questioners at various gatherings and even managed an improvised "*petit pathos oratoire,*" which carried the evening before an assembly of workers in Cherbourg (112/93). The only thing he chooses to quote from his small-town meetings is a response to the question of whether he would die at his post should the

new Assembly be invaded by armed rioters: "Yes, like you, I believe
danger awaits those who would faithfully represent you, but with
dangers there is glory and it is because there are dangers and glory that
I am here" (110/91).

From this invocation of political *grandeur* the text turns immediately to *bassesse*. The reader is offered a portrait of the type of the
political egoist in the person of L. J. Havin, who had escorted the
Duchess of Orleans on February 24, but by the next day had jumped to
the republican side and was now the provisional government's com-
missioner for La Manche. Tocqueville had always taken him for "one
of those rootless men of ambition, who got stuck for ten years in the
opposition whereas they had only intended to pass through it." "How
many of these men have I seen around me, tormented by their ability
and falling into despair because they see the best part of their lives
spent criticizing the vices of others without having a chance to indulge
a little in their own . . . Most have developed from this long abstinence
such an appetite for positions, honors and money, that it was easy to
predict that at the first opportunity they would throw themselves on
power with a sort of gluttony without even waiting to choose either the
moment or the morsel" (111/92). Havin is merely corrupted by ambition and greed; those members of the La Manche council who, just
weeks before had been in the pocket of one of Guizot's administrators,
are shown as shameless sycophants before this same Havin whom they
had treated with sneering condescension during the previous decade
when he was out of office. "Now they praised him, voted for him and
smiled on him; even spoke well of him among themselves for fear of
indiscretion. I have often seen larger *tableaux* of human baseness but
never one more perfect . . . later when things were reversed and they
were back in power, they pursued this same Havin with unheard
violence and injustice" (113/93–94).

Appropriately, after these portraits and tableaux of politicians corrupted by Paris, the narrative closes with two purely rustic tableaux. A
few days before the voting Tocqueville retreats to the family chateau,
"my poor and dear Tocqueville," which "perhaps I was going to leave
forever!" (113/94). The romantic paragraph that follows exhibits a
vocabulary and tone seldom found elsewhere in the *Recollections*. "As
I entered, I was seized with a sadness so great and so peculiar that it has
left in my recollections traces which today I still find marked and
visible among all the vestiges of the events of those times. I arrived

unexpectedly. The empty rooms, where there was no one but my old dog to greet me, the uncurtained windows, the piles of dusty furniture, the dark fireplaces, the stopped clocks, the bleak look of the place, the damp walls—all seemed to announce abandonment and presage ruin" (113/94). What had always been "a charming retreat" from public life now seemed to Tocqueville a "desolate wilderness." Yet amid the desolation of the chateau's current appearance images of happier days came to mind: "I saw, as if from the bottom of a tomb, the sweetest and gayest images of my life." The paragraph closes with a reflection from the perspective of 1850. "How much brighter and more compelling man's imagination is than reality. I had just seen the monarchy fall; since then I have witnessed the most terrible and bloody scenes; well! I tell you, none of these great *tableaux* caused then or causes now an emotion as poignant or profound as I experienced that day at the sight of the ancient home of my fathers and the memory of the peaceful days and happy hours that I passed there without knowing their price. I can say that it was there and on that day I really understood the full bitterness of revolutions" (113/94). Two things are striking in this evocation. First, the depth of feeling—the text is careful to remind us that those events either before or after (including the June civil war!), which one might have expected to move him more deeply, had far less effect than the ancient site of his aristocratic pleasures and privileges. Second, the tendency of Tocqueville's discourse to transform even the most vivid pictorial *tableau* into a *tableau* of moral exemplification.

The pastoral, however, does not end with Alexis de Tocqueville standing alone in his deserted chateau. Instead we are treated to a recessional and a closing *tableau vivant*. On election day, all the male inhabitants of the area around the village of Tocqueville were to walk together to vote at the town of Saint-Pierre. They lined up alphabetically, Tocqueville taking care to go to his appropriate place since "in democratic times one must be put at the head of people, not put oneself there." There were a hundred seventy men in procession, including the crippled and sick who came behind on horses or in carts.

When we got to the top of a hill overlooking Tocqueville there was a momentary halt; I knew that I was required to speak. I climbed to the other side of a ditch, a circle formed around me and I said a few words inspired by the occasion. I reminded these good people of the gravity and importance of the act they were about to perform; I advised them not to let themselves be accosted or diverted by people who might, when we arrived at the town, seek to deceive them, but rather march as a united body with each man staying in his place until all had voted . . . they shouted they would do it and so they did. All the votes were given at the same time and I have reason to think that almost all were given for the same candidate.

As soon as I had voted myself, I said good-by to them and got into a carriage to go to Paris (114/95).

The aristocrat has learned to make his obeisance to democracy; the small price of taking his alphabetical place costs nothing to his honor since it is by such gestures that a *grand notable* like Tocqueville will maintain his preeminence. But the text tells us more by giving us a closing *tableau* of great symbolic power. The virtuous aristocratic leader toward whom "the population was always well disposed . . . but now positively affectionate" pauses on the hilltop to offer a little civic homily as he leads "his people" to the solemn act of their first democratic communion. And because he is worthy to lead them, they in turn show themselves worthy of the franchise that has so gratuitously fallen upon them and give him all their votes.

Not only the themes and images of Chapter 4 are pastoral, but the tone and structure are as well. The images have been primarily those of unity: if Paris is preparing to tear itself apart over property, the countryside has achieved *fraternité* over property; if the peasants once wrested their land from the aristocracy in a bloody revolution, they now love their aristocratic landlord and want him for their representative. But it is also in the balanced forms of the language that this rustic concord makes itself felt. The chapter has a perfect *a b b a* form; its opening and closing parts dwell on the unity and fraternity of the classes whereas its two middle parts are back-to-back images of political integrity (Tocqueville) and the total absence of integrity (Havin and the commissioners). This equilibrium extends in many places down to the level of the sentence. Consider this simple passage from the opening paragraph on how the revolution went almost unnoticed in the countryside, a passage that slips in an aphorism on the political mentality of the peasantry: "The superior classes bent immediately under the blow; the inferior classes hardly felt it. Ordinarily, the agricultural classes receive political impressions more slowly and retain them more obstinately than any other classes; they are the last to rise and the last to sit down" (106/86). There is the steady rhythm here of the peasant and the country noble walking the land together, the same calm pace of the liberal aristocrat and his people as they walked the three miles from Tocqueville to Saint-Pierre. The text does not lose itself completely in its country idyll since fear and the threat of civil war are in the background. Yet even they are evoked at symmetrical points in the text. Just as the chapter alludes at the beginning to the external threat behind the unity of all property-owning classes, so at the very end of the chapter we are not left gazing at the solemn tableau on the hill, but are reminded that one must, after all, say good-bye to these *"braves gens"* and turn toward Paris, the symbol of anarchy and danger.

The following chapter describes what Tocqueville found on returning to Paris. After some opening paragraphs on the comic stupidity of the revolutionary leaders who "handed themselves over to the nation and at the same time did everything to alienate it," the text suddenly takes on an ominous tone as it describes the state of the city. "What was not ridiculous but truly sinister and frightening, was the appearance of Paris when I returned. I found a hundred thousand armed workmen, formed into regiments, without work, dying of hunger but their minds full of vain theories and chimerical hopes. I saw society cut in two: those who had nothing united in a common covetousness; those who had anything, in a common anguish" (117/98). Paris is as divided and anarchic as the countryside was united and orderly. In the pastoral chapter the only base figures are Havin and the commissioners—men who have been corrupted by their contact with Paris. In the city chapter the only men of integrity are the new deputies of the Constituent Assembly elected from the provinces, men whose inexperience is compensated by their disinterest and courage (123/104). Taken together, the two chapters became another instance of the kind of moral/political polarity at work in the portraits and *tableaux*: province versus Paris, order versus anarchy, good sense versus vain theories, contentment versus covetousness, fraternity versus fratricide. Moreover, in form, the city chapter is as agitated and broken up as the preceding one was balanced and unified. Chapter 5 is a kind of anti-pastoral, alternating between satiric passages on the provisional government or the Montagne faction in the Assembly and somber descriptions of the signs of social division and the coming war. The pastoral chapter exhibits a metaphorical unity in the way its themes can substitute for one another whereas the alternations in the antipastoral chapter are metonymical procedures in which one theme sets off another by contiguity.[21]

Thus, even at the level of its larger narrative units, the *Recollections'* informality and loose construction hides a deeper moral structure. If one were to treat the text only in terms of its superficial genre indicators, one might feel comfortable dipping into it here and there to draw out a portrait, a tableau, or an aphorism to serve as a documentary source or an illustrative citation. But the *Recollections* does not use these traditional components of the memoir and history merely to describe character, make a point, or demonstrate literary finesse; these genres function to instance a moral code whose systematic nature I will explore in Chapter 4 below.

21. For example, the passage satirizing the revolutionaries which opens this chapter ("There have been worse revolutionaries than those of 1848 . . . but none stupider. . . .") ends with a comic line from Molière epitomizing the radical's astonishment at the voter's ingratitude in electing a conservative majority ("Why don't you love me, impudent lady"), a line that touches off the somber beginning of the next paragraph ("What was not ridiculous but sinister and terrible was the appearance of Paris. . . .") (115–17/96–98).

3

PLOT

Plot, Story, Chronicle

As readers we not only begin to identify particular genres or themes on our first pass through a text, we also read for narrative coherence. Moreover, we may find that many of the stories historians tell about 1848 bear a striking resemblance to one of the traditional plot types found in literature. Thus a text like the *Recollections* can be studied for both its narrative structure and its plot type. In the twentieth century, plot has come to be seen as a signifying form applicable across genres, a position that has received its most influential expression in the work of Northrop Frye. Although the typological approach must also consider the *structure* of events, typologies like Frye's focus on the *meaning* of events, attempting to gather possible meanings under categories that help us see the similarities among stories and their connection with a few primary masterplots of our cultural tradition.[1] The purely structural approach to plot, on the other hand, disregards the traditional type categories and looks at plots as part of a more general phenomenon of storytelling. This approach has its exemplary formulation in contemporary narrative theory, which is less interested in

1. Northrop Frye, *Anatomy of Criticism* (Princeton, N.J.: Princeton University Press, 1957). There are, of course, a number of other typologies of content with a less existential orientation such as Ronald Crane's useful Aristotelian division into plots of action, plots of character, and plots of thought, in *Critics and Criticism* (Chicago: University of Chicago Press, 1957). One of the best-known typologies is the fourteen-category matrix of Norman Friedman, *Form and Meaning in Fiction* (Athens: University of Georgia Press, 1975).

developing typologies of plot than in canvasing the possibilities of narrative construction, focusing on the ordering conventions shared by writers and readers.[2]

I have been using the terms story, plot, and narrative interchangeably up to this point, but one of the most important contributions of narrative theory has been the distinction derived from the Russian Formalists between story and plot (*fabula* and *sjužet*). It is an operational definition that allows the narrative analyst to construct a chronological "story" that can be compared to the "plot" or "discourse" of the actual text, thereby setting in relief the various artistic elements that constitute the text. Of course, it is not only novels whose plots rearrange an implied chronological story, biographies and even historical narratives may open with a crucial later event and then return to a more chronological telling. The story/plot distinction has received many formulations, but its value is vitiated if it is viewed as a description of two existents, rather than as an heuristic device to tease out aspects of narrative structure which would otherwise go unnoticed.[3] Even if understood heuristically, however, the story/plot distinction obviously needs modification when applied to a historical text like the *Recollections* where the "story" that can be reconstructed from the "plot" of the text is in turn derived from an external "chronicle" of events.

The specific value of the story/plot distinction, like that of the

2. Narrative theory or narratology has spawned an enormous and ever growing literature. Among the recent general discussions I have found most useful are Shlomith Rimmon-Kenan, *Narrative Fiction: Contemporary Poetics* (London: Methuen, 1983), and Wallace Martin, *Recent Theories of Narrative* (Ithaca, N.Y.: Cornell University Press, 1986). The results of many of these efforts to arrive at the constitutive categories of narrative are often little more than modifications of Aristotle's beginning, middle, end—for example, "initial situation, transformation, consequent situation," or "adjective/verb/adjective." See Tzvetan Todorov *The Poetics of Prose* (Ithaca, N.Y.: Cornell University Press, 1977), 108–19.

3. Gérard Genette has gone beyond the story/plot polarity to suggest that there are really three aspects to be distinguished in narrative, namely story, plot, and the act of narration itself. In this way he has been able to reintroduce other aspects of traditional literary theory such as characterization, voice, point of view, etc. *Figures III* (Paris: Éditions du Seuil, 1974), 71–72, in English as *Narrative Discourse* (Ithaca, N.Y.: Cornell University Press, 1980), 25–26. Compare Barbara Herrstein-Smith's cogent objections concerning the source of criteria for determining "story" as opposed to plot or discourse: "Narrative Versions, Narrative Theories," *Critical Inquiry* 7 (1980): 213–36. There is also a valuable discussion in Jonathan Culler, "Fabula and Sjuzhet in the Analysis of Narrative," *Poetics Today* 1–3 (1980): 27–37, and in Chapter 9 of *The Pursuit of Signs* (Ithaca, N.Y.: Cornell University Press, 1981).

Weberian ideal type, is that it permits a comparison of the *selection, order,* and *duration* of events in the plot with their enumeration, sequence, and pace in the chronology of the story, which can be reconstructed from the actual narrative text. Although at first glance the chronicle implied by a factual text like the *Recollections* might seem to be easier to recover than the chronological story behind a fictional text, there are strong philosophical grounds for believing that the factual chronicle underlying historical texts is also a matter of construction and not just discovery. As the *Annales* school has shown, the very notion of an "event" as a discrete entity that can be described, named, and dated is the product of a certain epistemic set. And which of the events perceived on the basis of this set are then to be selected and how they are to be described also appear to be as much a function of the historian's guiding problem set and ideological orientation as is the literary theorist's reconstruction of the "natural" story line behind a given plot. Thus both historical texts and fictional texts have a similar relation to a "story" or "chronicle" which can be constructed on the basis of their discourse. This is not to say that there are no differences between fact and fiction, that it is as irrelevant to ask how many insurgents were actually executed after the June fighting in 1848? as it is to ask how many children had Lady Macbeth? I will deal with this referential aspect of the *Recollection's* treatment of the chronicle of 1848 in Chapter 6. At this point I will simply make use of the dual chronology preceding Chapter 1 to illuminate the *Recollections'* process of selection.

Selection

Even a cursory comparison of the general chronicle of 1848 (right-hand column) with the story contained in the *Recollections* (left-hand column) reveals the text's radical selectivity. Given the crucial importance of endings in determining the plot of a story, the most striking difference between the *Recollections'* account and the general chronicle of 1848 is that Tocqueville lets his book end in October 1849 rather than with the Napoleonic coup of December 2, 1851. The choice of a certain beginning and a certain ending in a temporal process determines a middle and with it the general shape of a story. By letting his account close with the fall of the Barrot cabinet in 1849,

Tocqueville chose a rather arbitrary terminal point as compared to the now traditional chronology of the Revolution of 1848. In one sense, of course, it was impossible for Tocqueville to have given his story the ending of December 2, 1851, since he stopped writing the text as we now have it at Versailles in the fall of 1851, a month before the coup. But why didn't he "complete" the *Recollections* once the coup put an end to the Republic; why didn't he reopen his account, or, like Marx, whose *Class Struggles in France* extends only to May 1850, why did Tocqueville not rewrite the story in the light of Bonaparte's coup as Marx did in *The Eighteenth Brumaire*? Despite the fact that Tocqueville's brief imprisonment was more an adventure than an occasion of suffering, his indignation and refusal of the new regime were unflinching and unforgiving from the beginning. Yet Tocqueville, forced definitively to the sidelines, did not reopen the text of the *Recollections* even though he could easily have added to it without violating his rule of keeping to an eyewitness account. For not only had he directly experienced the coup, he had returned from Sorrento a few months before the coup to serve as the official *rapporteur* of the Assembly committee that proposed a revision of the Constitution in an effort to avert a showdown between the Assembly and Louis-Napoleon. Moreover, as foreign minister in the Barrot cabinet, Tocqueville had even discussed with Louis-Napoleon various options for prolonging his presidency. Yet in the text of the *Recollections* as it was left for posterity we hear nothing of Tocqueville's work on this committee, his interview with the president, his arrest during the coup, or of the eloquent letter he sent to the London *Times* describing the coup and urging the British to reject it.[4]

The question of why the *Recollections* was left to close with the fall of a cabinet rather than the end of the Republic can be taken in two senses: one external and biographical, the other internal and textual. No doubt there was a major psychological factor behind Tocqueville's failure to immediately complete the story of 1848: a career reappraisal already begun in Sorrento in March 1850 when he wrote Kergorlay that he felt he was more likely to make a lasting contribution as a writer than as a political leader and proposed writing a book on the

4. Tocqueville's letter may be found in Roger Boesche, ed., *Alexis de Tocqueville: Selected Letters on Politics and Society* (Berkeley: University of California Press, 1985), 266–78.

First Empire.[5] From a psychological point of view it was obviously more attractive to launch a large-scale new project, which might indirectly contribute to future political developments in France, than to go back to record the ignominious end of one's parliamentary career. But there are also exigencies *within* the text of the *Recollections* as it stood in November 1851 which would have hampered any revision of the manuscript in light of the December coup had Tocqueville desired to complete the text. Reopening the text to include December 1851 would have affected its narrative structure, forcing him to rewrite the earlier parts in relation to this new ending. Even if he had left what was already written untouched, and simply added the new material, it would still have changed the narrative structure by shifting the center of gravity from the worker's revolt of June 1848 and Tocqueville's career to Louis-Napoleon and his conflict with the Assembly.

The most startling aspect of selection in the *Recollections,* apart from not extending its account to the coup of December 2, is the omission of all events from June 1848 to June 1849—the omission of an entire year from an account that covers a period of a little over twenty-one months! What has the *Recollections* omitted concerning that period? Had Tocqueville written the projected chapters based on an outline left among his papers, the narrative would have included (1) his role in the debates on the Constitution; (2) the government and character of Cavaignac; (3) a portrait of Thiers ("not better perhaps, but different than I had thought"); (4) a description of the movement of reaction and his vote "without hesitation" for all measures to "establish order and discipline in society and defeat the revolutionary and socialist party"; (5) the candidacy and election of Louis-Napoleon and the machinations of Thiers and others who decided to back him; (6) the transfer of powers and the Roman expedition; and (7) Tocqueville's observation of revolutionary activity in Germany. Without knowing how the transformation of these notes into rhetorical and narrative form would look, one cannot be certain of the effect they would have on the reader's perception of narrative shape. What can be estimated with some assurance, however, is the effect the omission of such a large segment has on the reader's experience of the text as it stands. Considering the effects of such omissions automatically shifts

5. Alexis de Tocqueville, *Oeuvres complètes* (M), 13, 2, 229–33 (*Selected Letters,* 252–28).

attention from the phenomenon of *selection* (inclusion/omission) to that of *duration* or *pace,* that is, the relative amount of text space/reader time given to events.

Duration

By itself inclusion of an item tells very little about its role in a text, since it may be merely alluded to or the subject of an extended account. Omission, on the other hand, is the zero degree of duration, though its effects are hardly zero in degree. Gérard Genette has expanded literary theory's traditional duration categories of "scene" and "summary" to five: *ellipsis* (omission), *summary* (compressed narration of events), *scene* (detailed dramatization, usually with dialogue), *pause* (a brief suspension of narrative time for either description or incidental reflection), and *digression* (where commentary, rather than slowing the pace of the story, halts it).[6]

Ellipsis

In the case of the major ellipsis in the *Recollections,* just described, the omission of an entire year creates for the reader an experience of temporal enjambment. The text leads the reader steadily from the February Revolution through the June Days of 1848, in all a period of four months; then with Part 3 it suddenly takes up a year later in June 1849 and continues its treatment of affairs until October 30, 1849, covering this five months at a level of detail comparable to Parts 1 and 2. The effect of this ellipsis on the reader is similar to that of the breaks in cinematic montage; the jump over a year's time forces us to assume that there has been a process of development but that for purposes of understanding the plot, the resulting situation is all that counts. If this particular gap in the text were the only instance of a major omission, it would hardly be worth attention. But in fact it is only the most extreme case of numerous ellipses. Going back over the dual chronology for

6. Genette, *Narrative Discourse,* 86–112. The category "digression" is not discussed in this work but in *Nouveau Discours du récit* (Paris: Éditions du Seuil, 1983), 22–25, where Genette speaks of this fifth type of tempo modulation as "*digression réflexive.*"

Parts 1 and 2 will reveal that despite the brief time period covered, the reader is not presented with a continuous account but an intermittent series. For example, after the description of February 24 there is no discussion of the numerous decrees and actions of the provisional government which form part of every standard history of 1848 (universal suffrage, length of work day, abolition of slavery, and so on). Nor is there discussion of the incidents over the dissolution of the elite companies of the National Guard of March 16 or the mass popular demonstration of April 16. Thus some of the most significant actions and events of the new revolutionary Republic are skipped over as the text moves directly from Tocqueville's general impressions of the days immediately following February 24 to his April election campaign in La Manche (pastoral chapter). Tocqueville does not hide the fact he has omitted some events: "I do not want to write the history of the revolution of 1848. I am only trying to recover the trace of my actions, ideas and impressions during this revolution; thus I skip over the events which occurred during the first weeks after February 24th" (100/79). Yet only a reader with a firm grasp of the chronicle of this period will realize how much of importance to the general history of the time is passed over with this remark. And even such a knowledge-able reader is not likely to hold the *omitted* events in mind but will continue to piece together the *Recollections'* narrative line as if those events had never occurred.

Pause and Digression

The two major ellipses considered so far are both marked so that readers at least know that a time period is elided even if they are unaware (without going outside the text) of the elided content. The phenomenon of pause also creates a temporal gap, but as its name indicates it is a brief suspension that merely slows narrative progression through a co-temporal description or reflection ascribed to the *same* space-time as the events narrated. These descriptions or reflections become *digressions* when they stop the narrative flow and switch to the time of writing for extended comment from the narrator's later point of view. In a memoir like the *Recollections,* both *pause* (co-temporal description/reflection) and *digression* (retrospective commentary) are a constant and characterizing feature of discourse, a feature examined in detail in my discussion of voice (Chapter 5).

Scene and Summary

Somewhat less frequent in the memoir genre is that standard convention of the nineteenth-century novel, the alternation of scene and summary, in which extended dramatic scenes carry forward the crucial actions of the plot and the intervening story time is filled in with descriptions and action summaries. Nevertheless, this typical device of fiction can also be found in the *Recollections*. The section on the Banquet Affair, for example, covers events of several months in a dozen pages, containing passages of summary narration punctuated by numerous digressions for commentary and at one or two points the fragments of a scene. The long account of the revolutionary day of February 24 or the accounts of May 15 or 21, on the other hand, are traditional scenes.

Pace

As in the case of selection, an attempt to *measure* the duration of the various scenes or *tableaux* in a text like the *Recollections* against the duration of events in the reconstructed story is complicated by the fact that one is also dealing with the "real" time of chronicle. But the differences between fictional texts like novels and factual texts like memoirs and histories is not as great with respect to duration as might first appear. Historical texts, whether narrative or analytical, never aim at the absurd objective of making text time strictly proportional to chronological time. Even in a realist novel the closest one comes to this is a scene of pure dialogue, and even then the printed dialogue cannot copy the variable pace of real speech. Rather, traditional realist narrative in both fiction and history has normally attempted to establish a *ratio* among the text spaces allotted to episodes which is *equivalent* to the ratio of perceived importance among factors (events, conditions, causes, motives) in the story/chronicle.[7] Such text units are jointed by connectives which create the impression of continuous duration. In this way writers and readers of traditional realist narrative have worked together to represent the pace of historical time, much in the way representational painters and their audience have developed be-

---

7. For a discussion of the problem of measuring pace in fiction, see Genette, *Narrative Discourse*, 86–95. Also *Nouveau Discours*, 23–24.

tween them conventions for constructing and deciphering a pictorial equivalent of visual reality. As in the case of the variability of color and light in painting, the variability of duration in a realist text is not a matter of *copying* time on some reduced scale but of developing within the text a parallel system of conventional equivalencies. It makes no sense—in fact it would be impossible—to compare a single painting with visual reality or a single text with real time in the absence of such conventions.[8]

In order that the pace or durational pattern of a text like the *Recollections* stand out in relief, therefore, it must be compared not to real time but to another text. Although the convention of the printed chronology is itself a form of text, it is less useful in revealing durational ratios than revealing selection since a chronology is a list, a simple on/off system. With respect to duration, a chronology can at most break larger events into a list of many small ones or, as we have seen, provide an indication of elements omitted or merely mentioned and thus at or near zero-degree textual duration. If we want a measure for events actually recounted, only a comparison with another discursive text can provide a useful scale.

The following chart (p. 50) compares the relative amount of text space devoted to major events by Tocqueville's *Recollections,* by the twentieth-century historian Georges Duveau's *1848: The Making of a Revolution,* and by Flaubert's *Sentimental Education.*[9] Duveau's text is chosen because it is a highly respected narrative which covers roughly the same period as Parts 1 and 2 of the *Recollections,* that is, from the Banquets to the end of the June Days. Flaubert's text has been chosen because it offers us an opportunity to observe the way a fictional text handles the same period. Since the total amount of space given to the period considered (February 22–June 26) varies in each text, I can compare only the amount of space devoted to certain happenings relative to the total space covering this period in the same text. Naturally, each text has agendas other than the representation of historical occurrence, for example, analysis, explanation, commen-

8. Ernst Gombrich, *Art and Illusion* (Princeton, N.J.: Princeton University Press, 1960). There are, of course, borderline cases where a visual or verbal near coincidence is achieved, e.g. *trompe l'oeil.*

9. Georges Duveau, *1848: The Making of a Revolution* (New York: Random House, 1966); Gustave Flaubert, *Sentimental Education* (Harmondsworth: Penguin Books, 1964).

tary, recollection of personal feelings and motives, narration of the public and intimate lives of fictional characters. But in each case all of this is part of the total text that the reader experiences. The *duration* of the represented historical events is experienced against the background of the duration of this other material—much of which is so closely connected or interwoven with the more purely representational passages that measurement is difficult. Hence, I cannot claim a fine level of quantification in my measurement of ratios of duration within each text. Nevertheless, the differences among the texts in the ratios of space allotted to certain occurrences is so extreme as to permit some useful observations about textual construction and its effect on the reader. The numbers in the columns on the right reflect the percentage of text space that each event complex occupies. Percentages were arrived at by taking as a basis that portion of each text which covers the period February 22–June 26. A zero indicates an ellipsis, an event not mentioned, a plus sign that the event is merely alluded to but neither described nor discussed.

The chart shows clearly that the *Recollections* gives zero textual duration to many actions of the provisional government and to the demonstrations of March 16–17; it merely mentions the shooting on the boulevard des Capucines, but devotes eleven percent of its space (eighteen pages) to about three hours of the Assembly meeting on February 24 and another ten percent (sixteen pages) to the few hours taken up by the invasion of the Assembly on May 15. In *Sentimental Education* Flaubert chose to give us in vivid detail (scene) the episode of the mob's invasion of the Tuileries on February 24 (omitted from the *Recollections* and *1848*), but merely mentions the important events in the Assembly that day. Moreover, almost all other events from the standard chronicle of 1848 are presented in Flaubert's novel in brief summaries or through incidental references by characters. Flaubert seems to have presented the invasion of the Tuileries in such detail in order to satirize the greed and vulgarity of the lower classes, as well as the cynicism of the bohemian Hussonnet and the naive romanticism of the young bourgeois, Frédéric, who is momentarily caught up in the enthusiasm. Tocqueville seems to have had somewhat similar motives of revealing greed, cynicism and naïveté in giving over so much space—with comic detail—to the actions of the mob in the Assembly on February 24 and May 15. Georges Duveau, on the other hand, not only gives extended treatment to February 24 and May 15

The Secret Mirror

Patterns of duration in three texts on 1848 (as percentage of text segment dealing with February 22–June 26, 1848)

Events	Recollections	1848	Sentimental Education
February 22–23: Banquets and street fighting	5	12	3
February 24: Fighting at Palais Royal/invasion of Tuileries	0	+	9
February 24: Failure of regency in Assembly	11	4	+
February 25–March 15: Actions and decrees of provisional government	1	13	0
March 16–17, April 16–20: Demonstrations and counter-demonstrations	0	8	0
March–April 23: Electoral campaign	8	1	21
May 15: Invasion of Assembly	10	7	+
May 21: Festival of Concord	4	1	0
June 22–26: Civil war in Paris	24	8	6

but gives equal prominence to the March 16 demonstration of the elite companies of the National Guard and the worker's counter-demonstration of March 17. The reason he treats these episodes at length is his conviction of their importance in transforming the fraternal illusions of February into the bitter class conflict of May and June, that is, the demonstrations of March 16 and 17 signal the beginning of a split between the petty bourgeoisie and the workers. As a professional historian of the twentieth century, he is *allowed* to see the importance of these events by his retrospective and encompassing view of the evidence, and his professional allegiance to the representational conventions of realist narrative *obliges* him to give them a comparable textual space.

The *Recollections*, as a memoir, stands midway between the textual

conventions of the novel and the traditional representational obligations of the narrative historian. Thus the *Recollections* can permit
itself some of the freedom afforded the work of fiction since the genre
conventions for the memoir allow it to dilate on personally witnessed
events or situations. For example, both the *Recollections* and *Sentimental Education* devote a proportionately larger amount of space to
their respective protagonists' electoral campaigns than Duveau does to
the entire electoral process in the spring of 1848. Tocqueville's section
on this electoral campaign is the first step in this text's story of his
emergence as a confident and skillful political leader. Correspondingly, Flaubert's long section on the electoral period is both a step in
Frédéric's political disillusion and a carnival interlude revealing the
fatuousness of the political clubs in particular and of political involvement generally. (Of course, both Tocqueville and Flaubert may have
found this first modern experiment in universal suffrage interesting in
itself.)

The looser obligations of the memoir with respect to selection and
duration, however, should not lead us to assume that the *Recollections'* intermittent treatment of events and its extreme variability in
handling duration are simply a matter of emphasis. The effect is deeper
and operates more subtly. As in Flaubert's novel, so in the *Recollections*, certain episodes are dilated in order to exemplify central themes.
Intermittent presentation combined with indices of variable duration
make the major episodes symbols of a set of corresponding social and
moral conditions rather than a causal chain. One's initial experience in
reading the *Recollections* is of a continuity over time. The presentation, after all, is primarily chronological and this sequencing has the
usual narrative effect on the casual reader: one thing following another becomes one thing following *from* another (*post hoc ergo prop-
ter hoc*). But a closer reading would allow one to see that there is a
consistent thematic that *vertically* connects the episodes, *tableaux,*
portraits, and commentary in the text. What the *Recollections* offers in
place of a continuous narrative is not a sequence of episodes, anecdotes and observations typical of the memoir genre, but *a series of
moral/political tableaux*. Thus the intermittent structure resulting
from *selection* and variable *duration,* though relieving the text of the
power (and burden) of a causally integrative or totalizing discourse,
generates a less obvious but equally effective strategy deploying a
series of exemplary moments.

Order

Although these exemplary moments are constituted in part by the pictorial and thematic codes that will be examined in detail in the next chapter, they are also constituted by their place in the chronological series, an ordering that has certain plotlike effects on the reader. At its most elementary level, order in narrative theory merely concerns the deviation of the order of actions in plot from their order in the reconstructed chronology of story. In the case of the *Recollections,* the text only deviates from strict chronological order at two symmetrical points: (1) at the end of Part 2 the activities of the Constitutional Commission, which began in May and ended just before the June Days, are gathered into a separate chapter following the account of the June civil war; and (2) at the end of Part 3, Tocqueville's actions as Foreign Minister are gathered into the separate chapter that concludes the text. Both chapters, moreover, lack the vivid narrative quality of the remainder of the work and strike the reader as somewhat anticlimactic. Tocqueville is aware of this and begins each of these topical chapters with a remark that he had reserved their material so as not to break the thread of his narrative (*récit*).

But the ordering of episodes in the *Recollections* concerns something more profound in its effect on the reader than these minor displacements from natural chronology. The order that contributes to the reader's experience of plot effect concerns the total *shape* given the episodes, their rise and fall or what the Classical tradition has called complication and denouement. Shape requires a principle(s) of intelligibility—thematic and indexical elements that can signify whether movement in the plot has taken place and in what direction (hence the metaphors of rising and falling). In a structural approach to narrative the identification of the text's selection of elements from the story/chronicle and of the textual duration given to them is part of the process of constituting the basic *units* of analysis. The crucial problem for such a retrospective structural analysis, of course, is how to identify and name these units.[10] It cannot be a question of finding the

10. The central texts on this issue are still those of Roland Barthes, although the studies of Greimas and Todorov also offer important insights. See Barthes's early discussion "Introduction to the Structural Analyses of Narratives" in *Image, Music, Text* (New York: Hill and Wang, 1977), 79–141. His more nuanced, later view is

smallest constitutive elements and describing how the text is built up from them since one would quickly end up with a heap of phrases, words, and syllables unless there were a criterion of division already available. Rather, one begins at the other end with the largest units and moves downward to their auxiliary units and elements. But even the largest units, the primary actions of the text, can be seen only as units in terms of an understanding of what the text is about. This central action or thematic can in turn be discovered *in the course of reading* only by projecting ahead various possibilities opened up by each episode as it appears, with subsequent passages confirming, others disconfirming, these possibilities as well as opening up new ones.

I have already presented enough of the *Recollections'* content to identify its three main topics: a primary topic, revolution from below over the issue of property; a secondary topic, the self-portrait of Tocqueville as a man worthy of his time; and underlying these, a moral conflict between grandeur and disinterest on one hand and pettiness, greed, and egoism on the other. Thus, from early on the reader begins to follow a dual plot whose themes are determined by a binary moral code. And since the prevalent model of narrative in our culture is a temporal sequence in which at least one transformation occurs, the reader is already prepared to find a transformation on both the primary and secondary plot levels from an initial situation to a consequent one. Because of the generally chronological rather than thematic ordering of episodes in the *Recollections,* the two levels are usually interwoven, though their points of transformation do not coincide. The following discussion of plot shape summarizes the main stages of narrative development on each topic level with a closer consideration of certain passages crucial to the reader's subsequent construction of plot type.

Political Level

The primary or political level of the plot tells the story of excess liberty turned by the greedy pursuit of equality into an agon of civil

---

scattered throughout *S/Z* (New York: Hill and Wang, 1974). See also Jonathan Culler's "Defining Narrative Units" in Roger Fowler, ed., *Style and Structure in Literature* (Oxford: Basil Blackwell, 1975), 123–42.

war leading to reaction. The *initial situation* on this plot level is described in Part 1 and the first two chapters of Part 2. Part 1 describes a petty class of greedy and inept politicians who stumble into a revolution and are sent packing by a mob of workers egged on by histrionic opportunists playing at revolution. The opening chapters of Part 2 complete this account of the initial situation by revealing the socialist "reality" behind the revolutionary theatrics of February. *The transformation* on the political level is contained in Chapters 3–10 of Part 2, which describes the polarization of the nation into a party of anarchy (workers and socialist theorists) and a party of order (aristocracy, bourgeoisie, peasants) leading to a civil war in which the victory of the party of order inaugurates a reaction against political liberty. The *consequent situation* on the political plot level is described in Part 3, where the futile efforts of Tocqueville and his friends to sustain a moderate republic include their implementation of further measures of reaction against political liberty.

Initial Situation. As we saw in our earlier discussion of the text's portraits of the bourgeoisie and its political leaders, the bourgeoisie's underlying greed and ineptitude become evident in the Banquet Affair, which was intended to be a libertarian reform campaign but instead generated a revolt that could not be controlled. Part 1 culminates in a vivid description of the revolutionary day of February 24 and the tumultuous scene in the Chamber, where a last attempt to save the monarchy by naming the Duchess of Orleans as Regent is thwarted by an invading mob. In order to indicate the reader's construction of the initial situation of the political plot, one must examine more closely this climactic scene along with the text's attempt to draw a moralizing conclusion to its account of February 24.

At the climax of the chaotic Chamber session of February 24, as the deputies debated whether to form a provisional government or vote in the Regency, a new wave of intruders poured onto the floor pushed ahead by two columns of armed men who "marched up onto the platform with a theatrical step, waving their flags and bawling out with much jerking and melodramatic gestures some revolutionary gibberish" (73/51). Sauzet, the Assembly president, declared the session over and put on his hat, which was the customary gesture for closure, but "with his knack of making the most tragic situations ridiculous, in his haste grabbed his secretary's hat and pulled it down over his eyes" (73/51). Meanwhile, Lamartine had managed to command silence long enough to begin an oration in favor of a republic, but before he could finish, the locked doors of the remaining galleries were suddenly smashed in and the balconies invaded by a mob, one of whom aimed a rifle at the president and speaker. The president murmured again that the sitting was over and "descended or rather slid onto the platform on which his chair stood. I saw him pass before my eyes a shapeless mass; I would never have believed that fear could so accelerate a fat body. . . . The remaining conservative deputies fled and the populace . . . jumped into their seats . . . crying "Take the places of the sell-outs!" (74/52).

The narrative is broken at this point, as Tocqueville turns the mirror on himself, still seated on his bench and strangely unmoved. The reason for his lack of emotion at the time, he believes, is the *form* taken by this revolt on February 24. Later in the course of the revolution he would see "two or three sights which had something of greatness about them" (*deux ou trois spectacles qui avaient de la grandeur*). The scenes before him on February 24 totally lacked *grandeur* because they "lacked truth." Instead they were acts of imitation in accord with the French, and especially Parisian, habit of mixing "literary and theatrical remembrances" with serious demonstrations. Unfortunately, in this case, "the imitation was so visible that the terrible originality of the facts remained hidden." Everybody's mind was so full of images of the first revolution that they "rather performed the French Revolution than continuing it" (75/53).

> Despite the naked swords, the bayonets and muskets, not for a moment could I persuade myself that I or anyone else was in mortal danger. . . . Bloodthirsty hatreds only came later; they had not had the time to be born; the peculiar spirit of the February Revolution had yet to show itself. Meanwhile, we sought without success to warm ourselves at our father's passions; we imitated their gestures and their poses as we had seen them in the theatre without being able to imitate their enthusiasm or feel their fury. A tradition of violent actions was being followed by frigid souls without being understood. Although I saw clearly that the denouement of the play would be terrible, I could never take the actors seriously; it all seemed a vile tragedy played by a provincial troupe. (75/53)

A little later, Lamartine tried to read the names of a provisional government above the noise of the crowd—"most of the names were acclaimed, some rejected by murmurs, others greeted with jokes, for in popular scenes as in Shakespeare's plays, the burlesque jostles the terrible" (76/54). After a while Lamartine began to be embarrassed at his position since "in a revolt as in a novel, what is most difficult to invent is the ending." But someone cried, "To the Hotel de Ville!" and off they all went. Tocqueville decided there was nothing more to be done and was about to leave when a column of National Guardsmen with fixed bayonets dashed into the hall, their leaders shouting, "Long live the Duchess of Orleans and the Regency" (77/56). Tocqueville himself now has trouble finding an ending. The ending he chooses is one of the few passages in the *Recollections* based on secondhand testimony. This ending recounts the fate of Odilon Barrot and Adolphe Thiers, the two politicians whose ambition and political misjudgment had done so much to bring about the revolution. Barrot is described to Tocqueville by a mutual friend as a man exhausted and beside himself who spent the entire day, often at the risk of his life, haranguing before the barricades in a vain attempt to save the monarchy. Thiers is described as fleeing from one neighborhood to another, out of his mind with fear and muttering disassociated lamentations. Tocqueville closes his account of February 24 as well as Part 1 of the *Recollections* with the remark that of the four who brought on the February Revolution, Louis-Philippe and Guizot were in exile and Barrot and Thiers half mad (80/58).

What is the effect of this ending to Part 1 on the reader's attempt to construe the narrative's initial condition and project a probable direction for the plot? It seems clear that the text sets out to tell a story that is serious, even tragic. Earlier passages in the text, quoted from Tocqueville's essay on the "Middle Class and the People" and his January speech warning of revolution, suggested the coming of a fundamental struggle over property that would shake society to its roots. Even in his ironic description of the February 24 invasion are reminders of "the terrible originality of the facts" behind the revolutionary theatrics, of the "tragic situation" that Sauzet renders ridiculous, and the "terrible denouement" which Tocqueville anticipates. And yet almost everything else about Part 1 undermines this seriousness with the result that the contrived moralism of Tocqueville's ending seems false. The portraits show everyone as morally unworthy and politically clumsy and the details in the scenes and tableaux of February 22–24 are either comic (Sauzet's hat), grotesque (representatives as greedy, snarling dogs pulled off the prey), or burlesque (the mob cheering, groaning, and wisecracking at Lamartine's list). Tocqueville's moral tableau at the end of Part 1 looks like a last-ditch attempt to turn his unruly text back into a cautionary tale, but his text keeps getting out of hand and dissolves moralism in satire and burlesque.

When we turn to Part 3, written three months later in Sorrento, the satiric tone has disappeared and the text opens with an analysis of the causes of the February Revolution from the perspective of the writer in 1850. Two things are happening to the reader here. On the one hand, the hiatus between Parts 1 and 2 is experienced as a major textual break between the narrative of the February Revolution in Part 1 and the narrative of the coming of the June civil war in Part 2. On the other hand, because the digression on the causes of February, which opens Part 2, begins to reveal "the terrible reality" behind the revolutionary theatrics of February 24, this chapter still constitutes part of the *initial situation* of the political narrative as a whole. Tocqueville says that the February Revolution was born of "general causes fertilized . . . by accidents." Among the causes, the two most significant for the reader's apprehension of narrative direction are: the "passion for material possessions" encouraged by the regime and infecting the workers, and socialist theories teaching that poverty results from "laws not providence." The "accidents" (secondary causes) include the clumsiness of the opposition, which wanted reform but produced a revolution, the excessive response to the riot, followed by the withdrawal of all force, and the "senile imbecility of Louis-Philippe" (84/63). As one might expect, the primary causes on this list also point forward to the June civil war, whereas the secondary causes or accidents only point back to February. In fact, this list of "accidents" provides a kind of summary of the selfishness, ineptitude, stupidity, and weakness catalogued in the portraits and tableaux of Part 1. The content of the list perfectly matches our analysis of the other signs of Part 1's satiric mode since, to borrow Hayden White's way of speaking, tragedy needs the metonymic order of cause and effect, but in Part 1 is subverted by satire which depends on the ironic discourse of accident, or, as the text puts it here in Part 2, this regime was not overthrown, it simply "fell" (83/61). With most of the reminder of Part 2, however, we will have an account of the coming of the "necessary and fateful" (178/165) civil war whose underlying causes are the same as those ascribed to February.

Chapter 2 of Part 2 begins with a description of the peacefulness and generosity of the common people of Paris in the first days following February 24 but quickly shifts to a long analytical digression on the second of the causes mentioned above: "It was socialist theories . . . which later on ignited real passions, embittered jealousies and finally stirred up the war between the classes" (95/74). After February 24, "a thousand strange systems" were proclaimed in pamphlets, speeches, newspapers and placards, all aiming at the elimination of one form or another of inequality. It was inevitable that "sooner or later the people . . . would discover that what kept them where they were was not the constitution of the government, but the immutable laws which constitute society itself. . . . And to speak of property in particular, . . . since all the privileges which covered . . . property had been destroyed, and property remained the main obstacle to equality among men, . . . was it not inevitable that the idea of abolishing it should occur to those who did not have any?" (96/75). In effect, the opening chapters of Part 2, by revealing the worker's materialist passions and acceptance of socialist theories, reach back over the satiric account of the revolutionary days of February to remind the reader of Tocqueville's earlier prediction of a class conflict over property, thereby completing the text's account of the initial situation to be transformed by the coming civil war of June.

Transformation. The text presents less a sequence of actions leading up to the June Days, however, than a series of *indices* concerning the antagonists and the social and moral values at stake.[11] As I pointed out in the discussion of the chronicle of 1848, events that other narratives make crucial steps in the coming of the worker's revolt (March 16–17, April 16) are ignored in the *Recollections.* The coming of the revolt is treated as if the underlying class conflict and moral qualities simply emerged of themselves over time. Thus the surface-level revolutionary theatrics of February 24 are depicted as giving way to an appearance of republican harmony in the first weeks after the revolt only to disappear in turn as real class interests and moral qualities begin to reassert themselves (99/78). If the approaching civil war is to be other than a cynical struggle between two greedy classes for material advantage, however, some new element must enter the narrative. This new ele-

11. On indices and their function see Barthes's "Introduction to the Structural Analysis of Narrative," *Image, Music, Text,* 92–97.

ment is provided by the pastoral interlude (Chapter 4) examined earlier. In the countryside the text finds uncorrupted peasants making common cause with their disinterested aristocratic landlord against the Parisian workers and their demagogic leaders. Thus, the pastoral chapter foreshadows the later coming together of all the worthy classes as a "party of order" which will save France from socialist anarchy. Moreover, we even find in Chapter 5 that under the threats and pressure of the Parisian workers, the "somber despair" of the bourgeoisie is gradually "turning into courage" (117/99).

At the same time that the text begins to rehabilitate the bourgeoisie in Chapter 5, however, it holds the revolutionary republican and socialist leaders up to sweeping ridicule, thus eliminating them as worthy dramatic characters and leaving the working class to stand alone against the combined forces of order (115/96). Tocqueville speaks of the coming battle between the haves and have nots as both inevitable and desirable: "I had always believed the February Revolution would not be stopped except all at once by a great battle fought in Paris . . . and that it would be best to seize the first opportunity to fight it" (117/99). By treating the June civil war as inevitable, however, the text relieves itself of showing *how* it came about. Thus, the next three chapters, dealing with Lamartine, the May 15 invasion of the Assembly and the May 21 Festival of Concord contain premonitions of the coming war but they do not mark new stages in the sequence of narrative actions. Nevertheless, they contribute to the reader's apprehension of plot through their tone and their indices of the social and moral values at stake.

The longest of these chapters is the wonderfully comic account of how the May 15 worker's attempt to force the Assembly to vote recognition of the Polish Republic completes the elimination of the revolutionary leaders from the story. As the shouting invaders, carrying red flags and the emblems of the Terror, packed the floor, the Assembly members sat silent and immobile. One after another of the club leaders, Raspail, Blanqui (looking like a "musty corpse"), Barbès (a cross between a "knight and a fool"), seized the podium and harangued the unresponsive Assembly, but no one could make the crowd of invaders quiet long enough for a vote (135–136/118–120). A fight broke out over the podium, a fireman in uniform won it but was struck dumb when he opened his mouth, Louis Blanc was carried around the hall "twisting and turning . . . [like] a snake having its tail pinched"

(137/121). Suddenly, the galleries cracked under the weight of the crowd and in the moment of silence that followed, the call to arms was heard in the distance. With cries of "we are betrayed," "to arms," "to the Hotel de Ville," the crowd began to disperse, but not before a club leader named Huber, who had just awakened from "a long epileptic fit," got onto the platform and shouted that the Assembly was dissolved. In the confusion that followed, Doctor Trélat, "a revolutionary of the sentimental type," approached Tocqueville to lament the event and the "madmen, real madmen who have brought this about! I have treated or prescribed for all of them . . . Blanqui is mad, Barbès is mad . . . Huber especially is mad" (139/122).

Not only do the elements Tocqueville selected for this tableau of May 15 contrast the "true" elected representatives of all France with the usurping Parisian mob and its demagogic leaders, but it sets up an implicit parallel with the text's earlier picture of February 24. There, the corrupt, conservative deputies of the old Assembly showed themselves doubly unworthy by their cowardly flight as the last wave of armed invaders arrived; here, the provincial notables of the new Assembly show their worth by courageously remaining seated in dignified silence amid the threatening revolutionary antics of May 15. There is also a contrast between the revolutionary histrionics on each occasion; February 24 was a "vile tragedy played by a provincial troupe," but May 15 is treated as pure buffoonery and burlesque. Once again the text has gotten out of hand and the predicted tragic agon over liberty/property is overwhelmed by exuberant satire. Although this satiric tone continues through the first half of the next chapter dealing with the incongruous Festival of Concord, signs of the coming agon return in the second half of that chapter to prepare us for the climactic moment of narrative transformation (146/130).

If these chapters leading up to the June Days are less a narrative sequence than a series of tableaux and indices, so are the two chapters (9 and 10) that recount the five days of actual fighting. A first set of indices emphasizes the class nature of the war and "the combination of greedy desires and false theories that engendered the insurrection and made it so formidable" (151/136). A second set concerns the determination and skill of the workers who "fought without a war cry, without leaders, without flags and yet with such marvelous coordination that it astonished the oldest officers" (151/136). Although the text has depicted particular workers as comic or depraved in keeping with classical stylistic rules, the indices of these two chapters on the civil war show little of the scorn or satire reserved for bourgeois politicians and social theorists. The world of domestic workers, however, is quite another matter, as indicated earlier in the discussion of the famous diptych of the drunken porter and the contented valet. The third set of indices, and the most natural ones for constructing a text dealing with a war, are those of worthy and unworthy leaders, courageous and cowardly fighters (166/152, 175/161). The act of courage that moved Tocqueville the most was the arrival from the provinces of men from all classes. Just before the end of Chapter 9, there is a lyrical passage on this human outpouring.

> By every route that the rebels did not control thousands of men . . . rushed to help us from all parts of France. . . . They belonged without distinction to all classes of society; among them were many peasants, many bourgeois, many great landowners and nobles, all intermingled in the same ranks. Irregularly and insufficiently armed, they threw themselves on Paris with unequalled ardor. (166/152)

So important for the narrative is the union of all classes that a similar passage recurs near the end of Chapter 10, emphasizing the presence of the aristocracy among this cohort: "The most obscure little squire from the backwaters and the elegant useless sons of the great houses all remembered that they had once formed part of a warlike ruling class" (177/164).

The account of the June civil war ends with a long commentary on the victory of the united forces of order and the *turn* this triumph produced in the larger story of 1848. The June Days "delivered the nation from oppression by the workers of Paris and restored it to itself" (178/165). Were the narrative to end here its plot would be that of a "romance" in Frye's sense, the triumph of good over evil, a moment of *grandeur* in which the hero, the morally worthy classes, would have saved France from "oppression" by the morally unworthy workers. Moreover, it would be a victory that, momentarily at least, had drawn all the other classes of society together, distracted the bourgeoisie from its materialist preoccupations, and revivified an aristocracy necessary to the vitality of the nation. But this celebration of the victory of order and *grandeur* over anarchy and greed is only momentary. "I realized at the time that the June fight was a necessary crisis but that afterwards the temper of the nation would in some way be changed." The text then makes a turn toward a denouement that renders the moment of victory especially hollow to the champion of liberty: "I, who detested the Montagnards and scarcely cared for the republic, but who adored freedom, I felt a great apprehension for it. . . . Love of independence would be replaced by fear and perhaps disgust for free institutions; after such an abuse of freedom such a reaction was inevitable" (178/165). Like many narrative turns, this one is described as inevitable; in the moral universe of the text, France, which has once again abused liberty, must pay for it by losing its liberties. In mid-paragraph, following the words just quoted, there is a shift of perspective from the recollected thoughts of the Tocqueville of 1848 to the reflections of the Tocqueville of March 1851 who has participated in that reaction and is now watching it from Sorrento, Italy, wondering if the retreat from liberty will not make 1848 a symbol of futility. "This movement of retreat began in effect after June 27th; at first it was very slow and invisible to the naked eye, then more rapid then impetuous and irresistible. Where will it end? I don't know. I think we shall find it difficult not to go back well behind the point we had achieved before February, and I foresee that all of us—socialists, Montagnards, republicans and liberals—will fall into the same discredit, until the particular recollections of the revolution of 1848 retreat and grow dim and the general spirit of the time regains its dominance" (178/165–66). This pessimistic prognosis, which ends the account of the June Days, forms a coda to the narrative of Part 2. Moreover, there is a sense in which the entire text of the *Recollections* has from the beginning been moving toward this moment given the prominence in the text's opening sections of Tocqueville's prediction of a revolutionary struggle over property. The fated conflict has come, the nation has survived, but victory for order and property has turned out to be a defeat for liberty. Yet the reader is not told enough about this defeat to make it a unit of narrative action. The Reaction and its likely continuation are merely predicted in a closing commentary.

Consequent Situation. Turning to Part 3 of the *Recollections,* the reader expects to find a narrative of the predicted reaction against liberty; instead, the text leaps over the year between June 1848 and June 1849 in order to recount the events of Tocqueville's five months as Minister of Foreign Affairs "while my memories are still fresh"

(196/185).[12] Although this ellipsis marks a transition in the focus of the narrative from external events to an account of Tocqueville's public role, it does include a brief report of the reaction predicted at the end of the account of June 1848. Part 3 opens with Tocqueville's precipitous return from a trip to Germany in May 1849 after receiving news of a crisis brought on by the election of a hundred and fifty Montagnards to an Assembly of over seven hundred members. The leaders of the conservative majority were terrified by their discovery that universal suffrage could go against them even this much, and decided that moderates of the stripe of Dufaure and Tocqueville were needed as part of the Barrot cabinet to help keep the Montagne faction under control. Once again the text shows everyone as unworthy; the Montagne members are treated as madmen of "savage temper" and the conservatives led by Thiers as cowardly self-seekers (201/191).

The major political action in the chronicle of this five months is the comically abortive revolt of June 13, 1849. The old Constituent Assembly, before dissolving in the spring of 1849, had passed a resolution forbidding French troops to attack the Roman Republic, but three days before Tocqueville and his friends were sworn in, Louis-Napoleon sent secret orders for an all-out attack on Rome in behalf of the restoration of papal government. This was a flagrant violation of the law and Ledru-Rollin of the Montagne faction called for impeachment of the president, and spoke of defending the Constitution "by arms" if necessary. Tocqueville had to reply for the government and though he had not known of the original decision to attack Rome nor did he approve it after the fact, vigorously defended it in what some thought was the best speech of his career (214–16/206–208). The demonstration and budding insurrection begun on June 13 were quickly extinguished and the Montagnard leaders were arrested or fled. "On the first occasion, the people led on more by appetite than opinion, had

12. Instead of ending with Chapter 10 Part II, the *Recollections* continues with an eleventh chapter devoted to the deliberations of the Assembly's committee which began drafting a new constitution in mid-May and ended its work just before the June fighting. Despite the fact that the story material of Chapter 11 is chronologically earlier than that of Chapters 9 and 10, it functions narratively as part of the third act of the political plot of 1848. The principle contribution of this chapter to the denouement of the political plot is that the work of the committee created the institutional framework for the conflict between Louis-Napoleon and the Assembly which becomes a central feature of Part III and its pessimistic tone matches the somber ending of the preceding account of the June Days.

fought alone, unable to induce their representatives to lead them. This time it was the representatives who could not induce the people to follow. In June 1848 the army had no leaders; in June 1849, the leaders had no army" (219/211). This ironic parallel with June 1848 reminds the reader that the turn toward repression adumbrated at the end of Part 2, has yet to work itself out in the text. The text finally returns to this aspect of its story by describing the accelerating demand of the Conservatives for additional measures of repression in the aftermath of June 13. If the Conservatives wanted order reestablished, Tocqueville writes, "we were their men, for we wanted the same as they, and we did it as well as they could desire and better than they could have done themselves" (224/219). After June 13, Lyon and several departments were put in a state of siege, six radical newspapers were suppressed in Paris, and many deputies arrested. But this new vigor did not satisfy the Conservatives who wanted to use the most recent victory "to impose repressive preventive laws." What follows next needs to be quoted in full:

> We ourselves felt the need to move in that direction although not wishing to go as far as they.
>
> For my part, I believed that it was wise and necessary to make great concessions to the terrors and legitimate resentments of the nation and that after such a violent revolution, the only way to save liberty was to restrict it. My colleagues agreed with me; accordingly we successively introduced a law to suspend the clubs; another to suppress the vagaries of the press with even more energy than had been used under the Monarchy; and a third to normalize the state of siege.(225/220)

The plight of liberty in the text of the *Recollections* is not only that the worker's revolt in June 1848 brought a reaction against liberty, but that in June 1849 a willing instrument of the Reaction was Tocqueville himself. In this passage on Tocqueville's sponsorship of further repressive measures, the two plot levels of the text come together. The political plot of excess liberty bringing an agon which leads to reaction finds in these passages the textual denouement of the turn against liberty announced at the end of Part 2. To fully appreciate the concurrent ironic turn on the self-portrait level, however, requires that one go back and trace the main narrative stages leading up to it.

Self-Portrait Level

On this level the plot of the *Recollections* tells the story of Tocqueville's transformation from a hesitant and marginal political figure into a confident and effective statesman. Of course, the major stages in this story are only part of the total self-portrait contained in the text's many indices of Tocqueville's character. Since my concern here is with narrative structure I will focus attention on Tocqueville's development as a political leader, but take note in passing of some of the text's other indices, notably those of aristocratic and libertarian identity.

Initial Situation. The initial situation of Tocqueville on the self-portrait level of the plot is that of an ambitious but somewhat marginal and diffident participant in French political life. Thus, the reader is not only told in the opening passages that Tocqueville lived "rather apart" in the parliamentary world of the July Monarchy but reminded in the account of the Banquet Affair of Tocqueville's aloofness and disdain for petty motives, and during the climactic scene of February 24, of how unmoved he was by the events before him. A small incident at the climactic moment on February 24 when the mob has prevented a vote on the Regency unintentionally indexes not only the marginality and futility of Tocqueville's actions, but also the powerful hold his aristocratic background had on him. Just after the passage on the theatricality of the revolutionary invasion, Tocqueville remarks that the only thing "which truly moved" him the entire day was the sight of the courageous Duchess of Orleans and her child. As he sat there amid the continuing uproar in the Chamber thinking of her "sad, gentle and firm looks," he felt so touched with pity that he suddenly jumped up and ran to find her.

> In an instant I pierced the crowd, cleared the lecture hall, ran down the coat room and found an open stairway to . . . the attics of the palace. A messenger I ran past told me I was on the track of the royal party . . . I went on and reached a landing; the noise of the footsteps ahead of me had just that moment stopped. I found a closed door in front of me, I knocked, it was not opened. Then I stopped, . . . astonished to find myself there; for, after all, I had no reason to attach myself to the fortunes of that family. They had offered me no kindness, nor even any sign of confidence. I viewed their arrival on the throne with regret, and if I

loyally helped to keep them there, it was in the public interest, not out of affection. Its only attraction in my eyes was that inspired by great misfortunes. If princes were like God who reads hearts and takes intentions for acts, surely they would have been grateful for what I wanted to do that day; but they will never know it, for no one saw me and I told no one.(76/54)

This tableau of Tocqueville before the door of royalty is surely one of the text's finest moments of mirror work, adding the author himself to that procession of distracted actors whose portraits and gestures line the narrative of the February Days. This noble woman and her child are the only sight that can move him, not just in the sense of touching his feelings, but can literally make him rise from his seat, bound up stairs and run down corridors. He can walk away in disdain from the heated political altercations of his closest friends (69/47); he can sit impassive as a mob invades the Assembly, a monarchy falls and a republic is proclaimed (75/53); but at the sight of this noble and courageous woman with her child he is on his feet. No doubt the text intends this tableau of Tocqueville standing outside the door ready for service as an example of noble disinterest. But for the twentieth-century reader, this spontaneous act of aristocratic generosity is likely to appear a beau geste that reveals both Tocqueville's practical ineffectiveness and the depth of his aristocratic loyalties.

The nadir of Tocqueville's disillusion, however, comes at the beginning of Part 2 in the text's account of his feelings on the afternoon of February 24 when he arrived home from the Chamber after the failure of the Regency. Tocqueville compares the pain he felt on the afternoon of February 24, 1848, with that he felt at the 1830 Revolution and the mirror of the text reveals him in a kind of double exposure.

1830

July 30th, at dawn on the exterior boulevards of Versailles, I saw the carriages of King Charles X, their emblem already scratched out, rolling slowing, in line, with a funeral air; at this spectacle I could not hold back my tears . . . I felt an hereditary affection for Charles X up to the end, but this King fell for having violated rights which were dear to me, and I hoped that the freedom of my country would be revived rather than extinguished by his fall.

1848

Today that freedom appeared dead; these princes who fled were nothing to me, but I felt my own cause was lost.

I had passed the most beautiful years of my youth in the midst of a society which seemed to become prosperous and great in becoming free; there I had conceived the idea of a moderate, regular freedom, restrained by beliefs, mores and laws; I had been touched by the charms of that freedom, it had become the passion of my whole life; I felt that nothing could console me for its loss . . . and I foresaw that the outcome . . . for us was a life miserably consumed by alternative reactions of license and oppression. (86–7/65)

Placed side by side these passages reveal a nostalgia for aristocratic rule and an anxiety over place yet, at same time, sound the theme of liberty with great pathos. Here, where Tocqueville's devotion to aristocracy and to liberty meet, we touch one of the affective cords of the *Recollections*. These indices of Tocqueville's marginality and ineffectiveness and the misery he felt during his parliamentary career are finally drawn together for the reader in an explicit self-examination at the end of Chapter 3, Part 2. Now, as he faces the decision of whether to seek a seat in the new democratic Assembly he reflects on the reasons for his previous unhappiness: "I lacked the qualities to play the brilliant role of which I dreamed" (102/81). He had hoped to be as successful an orator as he had been a writer but found that the talents of the writer hindered those of the speaker and he was regarded as "correct, sometimes profound, but always cold" (102/82). He was also hampered by his disdain of such "petty practices" as tactically supporting measures he did not believe in or cultivating the acquaintanceship of men whose aid he might one day need—he could not stand mediocrities and could not even remember their names from one day to the next. He hated cloakroom argument and walk-around politics where one must repeat the same case over and over, but above all, he was repelled by the "mediocrity and monotony of parliamentary events and the petty passions and vulgar perversity of the men who thought they were the parliamentary leaders" (103/83). This disgust with the egotism and mediocrity of his time had two results: on the one hand, "a morose isolation" which was increased by people mistaking his boredom and reserve for arrogance and, on the other hand, a discouragement and self-doubt resulting in a performance "far below the level of my natural ability" (104/83).

Transformation. The narrative transformation on the self-portrait level occurs in two stages. The first stage coincides with Tocqueville's decision at the end of the self-examination just cited to run for a seat in the new Assembly. In the days following the February Revolution, Tocqueville, to his surprise, had begun to discover in himself "a certain relief, a sort of joy, mixed with all the sadness and fears provoked by the revolution" (102/81). Although the new society was disorderly, "political skill was less necessary than disinterest and courage; character more important than the act of smooth talk or managing men." Above all, the issues were no longer petty and obscure but crucial and clear: "this way the salvation of the country; that way its destruction" (105/85). Thus, Tocqueville decided to throw himself into the arena and "devote to the defense, not of some government, but of the laws that constitute society itself, my fortune, my peace and my life" (105/85).

The transformation announced, the text loses no time in showing the new Tocqueville in action as Chapter 4 (the pastoral) describes his confident campaign in La Manche. Even on his return to the "sinister and frightening" atmosphere of Paris in Chapter 5, his confidence and activism continue. Tocqueville feels at home in the Constituent Assembly filled with new men since he is now part of a victorious majority whose aim he shares. Throughout the next four chapters, which lead up to and recount the June Days, Tocqueville is an active participant whether in his place in the Assembly or in the streets following the progress of the battle. In this central section of Part 2 the self-portrait level of the plot reaches a kind of plateau and recedes into the background as the text focuses on developments on the political level. Nevertheless, for the reader who has been alerted to the indices of Tocqueville's profound feeling regarding aristocracy (pursuit of Duchess of Orleans, tears for Charles X, moving adieu to the ancestral chateau in Chapter 4), there are additional markers in the chapters on the June Days. Not only was Tocqueville touched "with emotion" by the general phenomenon of the aristocracy coming together with the other classes to play a crucial role in the climactic June battle, but he was "moved to tears" by the arrival of his white-haired cousin, Le Peletier d'Aunay, armed only with "a small ceremonial sword" (167/153), and he closes his narrative of the June fighting with an invocation of the death of Chateaubriand "who perhaps best conserved the spirit of the old races" (177/164).

With the account of his five months as Minister of Foreign Affairs in Part 3, we come to the second and climactic stage in the narrative transformation on the self-portrait level. Although the Barrot cabinet formed in June 1849 was only a cabinet of expediency designed to keep the Montagne faction under control, Tocqueville did not hesitate to join it. The idea of "taking a post that so many feared to take and of rescuing society from its wretched situation flattered both my integrity and my pride" (202/193). The task of "saving the Republic," that is, of keeping it "regular, moderate and conservative" (202/192), was obviously going to be difficult since those who believed in the Republic "were incapable or unworthy of leading it" and those who could have "established and led it, hated it" (210/202). Unfortunately for Tocqueville and his moderate colleagues, the easy defeat of the June 13 insurrection and the arrest of many of the Montagne deputies meant the coalition cabinet was no longer needed as a buffer. The text now focuses on Tocqueville's efforts to keep the cabinet in power by buying Legitimist support, a policy that made him the cabinet's chief liaison to the Legitimist party, owing not only to his having proposed the alliance but also to his background. "I was a hundred times more at ease dealing with aristocrats whose interests and opinions were entirely different from mine than with the bourgeoisie whose ideas I shared and whose interests were similar to my own" (223/217). Yet Tocqueville is now ready to make concessions even to the bourgeoisie on what they desired most since the revolution had not destroyed their passion for government positions but only "made them hungrier" (226/221). Tocqueville also shows us in these passages how he learned to manipulate the leaders of the "rue de Poitiers" group by overwhelming them with deference and "asking them for advice, which I almost never took. . . . This trick was especially effective with M. Thiers" (237/233). If Tocqueville writes with relish of his success in handling Thiers and company or the run-of-the-mill bourgeois politician, he is no less satisfied with himself for his efforts to play upon Louis-Napoleon's ambition. Although clearly seeing Napoleon as "the greatest and most permanent of dangers," Tocqueville "hinted that if he governed France quietly, wisely and modestly . . . he might be re-elected despite Article 45" (230/225).

The mirror of the text lets us see a Tocqueville who has finally gained the ability he always lacked under the July Monarchy to cultivate those he does not agree with, manipulate opponents by flattery, give impassioned speeches from the floor on matters he does not believe in, and even remember the names of politically important mediocrities. Moreover, as the defender of a "moderate, conservative and constitutional" Republic who detests manipulative politicians, Tocqueville is not above "hinting" to Louis-Napoleon that a violation of the Constitution is all right in the circumstances. In short, the mirror reflects a Tocqueville who has been transformed into a politician and a rather shrewd one at that. Under the July Monarchy, Tocqueville had felt "discouraged and anxious in the presence of minor responsibilities." "I now felt a tranquility of spirit and peculiar calm faced by greater ones, . . . Previously the idea of a setback had seemed unbearable; now the prospect of a crashing fall in one of the greatest theatres of the world did not trouble me at all, which made me realize I was more proud than timid" (235/231). At last Tocqueville has come face-to-face with *grandeur* and this experience "emboldened me for the rest of my life," giving "perhaps the greatest good in this world, confidence in myself" (236/232).

Consequent Situation. On a first reading the long final chapter recounting Tocqueville's views and actions as Minister of Foreign Affairs strikes one as anticlimactic. Yet careful attention to these pages in the light of the initial situation and transformation already established by the text will add an important confirmation and a surprising conclusion to the self-portrait plot level. It is clear that Tocqueville faced the same dilemma in foreign affairs as at home: how to steer a middle course between absolute monarchy and republican excess and how to join in the Reaction without denying "the principles of our Revolution, liberty, equality, clemency" (243/240). The text scores the selfish and cowardly behavior of the German revolutionaries as well as the abuses of the Prussian victors whose summary executions, suspension of liberties, and attempts to dominate the monarchic government of Baden it had just restored drew a letter of protest from Tocqueville (244/242). The other case where Tocqueville at least used diplomatic pressure to forestall a reaction worse than return of the status quo, was Piedmont where the Austrians' victory at Novara left the Piedmontese at their mercy. Tocqueville, convinced that "Piedmont was too close to us for us to allow her to lose the independence that kept her separate from Austria, or to relinquish the new-found constitutional institutions that linked her to us," got the Cabinet and

President to agree on a stern communique backed by threat of force and the Austrians softened their demands (251/250).

In these instances we cannot tell whether the defense of liberty or French "sphere of influence" concerns are uppermost to the author. In the handling of the Swiss and Turkish refugee affairs, on the other hand, Tocqueville's verbal commitment to constitutionalism and liberty clearly seem of less concern than propitiating the reactionary powers. The success of the armies of repression had led thousands of refugees to pour into Switzerland from all over Europe, and when the Swiss granted them asylum, Prussia, Austria, and Russian threatened to invade. Tocqueville convinced the reactionary regimes to join France in denying admission to all refugees so that they could not emigrate to England or America and the Swiss, we are told, faced with the care and feeding of some twelve thousand "adventurers," suddenly discovered "the drawbacks of the right of asylum" and expelled the refugees (245–46/243–44). Even in the crisis provoked by the sultan's having granted asylum to Dembinski and Kossuth and the tsar's subsequent threat to invade the Ottoman Empire if they were not expelled, Tocqueville's attitude was not favorable to asylum. Tocqueville instructed his Russian ambassador to assure the tsar of France's peaceful intention and ask if "Kossuth's skin" was really "worth a general war?" To almost everyone's astonishment the "great Emperor retreated" and the French, thanks in part to Tocqueville's cynical treatment of the right of asylum, received credit for having shown greater diplomacy in the affair than the British. "Just as we learned of the end of this dangerous quarrel, the Cabinet, which had thus seen a happy ending to the two external problems that menaced the peace of the world, the Piedmontese and Hungarian wars, was itself about to fall" (263/262). With these lines the text of the *Recollections* comes to an end.

Reversals

How does the reader understand the overall ordering of narrative episodes in the *Recollections*? Although "unfinished" and lacking any final commentary, the text itself offers explicit clues as to how Tocqueville wishes it to be read. Thus, on the political level, the turn to reaction after June is called not only "inevitable" but also a "just resentment" of the nation after such an "abuse" of freedom. And on the self-portrait level, Tocqueville's sponsoring of repressive measures and his use of manipulation in domestic and foreign affairs is treated as part of his personal triumph over pride and self-doubt. Yet the reader cannot help noticing certain structural and indexical features that suggest a reversal rather than the simple moral progression described in the text's self-interpretation.

On the political level of the plot there is, of course, an obvious reversal. The opening pages of the *Recollections* foretell the story of a fundamental struggle over the order of society in the name of equality and liberty, but when the victory of ordered liberty finally comes, the text announces a reaction against liberty destined to set the nation back behind where it had arrived before 1848. Although it does not narratively develop the theme of reaction immediately after its account of the June victory, the political history in Part 3 of the text does confirm it with the references to the repressive measures taken by the Cabinet after June 13, 1849. A more subtle reversal also occurs in Part 3 when the victorious party of order is described as coming apart in an ironic return to the pettiness and greed characteristic of the bourgeois July monarchy.

On the self-portrait level the reader may also discern a reversal, one that coincides with the political denouement of the repression of liberty. Thus, when the Barrot cabinet curtails freedom of assembly and of the press "with even more energy than . . . under the July monarchy," Tocqueville's earlier prediction of a retreat from freedom going back "well behind the point we had achieved before February," is fulfilled in his own text and in part by his own actions. From the one who earlier writes "I . . . who adored liberty" (178/165), we now have "the only way to save liberty was to restrict it" (225/220). Nor, is the severity of the measures adopted after June 13 something reluctantly agreed to by Tocqueville; it was his own idea ("My colleagues agreed with me"). The prose in this passage is clipped and vigorous, moving without hesitation or qualification—except to suggest that the conservatives wanted even more repression. Finally, as confirmation of Tocqueville's willingness to compromise political liberties, we have his ambiguous performance as foreign minister vis-à-vis the reactionary powers and the defeated revolutionaries' right of asylum.

Whether this reversal in Tocqueville's commitment to liberty is to be understood as tragic or ironic is more difficult to say. Some readers, who share Tocqueville's social and economic conservatism or who hold a deterministic view of class, may be inclined to take the text at face value on both its plot levels. Whether one ideologically agrees with Tocqueville or sees his liberalism as a mere cover for class interest, however, that such repressive measures are proposed by the same pen that has just proclaimed the love of liberty must at least tempt one to an ironic reading. Moreover, there remains for all readers the final reversal of the text, the fall of the cabinet and with it the failure of Tocqueville's high hopes of keeping a moderate and liberal Republic going. He has made common cause with the bourgeoisie whom he despised, assisted in the suppression of liberties he adored, flattered Louis-Napoleon's ambition to subvert the Constitution, and, having risked all this to "save" the nation, falls from power after only a few months with the fundamental domestic conflict no closer to resolution than before. Not only does this fall cast its shadow back over the entire narrative on both the biographical and political levels, but the informed reader cannot help thinking of the fall of the Second Republic itself which came just a month after Tocqueville wrote his final sentence. In the Napoleonic coup of December 2, 1851, the entire effort of 1848 is reversed and Tocqueville's earlier prediction of the "same discredit" descending on all parties and all actors alike comes true.

It is one thing to argue that the reader inevitably looks for closure in narrative; it is quite another to suggest this closure takes the form of "naming" plot types. One of the reasons for the reader's uneasiness in naming the plot of the *Recollections* is not only that literary theory lacks agreement on the basic criteria for a typology of plots, but also that we are all too aware of the deep layer of cultural accretions surrounding traditional terms like tragedy, satire, and so on. Although this accumulation of connotations would seem to demand an effort at rigorous definition and systematization, to the extent such an effort succeeded, the resulting matrix would be correspondingly remote from the rich associations that readers intend in their intuitive nomination of a narrative as tragic or satiric. Plot categories are not only terms of analysis but names of traditional story forms so deeply rooted in culture that they are part of almost everyone's literary competence. Considered from the point of view of literary competence, a particular shape such as tragedy must be regarded as a general set of expectations which can range from the mere recognition of misfortune and fatality to the application of a complex set of rules. As readers we are not forced to claim that Tocqueville intended his narrative to have a tragic or satiric shape, or that each reader simply imposes a designation on it. Rather, our naming is motivated by the resonance of the text's narrative order and indices with a shared cultural tradition.

Although I have been able to indicate some lineaments of a tragic plot on the political level, even the tragic structure of the narrative seems tinged with irony since it is the noble aim that is reversed at the moment of success. Along the way, moreover, this story constantly threatens to turn from ironic tragedy into pure irony as the satiric moments of the text show almost everyone to be unworthy of the drama in which they are playing. The self-portrait level of the plot, on the other hand, shows Tocqueville as a moral type of the man of integrity, one of a handful of individuals ready for disinterested service to the cause of liberty and greatness. Although he and his friends failed on the stage of history, the text implies that the secret mirror of the *Recollections* is there to reflect their true historical worth. Yet the reader can see in the multiple reflections of the text the extent to which Tocqueville and his friends "fall" into both the Reaction and the manipulations of conventional politics. If the main story-line can be read as an ironic tragedy, the secondary story-line seems to end in tragic irony. And the reader's knowledge of the Napoleonic coup, which briefly landed Tocqueville himself in prison just a month after finishing the *Recollections,* intensifies the sense of irony as one reads a text whose author could not know it as he wrote.

Which way is it, then, in the last analysis? Irony dominating tragedy or tragedy dominating irony? On the basis of what Tocqueville writes elsewhere, it would be hard to place him in the camp of the ironists of history; his total historical vision and deepest convictions as a constitutional liberal and moralist are certainly more compatible with the tragic sense of existence. But his text, this particular text, is not so clear. It seems to *intend* a story rooted in universal moral law, a cautionary tale of human excess and chastisement; but in the process of writing, another spirit asserts itself and steadily undermines this morality play. Satire and comedy take the center of the stage; greedy desire and revolutionary romanticism rear their heads everywhere and mock the gestures of *grandeur* which appear as theatrical when executed by aristocrats as by the people.

Plot versus Genre

This tension between the tragic and ironic dimensions of the *Recollections'* narrative shape is not the only complication in its diachronic development. The reader's difficulty in finding a coherent plot in the *Recollections'* narrative is one sign of the residual validity of the fact/fiction distinction. The "plot effects" to which we have called attention are not, after all, intended by the author in the strong sense we might expect in a work of fiction, nor are they consciously sought for on the part of the reader. They are secondary effects brought about by the reader's intrinsic relation to time and narrative.[13] Although the memoir conventions permitted Tocqueville to omit a greater part of the story of 1848 than he could have allowed himself in a continuous history, the text is, nevertheless, a history of 1848 in the sense that it can select by omission or at points eschew chronology in presentation, but it cannot invent episodes or conjure evidence. Moreover, the reader is told at the beginning of the text that the device of the secret mirror will reflect truth in spontaneity rather than through a literary construction, thereby further disarming the readers' expectation of literary effects. By seeking out the plot effects that work covertly on the reader, I have had to deliberately subvert normal genre conventions for "factual" works in order to bring forward the autonomy of writing.

But this subversion of normal genre conventions points to the most serious objection to a structural and typological analysis of the "plot" of a memoir, namely, the argument that the genre conventions for nonfiction texts like memoirs (and, a fortiori, for history) are such that our discovery of plot structures—and plot types—is simply the result of having gone looking for them rather than a natural emergence in the reading process. This is a particularly serious objection since it is grounded in the *experience of reading,* which I have taken as one of my methodological guides. The *Recollections,* by its title and reputation, the character of its opening paragraphs, the early portraits and aphorisms, clearly announces itself as a *memoir* and arouses in the reader the expectations of informality that go with the memoir genre designa-

13. On temporality as the root of the narrative impulse see Paul Ricoeur's *Time and Narrative* (Chicago: University of Chicago Press, 1983), 52f.

tion. But it is the lack of a continuous narrative that makes an analysis of the text purely in terms of the memoir genre seem most compelling. The omission or mere mention of otherwise important events, the hiatus of an entire year in order to get on with an account of Tocqueville's time in the cabinet, the generally episodic texture and the wide durational variations of the text compared to a narrative history like Duveau's—all these appear as perfectly normal phenomena if we read the *Recollections* strictly as a memoir. The *Recollections'* only principle of unity in this view is its genre: as a memoir it is an account of what one person saw, thought, and did during the Revolution of 1848. In Aristotle's terms, the *Recollections* possesses only the lowest form of literary unity, the form common to epic (episodes unified by having the same character) and to history (episodes unified by occurring in the same time period).

Nevertheless I believe we can legitimately look for plot *effects* on the reader despite these genre expectations. The memoir effects are those of a first reading, shaping one's initial impression of the text. The *Recollections is* a memoir and one cannot forget that. But it is also, by virtue of its chronological ordering of episodes and its narrative devices, a story that betrays the form of plotting. These plot traces (initial situation, transformation, consequent situation) are the matter that the readerly desire for coherence begins to order. Out of the shaped but open possibilities of the text's episodic embodiment of the events of the Revolution and of Tocqueville's public life, the reader seeks a consonance. Hence, even a paragraph or a sentence of the text can come to have great weight. Such an element is the announcement of a turn to reaction at the end of the June Days, or the paragraph on Tocqueville's advocay of repressive measures, or the final sentence of the text as a whole: "and the cabinet was about to fall."[14] Nevertheless, neither this final trace of irony at the end of the text nor the tragic-ironic closing lines of the account of the June Days provide the reader with a

---

14. As Victor Shklovsky argued long ago about the picaresque novel, an episodic text can receive its meaning either from a final chapter or from a sentence describing some natural phenomenon, say an indifferent sky, which synecdochically sums up the entire work. Had Tocqueville chosen to complete his text with a projected fifth chapter on the Roman affair, he might have given us a "final" commentary or at least another paragraph like the ironic turn at the end of the June Days. As it is, this text ends with a "fall." "La Construction de la nouvelle et du roman," in *Théorie de la littérature*, ed. Tzvetan Todorov (Paris: Éditions du Seuil, 1975), 176–77.

definitive clue to the meaning of the text. There is too much else going on, too many satiric portraits and comic dilations, too many levels of reflection and commentary, too much of an episodic texture. Thus the tension between tragic structure and ironic mode in the text is complicated by a second tension between the expectations of episodic structure aroused by the text's indices of the memoir genre and the plot effects generated by its indices of narrative coherence. One can deny this tension in behalf of a purely memoirist reading only by "naturalizing" the memoir genre conventions and treating them as natural kinds whose boundaries are inviolable. In terms of plot Tocqueville's text remains a texture of discordances which the reader continually tries in vain to reduce to a single form of concordance.[15]

15. The term is Frank Kermode's in *The Sense of an Ending* (New York: Oxford University Press, 1967), 18. It becomes central to Ricoeur's discussion in *Time and Narrative*, 42–51.

4

CODE

In the preceding analysis of genre and plot in the *Recollections,* I have constantly referred to an implicit set of moral polarities. The pictorial and thematic codes I will now investigate are those of *this* text and not a system of ideas put together from a comparative study of various works of Tocqueville. The traditional procedures of the history of ideas come so naturally that any difficulty in comprehending a text like the *Recollections* immediately tempts us to compare passages from it with Tocqueville's other books, letters, and speeches in an effort to arrive at his "view" on a particular issue. This procedure is premature and one-sided, because it undervalues the relative autonomy of writing by lifting out terms for comparison before facing the complexity of the text itself. By examining pictorial and thematic codes, I will try to uncover the systematic set of constraints *within* the text which governs the way events are depicted and named.

The term *code* has a broad range of meanings in semiotics, and here its more general usage is intended.[1] A code is simply the set of elements employed in a particular area of practice in order to signify. The semiotician is not initially interested in what the code refers to or in its origins but in the *interrelations* of the set of terms composing it. From a semiotic point of view, for example, clothing constitutes a code by

1. Umberto Eco, *Semiotics and the Philosophy of Language* (Bloomington: Indiana University Press, 1984), 164–85. I have chosen to restrict the meaning of "code" here to the pictorial and thematic system of the *Recollections,* even though a wider usage is possible according to which one could speak of "codes" for genre, plot, and voice as well.

78

virtue of the differences among sets of items, for example, dark suit + white shirt + tie versus slacks + open shirt + sweater versus jeans + T-shirt. These and other combinations form a set of relations which can signify by virtue of conventional uses. Thus to wear a certain combination in the "wrong" setting can signify nonconformity, boorishness, insult; just as wearing the "right" combination can signify conformity, social sophistication, or compliment. One code can be employed within another, for example, clothing codes are normally nonverbal, but they can be used as part of a verbal code—white collar versus blue collar. In the case of the *Recollections* I consider first a few aspects of the cultural code that guides the visual descriptions of persons and events in the text. This prepares the way for a more systematic examination of the set of thematic elements from which the text is constructed, focusing on the pattern of binary oppositions that appear to constrain what the text is able to say.

Blanqui's Linen

In the *Recollections* Tocqueville reports that he spent a great deal of his time walking the streets of Paris simply observing and reflecting. Of course, he did this with a "serious" purpose and makes it a maxim "to always be in the seat where he belongs" when the Assembly is in session (70/48). Yet in the Assembly on days of crisis the text shows him as more often an observer than an actor in the dramas that take place there. He notices everything; the clothes, the gestures, the emotions, the symbols and echoes of tradition and ideology. As he says in a comment on his encounter during June with an enraged old woman and her cart, in times of violent crisis there are actions having no direct relation to politics which take on an aspect of disorder and anger "which does not escape the attentive eye and is a sure sign of the general state of mind" (160/145). Such general reflections are the discursive point of Tocqueville's deeply ocular relation to history in the *Recollections*. Tocqueville is no *flâneur*, in the *Recollections*, sauntering the streets of Paris in detached amusement, but is a secret mirror that captures the moral likeness of everything it turns on.

This mirror of recollection not only produces the dramatic *tableaux* and portraits already discussed but also *tableaux* in the more usual sense of pictures as scenes. T. J. Clark's penetrating questions and discoveries about the art of 1848 help us see some of Tocqueville's verbal pictures in a new light. Two things from Clark's study are especially appropriate to the *Recollections:* the question of the image of the Republic and the problem of representing the new forces of politics, the workers and peasants. Numerous artists greeted February with enthusiasm, high hopes, and a call for an end to individualism, for democratization of state patronage and salon juries, for an "art of the Republic." One result of this agitation in the art world was a state competition for an image of the Republic, a competition that turned out to be a fiasco since, by the time the competition had run its course, the Republic had "careened through the days of June" and into the time of reaction.[2] Even attempts to represent so specific a matter as the barricades take a strange form; pictures of it seldom show a real barrier but only a scattered pile of stones and timbers, a kind of stage on which symbolic figures can play their part. The finest painting of the barricades, done by Meissonier in 1849, is a stark depiction of silence and death, a dark, empty street, a low pile of paving stones and a dozen twisted bodies.[3]

If one compares this kind of realism with Tocqueville's description of the barricades, one can see what cool detachment his observing eye could guard. On the second day of fighting, driven by "an acute curiosity," he set out to see the battle for himself. "I found traces of the battle . . . from the Port Saint-Denis on; there one walked amid the debris of the retreating insurrection: broken windows, shattered doors, houses pocked by bullets or pierced by shells, trees cut down, paving stones piled up, and behind them, straw mixed with blood and mud, such were the sad vestiges" (171/158). In this description of a landscape without people, focusing on material damage, there is anonymity and the most banal of sentiments ("sad vestiges"). Finally, Tocqueville arrives at a street where his friend General Lamorcière is directing a mop-up operation; the reader gets a description of real fighting and death: "The men who were hit in front of me seemed pierced by an invisible shaft; they swayed and fell without one being able to see anything more than a little hole in their clothes; whenever I

2. T. J. Clark, *The Absolute Bourgeois: Artists and Politics in France, 1848–1851* (Princeton, N.J.: Princeton University Press, 1973), 31–71.

3. Ibid., 28–29. On the barricade in the French revolutionary tradition see also Georges Duveau's *1848: The Making of a Revolution* (New York: Random House, 1966), 161–81.

saw occurrences of this kind, it was less the sight of physical pain than the *tableau* of moral anguish which struck me. It was a strange thing, in effect, and frightening to suddenly see faces change and the fire of the eye go out in the terror of death" (173/159). The discourse is distanced and remarkably calm. Although fear is mentioned, the language itself is that of an observer moved, if at all, only by the disappearance of the function of sight. Even the "terror of death" is a rather conventional metaphor. We do not hear the crack of gunfire, the cry of pain, the rattle of death; we see only a little hole and a look of surprise as the fire of vision goes out.[4] The entire experience is ocular and estranged: "a *tableau* of moral anguish." At the beginning of his account of the June Days, Tocqueville writes with admiration of the careful workmanship of the barricade builders who went about their task "with the methodical skill of engineers, not taking up more paving stones than were needed . . . for a tidy wall" (153/138). Near evening of the day he made the observations on death just considered, he saw these same barricades: "As I passed by the little streets at the entry of which, the day before, I had seen such solid and neat barricades constructed, I now saw that the cannon had disarranged these pretty works, but one could see the traces" (176/163). "Pretty works" have merely been "disarranged"; now the text does not even mention the bloody straw to remind us of the hatred and desperation of the real fighting of June. Tocqueville's barricade, like those of the painters of 1848, has also become a stage, but an empty one where order has banished anarchy from the scene.

In one sense the absence of actual workers from the text's account of the fighting is only natural; in war one seldom sees the enemy. But it is not only at the end of the fighting that the workers are anonymous and all but invisible. They are seldom personally or concretely present anywhere in this text which, nevertheless, makes their revolt its central action. As Tocqueville put it in the account of his conversation with George Sand: "It was the first time I had a direct and intimate contact with someone who could and would tell me some of what was happening in the camp of our adversaries. One side never knows the other:

---

4. A painting in the Musée Carnavalet depicts the kind of moment Tocqueville describes. One sees a soldier with his body bent back, about to drop his rifle—we have to look a moment to find the little hole where the bullet entered his chest. The painting is reproduced on the cover of the Larousse pictorial history of France, *L'Histoire de France* 24 (June 1984).

they approach, they press, they grasp each other, they do not see each other" (150/135). Although few painters "gave faces to the People in the nineteenth century," according to Clark, there were Daumier's paintings of saltimbanques, Millet's depictions of peasant workers, and, of course, Courbet's *Burial at Ornans,* which looks straight at peasants and the bourgeoisie with a steady realism that outraged the right and discomforted the center.[5] In the *Recollections* one might have expected to see some real peasants; after all, Tocqueville's chateau was in their midst and he collected rents from them. But the only picture of peasants is the grand pastoral tableau of election day at the end of Chapter 4 of Part 2. We are shown the peasants beloved of bourgeois and Legitimist myth in 1848, filled with affection for the great lord who leads them, hanging on his words and obeying his directions. Yet they are completely anonymous in the text's description of them. Neither there nor anywhere in the pastoral chapter are we given a portrait of a peasant type or even a description of their problems and aspirations. The text ignores the great battle for the countryside that was actually going on as Tocqueville wrote in 1850, a struggle that belied the myth of the contented and conservative peasant.[6]

But it is the workers who are the focus of the *Recollections'* story in 1848–49. I have already noted that in keeping with the aesthetics of classical poetics the text often treats workers as comic or burlesque—or as menacing when aroused by greed and envy. In either case they are socially too low for either tragedy or satire. But what kind of visual representations does the text give us? We see workers on three occasions: during the days of the February Revolution, during the May 15 invasion of the Assembly, and during the June civil war. It would not be an exaggeration to say that Tocqueville never "saw" the Parisian worker unless the latter forced him to look, by either an attack or a threat. In February when the people invade the Assembly and prevent

5. Clark, *The Absolute Bourgeois,* 29. On Courbet see the second volume of T. J. Clark's study of painting and the Revolution of 1848, *Image of the People: Gustave Courbet and the 1848 Revolution* (Princeton, N.J.: Princeton University Press, 1973), 77–102.

6. The closest the text comes is its comment, in ridiculing the radical republicans for their stupidities, that they missed a great opportunity in not exploiting peasant resentment of bourgois bankers and moneylenders who constantly threatened their property (116/97). This is one of the many places where Tocqueville's and Marx's observations on 1848 agree in detail despite their opposed political views.

the naming of the Duchess of Orleans as Regent, the text shows us little about their appearance. They are armed and shout revolutionary slogans, but Tocqueville says he never felt anyone was in mortal danger and he can enjoy the Shakespearean jostling of the terrible and the burlesque when they shout their approval or emit groans of protest and wisecracks as the names of the Provisional Government are read.[7]

The invasion of the Assembly on May 15 was more frightening than February 24, and the text shows a greater interest in picturing "the people," though the language remains rather general, concentrating on the intentionality one could read from their faces. The text also gives a curious attention to their clothes.

> Their looks were astonished and ill-natured rather than hostile; with many a sort of gross curiosity dominated all other sentiments, since, even in our bloodiest revolts, there are always a multitude of half rogues, half gapers who think they are at the theatre. . . . I saw some drunks among them, but most seemed merely in the grip of a feverish excitement produced by the pressure and the cries from outside, the stuffiness, the crowding . . . ; they were dripping with sweat, although the nature of their clothes should not have made the heat uncomfortable, since many were very loosely clad. (134/117)

Tocqueville also noticed at this time that "the spirit of the people can receive and reflect images with great vividness and clarity" and recounts the comparison, made by "a man in a smock" between the Dominican, Lacordaire, and a vulture, owing to the way Lacordaire's long neck stuck out from the cowl of his habit. The description of May 15 also includes portraits of two individuals from "the people" who seize the podium; one is the comic incident of the fireman in his hat who demands to speak but is struck dumb, the other the description of the appearance of the revolutionary, Louis-Auguste Blanqui. The description of Blanqui is so malevolently vivid, that its crucial lines bear quoting in full: "his cheeks were withered and sunken, the lips white, a

---

7. Although the text tells us Tocqueville spent all his time on the first day after the revolution in the streets mingling with the "victors," it adds that he did not speak to them but only watched and listened. Even then his purely specular approach produces no tableau but only a general reference to the sight of the "have nots" guarding public buildings. And when he says, "I knew the common people well enough," it does not lead to a picture but to an ironic generalization about the workers' code of honor for days of revolution which allowed destruction and killing but not theft (93/72).

sickly, malign, foul look, a dirty pallor, the appearance of a musty
corpse, no linen visible, an old black frockcoat clung to his thin and
emaciated limbs, he seemed to have lived in a sewer and just emerged"
(135/118) The adjectival excess and reduncancy here is unlike
Tocqueville's normal style and gives credence to his claim that the
memory of Blanqui continued to fill him with "disgust and horror."
Here we certainly have vivid stylistic evidence of the linkage, in the
feelings of the well off, between the *classes laborieuses* and *classes
dangereuses*. T. J. Clark quotes Tocqueville's description of Blanqui to
illustrate his point that "when blindness is breached by extreme circumstances the result is pathos" and suggests that Tocqueville's little
picture of Blanqui is a "prejudice which clearly believes itself to be
description."[8] That there is prejudice in Tocqueville's depiction of the
working class is obvious, but the question one needs to ask about the
text is not simply whether Tocqueville was accurate, but whether there
is a visual code at work here which informs both his seeing and his
discourse.[9] Tocqueville was finally being forced to look at "the people,
proper, that is, those classes that work with their hands" (91/70), and
one of the more striking things about his descriptions is the frequent
notation of the workers' costume, especially the blue smocks and the
absence of "linen" (which meant both "white" shirt and under-
clothing generally).[10] The only other pictorial descriptions of workers
come in the account of the June Days and also make a textual mark
beside costume. "I encountered, at the opening of the rue Saint-Honoré, a crowd of workers who listened anxiously to the canon . . . all in
smocks, which for them, as everyone knows, are their fighting clothes
as well as their working clothes" (157/142). A little later we read:
"everywhere groups of workers in smocks listened to the call to arms

8. Clark, *The Absolute Bourgois*, 16.

9. There may be more visual truth than we might imagine in Tocqueville's report on
Blanqui, who had been rotting in a dank fortress for eight years and had been out of
prison for only about two months as of May 1848. Samuel Bernstein, in *Auguste
Blanqui and the Art of Insurrection* (London: Lawrence and Wishart, 1971), describes
Blanqui's appearance on returning to Paris after February 24, as thin, emaciated, and
"jail blanched" (137-59).

10. The emphasis on "linen" is a bid odd. Where were these people supposed to
acquire linen and the habit of wearing it? Compare the passage in which Tocqueville
describes how his friend Corcelle, on the day the barricades went up, was stopped and
forced to assist by the workers who noted his "black suit with a very white shirt" (*au
linge très blanc*) (153/139).

and the cannon, with a sinister air" (159/145). Amid the "disgust and horror" aroused by the memory of Blanqui's corpselike appearance there is also time to note that he bore "no visible linen." It is as if forced for the first time to look at workers, the eye has trouble getting beyond the costume, the mere index.

But there is something besides costume in these pictures: the look. The text describes the curious looks on the faces of the invaders of May 15, the look of joy on the faces of the group on the rue Saint-Honoré at the progress of the insurrection and in a later, more general observation, it marks the workers' "sinister air." Although these are still determinations from a middle instance, the text does offer three moments when Tocqueville comes face-to-face with "the people." The first is his encounter with the porter, that "socialist by birth," who had boasted of killing him. Tocqueville, pistols in his pockets, "looked him in the white of the eye" and ordered him to go ahead, lighting the way. Only at the end of the little story do we see the porter's face again as he finally decides to lift his hat (170/156). Then, of course, the text introduces the "contented face" of Eugène, even quotes the valet's responses to his master's question, the only "worker" we hear from in the text apart from the one who wants to wring Lacordaire's vulturelike neck.[11] Although domestic servants are a special case, we know from numerous writings of the nineteenth century that they too are often as invisible to their masters as the anonymous wearers of the blue smocks. Only the revolt of the workers makes either the porter or the valet catch Tocqueville's eye and receive a brief portrait in the text. But there is one other face-to-face encounter in the text. Tocqueville, on his way into the Assembly during the June fighting was blocked by an old woman with a vegetable cart and when he ordered her aside she suddenly rushed him "with such a frenzy that I had trouble defending myself. I was horrified at the hideous and terrible expression on her face where the demagogic passions and the fury of the civil war were vividly painted" (160/145). This is the closest Tocqueville ever approaches the lower classes in the text.

What ideas and conventions of representation determine these pic-

---

11. There is one other "good" worker in the text, Corbon, who had been appointed to the Constitutional Commission ("for they put workers on everything then"). Despite the ironic tone, Tocqueville not only grants that Corbon had a sound mind and firm character but tells how the other members of the committee gave him the dirty work of telling the committee chairman, Cormenin, they wanted his resignation (193/182).

tures of workers in the text? The ideas are not hard to find; the text offers them up like Homeric epithets on numerous occasions when it mentions the people or the workers: "ridiculous socialist theories" combined with "greed" and "envy." The "people" *are* seen in this text but they are seen in a mirror that can reflect only a moral or political distortion of their appearance. Tocqueville was an attentive observer, a man of great curiosity, but he had a particular set of prejudices when it came to workers just as he had when it came to the bourgeoisie. Even so, he lived and worked with the bourgeoisie every day, and if he gives no quarter in his satiric treatment of them, nevertheless, we feel his pictures are caricatures rather than stereotypes. Not so the pictures of workers. Finally constrained to look at them in 1848, Tocqueville resorts to the most conventional images and types. When the "people" are not playing their traditional stage role as figures of comedy or burlesque, they are pictured as either the contented and obedient servant or the greedy and rebellious workman, the one ready to die for his master, the other ready to kill him and take his place. Just as the dramatic *tableaux* of gestures give us moral types, the pictorial *tableaux* of the lower classes give us stereotypes. Although the text of the *Recollections* is the record of remembered observations, this visuality does not have a sensuous, intimate quality but is almost always depiction from a distance. There is neither the evocative concreteness of romantic prose nor the careful discrimination of realist description. The specific detail (costume, look) is cited less for itself than as an *index*. Only in some of the text's more excessive satiric or emotional moments does it permit itself to pile up details that serve no immediate indexical purpose. Here again the *Recollections* turns out not only to contain a series of *tableaux* in a gallery of portraits and morally typical scenes but to be itself a single *tableau* or table of types. To better understand the structure of this table, one must move on from its pictorial conventions to decipher its thematic code.

A Table of Virtues and Vices

Although the approach used in the following analysis of thematic codes is borrowed from structuralist thought, it makes no pretense of being structuralist in the technical sense. For one thing, the primary ordering devices in the *Recollections,* comparison and antithesis, are drawn from the old rhetoric. The discovery of binary oppositions throughout the text, therefore, may not reflect as much Tocqueville's psychological makeup or an unconscious universal as the pervasive operation of rhetorical commonplaces and figures that had become for him so much a part of the act of writing that they appear spontaneously almost everywhere in his works.

The pairs generated by the code of the text are almost endless, but they can be ranked in a rough hierarchy. At the bottom are the particular characters and the types they represent as in the portraits. Then come the more restricted polarities of Paris/province, bourgeoisie/aristocracy, republic/constitutional monarchy, workers/peasants, manipulation/honesty. Following this are the more general levels of centralization/decentralization, anarchy/order, equality/liberty, greatness/greed, literature/truth. Often one side of a polarity contains another polarity within it. For example, what makes the Republic of 1848 seem better to Tocqueville than the July Monarchy is that it raised the fundamental issue of anarchy versus order, but within the party of order Tocqueville soon perceives the unworthy conservatives still obsessed with their material well-being as opposed to those worthy moderates who put the nation's welfare ahead of their own. And within that group of moderates in turn are those flawed by ambition or rigid ideas (Barrot, Dufaure), as opposed to the few men of disinterest and talent of whom Tocqueville saw himself as the natural leader. It is as if the text is ready to divide itself into opposites at almost any point and then continue on the same pattern whenever a new level of detail is reached.

Identifying a set of primary oppositions in the *Recollections* which can serve as the dominant terms in the table is not an easy task since Tocqueville not only refrains from explicitly identifying an *idée mère*, but often uses his key concepts in ways that do not draw attention to themselves. This is the case with the most important substantive opposition in the text, the one that I believe underwrites and unifies many of the others, the opposition of "greatness" (*grandeur*) and "greed" (*cupidité*). I have systematically brought its occurrence to the surface as I analyzed the function of constituent genres and as I followed the text's narrative development. The first time I read the *Recollections,* however, I hardly noticed this pair and doubt if most twentieth-century readers would. On that first reading I was struck only by Tocqueville's comment that Louis-Philippe's politeness was "with-

out . . . greatness, the politeness of a shopkeeper rather than a prince"
(*sans . . . grandeur, une politesse de marchand plutôt que de prince*),
but considered it amusing rather than significant. Similarly, I noticed
the text's references to the workers' "greed" and "envy," but only
thought this the kind of callousness one might expect from a nineteenth-century economic libertarian. Easier to sense on a first reading,
though it too is seldom explicitly formulated, is the opposition of
"liberty" and "equality." But I doubt if a reader not already familiar
with *Democracy in America* or with Tocqueville's ideas as presented
in general histories of political or social thought would have immediately noticed that this pair is also at work throughout the text, since
it is seldom made an explicit theme. If, after a closer reading of the text,
one comes to the conclusion that even this classic pair is subordinate to
the moral opposition between *grandeur* and *cupidité*, it is because one
looks to the way this particular text works, rather than attempting to
synthesize the "ideas" in it with those of Tocqueville's writings as a
whole.

   In normal French usage, however, the general contrary of *grandeur*
is not greed (*cupidité*) but pettiness (*petitesse*). As we have seen, the
Recollections does make considerable use of the *grandeur/petitesse*
opposition in its early treatment of the bourgeoisie. Yet what Tocqueville finds petty about bourgeois values is precisely the bourgeoisie's
avid materialism, its insatiable desire for places and advantages, its
willingness to put individual comfort and gain above the welfare of the
nation. One could say that for Tocqueville *cupidité* is the peculiarly
democratic or egalitarian form of *petitesse* in capitalist society.[12] In
the *Recollections*, the bourgeois pursuit of material well-being (*le goût
du bien-être*) becomes, at its most intense, just the kind of "immoderate desire" for possession which the Western moral tradition calls
greed (*cupidité*).[13] Another bit of lexical evidence for the choice of

   12. Despite Tocqueville's adherence to economic libertarianism, he was never comfortable with the moral values of the new capitalist society and retained the aristocrat's
disdain for commercial careers. See his letter to Kergorlay of January 15, 1855,
Oeuvres complètes (M), 13, 2, 292–94.
   13. *Cupidité, convoitise, concupiscence,* can all mean "immoderate desire," but the
latter two have primarily religious associations in French, whereas *cupidité* is distinguished from them as particularly signifying an immoderate desire for wealth. It is
found in both its wider and narrower senses in the eighteenth- and nineteenth-century
writers with whom Tocqueville was familiar, for example, Montesquieu, Rousseau,

cupidité rather than *petitesse* as the opposite of *grandeur* in the *Recollection's* code is the important positive role the text gives to the precise antonym of greed, "disinterest" (*désintéressement*), the willingness to sacrifice self-interest, possessions and comfort for the civic good. Thus, the *Recollections'* discourse operates from a binary matrix dominated by *grandeur* versus *cupidité*, each pole of which draws into focus a complex of related moral values. On the one hand, greatness (*grandeur*) in this text embraces disinterested service of the public good, high intellectual and moral aims (élévation), the magnanimity of a noble character, and the glory (*gloire*) that belongs to those who sacrifice themselves for the good of the nation. On the other hand, greed (*cupidité*) in the *Recollections* embraces the more extreme forms of the desire for personal gain at public expense (*égoïsme*), the taste for material possessions and comforts (*goût du bien-être*), a willingness to lower oneself in the drive to get ahead (*bassesse*), and an absorption in the petty schemes and concerns of bourgeois life (*petitesse*). From these two moral poles one can work outward toward all the other leading substantive terms and concepts of the text. Thus, *grandeur* leads through *désintéressement* to "aristocracy" in general and to Tocqueville and his friends in particular, whereas *cupidité* leads through *égoïsme* and *bassesse* to "bourgeoisie" in general and to Havin and Thiers in particular.

If the text is ordered by such a matrix of oppositions one should be able to show its structure. In other words, it is time for the obligatory chart that will allow us to see what the text is saying. (See p. 90.)

Framed at one end by the substantive polarity of greatness/greed and at the other by the formal polarity of literature/truth, the remaining moral-political and formal polarities are listed roughly in order of their first narrative appearance within each category. Beginning with the category of classes, it is clear that Part 1 opens with a striking contrast between the behavior of the aristocracy compared to that of the bourgeoisie in the coming of the February 24 Revolution. The confused and cowardly actions of the "bourgeois" king, the opportunism of the middle-class revolutionary leadership, and the pusillanim-

Chateaubriand. For citations see E. Littré, *Dictionnaire de la langue française* (Paris: Hachette, 1881), 1:933, and *Le grand Robert de la langue française* (Paris: Le Robert, 1985), 3:112.

The *Recollection's* thematic code

Type of Polarity	Binary Operators	
	Greatness	Greed
Controlling substantive polarity	Greatness	Greed
Classes and groups in order of appearance	aristocracy	bourgeoisie
	peasants	workers
	party of property and order	party of poverty and anarchy
	contented domestics	ambitious domestics
	moderate republicans	reactionary opportunists
Political ideas, moral qualities and exemplars	liberty	equality
	reform	revolution
	serious spirit in politics	literary spirit in politics
	immutable laws of society	ridiculous socialist theories
	honesty	manipulation
	disinterest	personal ambition
	courage	cowardice
	statesmen	politicians
	(Barrot)	(Lamartine)
	(Tocqueville)	(Thiers)
	(Louis-Napoleon)	(Louis-Philippe)
	supportive wife	hysterical wife
	(Marie de Tocqueville)	(Alexandrine de Tocqueville)
	femininity in women	masculinity in women
	(Duchess of Orleans)	(George Sand)
Institutions and social tendencies	constitutional monarchy	democratic republic
	Army	National Guard
	the provinces	Paris
	local autonomy	centralization
Literary forms	mirror	painting
	reality	theatre
Controlling formal polarity	Truth	Literature

ity of the bourgeois conservatives in the Assembly are starkly contrasted to the dignity and courage of the Duchess of Orleans and to the behavior of Tocqueville himself. (There are, of course, aristocrats in the text who have sold out to the bourgeoisie, which puts them on the side of egoism and greed.) The opening chapters of Part 2 describe the fear provoked by the anarchic Parisian workers which leads to an unexpected solidarity between the conservative and sensible peasants and the *notables* of the provinces. The outcome of the elections is the production of two parties, the party of order made up of all those with some property to defend and the party of anarchy made up of the propertyless and their leaders among that handful of bourgeois and nobles whose minds are full of "chimerical" socialist ideas. At the height of this confrontation of order and anarchy two symbolic figures from the domestic wing of the working class appear on stage, one representing the morally worthy and psychologically sound type who is contented with his lot, the other the morally unworthy and psychologically disturbed type, ambitious to take his master's place. With Part 3 the places shift; the party of anarchy is driven from the scene and the party of order divides into a small group of statesmanlike moderates on one side and a quarreling mass of antirepublican opportunists on the other. The text ends with the fall of the virtuous moderate republicans and the victory of the reactionary opportunists who will go on to resolve the unsettled state of affairs with Louis-Napoleon in a way the text anticipates but cannot know. What is clear from the way the text has been structured up to its last line is that whatever particular group wins will belong to the unworthy who are driven not by the quest of greatness but by the lust for material gain and comfort.

When we come to the category of political ideas, moral qualities and their personal exemplars, the chronological progression is not as clear, though it can be argued that there is a rough predominance of certain ideas and certain qualities in particular sections as the narrative progresses. The liberty/equality opposition, which is so fundamental to Tocqueville's thought, generally can be sensed from the beginning even though it is only the drive toward social and economic equality through the abolition of private property which is explicitly treated in the opening passages. But it soon becomes clear that Tocqueville sees himself and a few of his friends and political allies on the center left as the sole champions of true liberty. They alone are prepared to support a Republic they do not particularly desire because it is the only liberal political institution with some claim to legitimacy. And toward the end of the narrative, when the possibility of maintaining a Republic against the forces of personal despotism on one side and bourgeois greed on the other is especially bleak, he writes, "I, . . . who adore liberty," and we feel he is close to meaning "I *alone* who adore liberty" (178/165). Of course, he shared his colleagues' desire to enhance liberty under the July Monarchy through electoral reform, but feared they might bring on a revolution by the means they chose (the "agitation of the banquets"). The reform/revolution pair plays less of a role in the *Recollections* than one might expect given its author's liberal sentiments. This is because it was the botched effort at reform, the "anarchic" instrument of the banquets, that led to the February Revolution. Once the revolution is underway, the text never treats seriously any suggestions that reform might be a way to mollify revolutionary passions. The June civil war is treated not only as inevitable but as a welcome opportunity to bring the clash of ordered liberty and anarchic equality to a crisis (117/99).

The next pairs (honesty/manipulation, disinterest/personal ambition, courage/cowardice) were the moral qualities in conflict from the time of the Banquets and the actions of those exemplifying them were among the chief "accidents" that brought on the February Revolution. The individuals who populate the text are so numerous and play such varied roles at different points in time that it would be difficult to make much of them in a structural analysis. After all, the point of structural analysis is to dissolve or, what is really the same operation in reverse, to constitute the individual as individual. I have mentioned four pairs of individuals, however, in order to show how such a constitutive analysis might be pursued. Rather than try to achieve their reformist ends by direct and honest means, Thiers and Odilon Barrot engaged in political manipulation. Barrot is represented as a man of integrity and courage whose only flaw is an ambition that sometimes interferes with disinterested service. By contrast Lamartine is described as the type of man whose ever dominant quality is personal ambition, and Thiers appears almost as a caricature of the cheap politician who, in addition to exhibiting a shameless lack of principle in his personal lust for power, is an abject coward.

It might seem surprising that among the many persons who could have been paired in illustrating the binary structure of the *Recollections*, Louis-Napoleon and Louis-Philippe would appear on the sides they do. The apparent irony of putting the clever and courageous Louis-Philippe on the same side as the unworthy, greedy middle class and the ambitious, erratic, sometime buffoon Louis-Napoleon on the side of the worthy, heroic, aristocracy is not as great as it might at first seem. In Tocqueville's portrait of Louis-Philippe, it is clear that for all the virtues allowed, Tocqueville harshly condemns him—indeed bitterly lays on his "senile imbecility" a large share of the blame for the success of the February Revolution. On the other hand, whereas Tocqueville finds Louis-Napoleon, for all his limitations of intelligence, his low tastes, and a "trace of madness," better than either Napoleon's friends or enemies believed, he blames as much the circumstances as Napoleon himself for the character of his presidency. Moreover, with respect to a series of qualities, the text finds the king and president to be opposites—to the advantage of Louis-Napoleon. The most important of these qualities is that Napoleon believes in himself whereas Louis-Philippe no longer believes in anything and rigidly goes through the motions of the corrupt system he and Guizot have constructed. Moreover, it is striking that Tocqueville describes himself as unable to even get a word in during a conversation with Louis-Philippe, but is always listened to politely by Louis-Napoleon and believes the president might even be persuaded by him. Had Tocqueville reopened the text of the *Recollections* after the coup of December 1851, he would no doubt have altered his portrait of Louis-Napoleon. As it stands, the president is shown—*insofar as* he invites comparison to Louis-Philippe—to be a man "worthy" of his time. That a man who is described as exhibiting so many intrinsically unworthy qualities, not to speak of a trace of madness, appears in our table where he does, shows the power of the oppositional order within the text.[14]

Two polarities control the role of women in the text. The first opposes the supportive and courageous wife (Marie de Tocqueville, Clementine de Beaumont, Mme de Lamartine, wives of workers) to the hysterical and cowardly ones (Alexandrine de Tocqueville and a Mme Paulmier). The second polarity cuts across the first and opposes femininity as seen in the aristocratic and bourgeois women and masculinity as seen in the workers' wives who are mentioned because they take an active part in warfare and whose daughters are singled out for the "virile way" they wear their virginal white dresses in the Festival of Concord and the strength of their arms when they pelt the Assembly

---

14. In letters written at the time a more negative portrait appears. See Tocqueville's letter to Beaumont of November 28, 1849. *Oeuvres complètes* (M), 13, 2, 252 (*Selected Letters*, 243). Yet even as Tocqueville was beginning work on the *Recollections,* he took time out as President of the *Conseil général* of La Manche to accompany Louis-Napoleon on his official visit to Cherbourg and the two exchanged public cordialities; André Jardin, *Alexis de Tocqueville: 1805–1859* (Paris: Hachette, 1984), 430–31.

members with fraternal bouquets (145/129). Although women generally do not play a leading role in the text, two prominent women appear as embodiments of femininity and masculinity in women. The Duchess of Orleans appears as the type of the noble wife (widow dressed in mourning) and mother (courageously representing the claim of her child); George Sand appears there not only as a liberated woman of questionable virtue (the text mentions her recent liaison with Mérimée) who pursues the more properly masculine profession of writing, but as filling her works with unfeminine women. Moreover, the two women also connect with the other polarities in our table since the duchess represents the last hope for a constitutional monarchy, whereas George Sand is identified with the workers and socialism (149–50/133–35).

Rather than ponder the accuracy of the *Recollections'* portraits or why Tocqueville despised one figure and admired another, we can read the text as ordered by a series of oppositions that require these individuals to appear as they do. The most striking discovery is that the figure of Tocqueville himself becomes a type—the man of integrity, the disinterested statesman, and finally the skilled politician able to manipulate others for the good of the country. Yet, like the other figures in the text, he is a type only as one-half of an oppositional pair. Thiers cuts a figure throughout the text that is not only morally despicable but humanly ridiculous; he is greed and cowardice personified, whereas Tocqueville has the liberty and greatness of the nation as his highest aim and pursues it with honesty, disinterest, high principle, and exemplary courage. One can see in the polarity Tocqueville/Thiers an embodiment of all the values at war in the text.[15]

The pairs that make up the last two categories—institutional arrangements and cultural forms—do not lend themselves as easily to the narrative development suggested for the first two. Certainly the text begins with the conflict of constitutional monarchy and republic

15. The text does not hide the strong element of ambition in Tocqueville's desire to play a leading role or the element of pride involved in his lack of success under the July Monarchy (235/231). Within the system of the *Recollection's* thematic code, however, the ambition of a Lamartine or Thiers is seen as directed toward personal aggrandizement at the expense of the nation whereas the text treats Tocqueville's ambition as aiming at the salvation and *grandeur* of the nation and ready to be sacrificed to the nation if need be (105/85) (126/108).

and with the loyal, if fatefully erroneous, obedience of the Army and its generals as compared to the vacillation and collusion of the National Guard. The contrast of Paris and the provinces as the place of unstable and stable insitutions, debased and wholesome values, comes to the fore in Part 2 and the closely related contrast of local autonomy and centralization is invoked soon after and plays an explicit role as an issue before the Constitutional Committee. The contrast of the demagogic Republic and the moderate Republic is, of course, the constant counterpart of these pairs.

Finally, we have the formal and stylistic pairs. Mirror and painting, truth and literature, as invoked at the very beginning of the text, are two expressions of the same phenomenon: the mirror captures what is true because unlike painting or literature it is not consciously arranged. These two pairs are soon followed in the text by the opposition between reality and theatre, a polarity explicitly operative in Part 1's account of February 24 which returns again in Part 2's treatment of May 15 and the Festival of Concord. Of these three interlocking polarities it is truth versus literature that underwrites the formal categories of the *Recollections* throughout the text in much the same way that the opposition of greatness versus greed informs the text's other moral-political categories. The noxious influence of "literature," according to the text, is not simply that the French "mix literary and theatrical memories with their most serious demonstrations," but the more general effect of what Tocqueville calls "the literary spirit in politics"—the preference for what is "interesting" over what is "true" (88/67). Thus Cormenin, an aristocrat turned radical, exclaimed to Tocqueville on election day in April 1848 how fascinating it was to see a country let its "domestics, its poor and its soldiers vote." "He talked," Tocqueville observes, "as if it were an experiment in chemistry" (193/183). The whole country, the text complains, had taken "to judging politics like a man of letters" (88/67). In Part 2 we are shown the literary spirit dominating the politics of 1848 in an even more direct manner through the "innovations" of the socialists writers and, above all, in the person of the poet Lamartine, the leader of the provisional government, whose portrait in Chapter 6 is built around the opposition of literature and truth: "I have never known a mind less sincere, or one that had a more complete disdain of truth. When I say disdain I am wrong; he never honored truth enough to bother about it at all. In speaking or writing he could follow it or leave it without noticing, caring only for a certain effect he wanted to produce at the moment" (126/108).

Differences

If the text is looked at solely from the point of view of its vertical or synchronic axis, one could say it is "about" difference and the importance of maintaining it. The world it generates is a world of threatened difference: political differences, social differences, economic differences, sexual differences, moral differences, representational differences. Although one side of the system of polarities is obviously the "superior" or "good" side, nevertheless, it cannot generate a text without the other side. Without greedy, manipulative politicians, without envious workers in thrall to egalitarian theories, without theatrical and literary models, there would be no story, no *Recollections*. Thus, a second thing the text is about is how the clash of differences seems to endlessly generate further differences. The contraries not only systematically depend on each other but can turn into each other or, in the moment when one overcomes the other in the text, the successful pole can divide into a new opposition.

But the textual dialectic here is not like Hegel's or Marx's, where higher and higher stages of opposition are produced leading to an apotheosis; in Tocqueville's text the same fundamental struggle occurs over and over again, only under new forms. If the corrupt order of the July Monarchy is overthrown in the name of ordered liberty (reform) and ordered liberty is in turn threatened by anarchic equality (revolution), the victory of ordered liberty sets order against liberty (reaction). The text must end somewhere; it happens to end with the fall into reaction, but that cannot be the resting place of the code itself since the dialectic of the code governing this text does not permit a final victory of one side of the polarities over the other—that would be the end of difference and the end of discourse. Because the *Recollections* must end, it cannot give us the next state, but the system of thematic codes allows us to anticipate it; the next stage will be an opposition in which "order" turns into a petty Napoleonic despotism opposed in the name of liberty by those able to rise to the call of greatness (compare *The Old Regime and the Revolution*). The thematic code of the *Recollec-*

tions is a system of differences signifying an eternal conflict, requiring history to be written as a tragic burden from which we will never be free.

Our analysis of the codes at work in the text has now added a vertical axis to the horizontal analysis of plot, a synchronic axis intersecting a diachronic and dynamic one. The *tableaux* along with the thematic codes that inform them, give us a series of signifying *clichés* linked in encyclopedic cross-reference. This system echoes the medieval use of the mirror (*speculum*) to designate an encyclopedic structure, as opposed to allegory where narrativity dominates analogy. I have already noted how Beaujour bases his argument for the autonomy of the "self-portrait" as a genre on the *topical* character of the self-portrait as opposed to the chronological structure of autobiography. I mention Beaujour again not simply to assimilate the *Recollections* to his concept of the self-portrait but because his analysis can help us articulate the *Recollections'* particular intersection of the spatial and temporal, of rhetorical form and narrative sequence, *tableau* and plot. Moreover, I have tried to show in the analysis of the synchronic oppositions how they make their own tropos toward the horizontal. Whether they turn of themselves (code generating plot) or are drawn heliotropically (plot generating *tableaux*) need not be decided in the abstract. A text is not a construction made up of an underlying skeleton and its stylistic clothing, so much as it is a texture produced by the interweaving of synchronic and diachronic devices. The desire to make one axis the basis of the other reflects an anxiety to escape the pliability of the text for the security of the work.

Ambiguities

In one sense my binary analysis works too well. By explaining so comprehensively what is there, it can make one forget what is not there, for example, the concept of justice. Justice appears in this text, if at all, only in the refraction of the ridicule heaped on "false socialist theories." The ambivalence of the text with regard to a possible justification of the workers' revolt and with regard to the role of women is especially revealing and will lead us in turn to reexamine the text's reigning substantive and formal polarities, greatness/greed and truth/literature.

Workers

This text never seems to decide whether the workers are driven more by need or by greed. The only passage that directly touches the matter of justice hardly suggests the possibility that there is even an issue to consider. The passage is from the account of the causes of the June Days which ascribes the tenacity of the workers in battle to a combination of "greedy desires and false theories." The passage continues: "These poor people had been assured that the goods of the rich were somehow the result of a theft against themselves. They had been assured that inequality of fortunes was as contrary to morality and society as to nature. Needs and passions aiding, many of them believed these things" (152/137). Here the "false teachings" are clearly the work of outsiders; we have already noted that one of the "causes" of the revolution in the text is the bourgeois regime's infecting the working class with its own materialistic obsessions (85/62). But what of the "needs" of the workers acknowledged in this passage? The idea of need also appears elsewhere in the text from time to time but it always seems to get squeezed out as if there were no room for it in the thematic matrix that controls the text. To the extent the text is organized by a system of polarities dominated by the greatness/greed pair it is easy to see why equality in the *Recollections* never means an ideal of justice or fairness but simply the desire of those who have less to equal those who have more, with the result that the battle against anarchy becomes a moment of *grandeur* in which the ugly monster of greed and envy is slain and the nation freed from "oppression by the Parisian workers." Nor do the pictographic codes that control the constitution of *tableaux* in the text allow the visualization of workers' need. The look on the workers' faces is described as sinister, angry, terrible, or joyous depending on how their struggle against the "forces of order" is going; it is never hungry or pained or justly indignant. Nor do we ever see on the workers' bodies the signs of hunger and need; we only see their smocks or their lack of linen. The sole figure representative of the working class in the text to bear the marks of suffering and deprivation is Blanqui, and Tocqueville reacts to him only with horror and disgust.

Yet even though our description of the thematic code and our analysis of pictorial stereotypes seems to explain exhaustively the ordering of themes and images in the text, "need" and "greed" continue to interfere with each other and make us doubt that the issue can be so easily decided. Most revealing of Tocqueville's ambivalence over the place of need are two passages where the textual variants show he had difficulty making up his mind. At the end of the account of the June Days we read that socialist theories continued "to penetrate the spirit of the people *in the form of greedy and envious passions,* sowing the seeds of future revolutions" (178/165). There is a variant to the last half of this which reads "to penetrate the spirit of the people, *helped by the miseries of the poor and by their envious greed*" (308/ 165). Here it seems that the marginal, "second thought" was ready to grant need a place at least equal to that of envy and greed. Near the beginning of Part 1 there is another hesitation and variant, but here "need" occurs in the main text and is eliminated in the variant. The phrase in question is found at the end of a characterization of the middle class, which is accused of "easily forgetting, in its petty comfort, the needs of the people." (31/5) In place of forgetting "*the needs of the people,*" the variant has the middle class forgetting "*la grandeur de la nation*" (295).[16] Certainly, phrases like "needs of the people" or "dying of hunger" or "wretched existence of the poor" strike us as stock usages, as stereotypical as the text's other references to the working class or the peasants. Nevertheless, the presence of these synonyms for need disturbs the symmetry of the polarities that dominate the text.

The reader accustomed to approaching texts from the perspective of the traditional history of ideas may be impatient with our analysis at this point. Why make so much of these variants in Tocqueville's text when we can easily settle what Tocqueville *meant* by going outside the text? For example, on the specific question of need versus greed there is an April 1848 letter to the English economist Nassau-Senior in which Tocqueville asserts flatly that "not needs, but ideas brought about this great upheaval: chimerical ideas on the relative condition of worker and capital."[17] Or, for a more general picture of Tocqueville's views on why the state should not directly aid the poor one can go to his

16. This variant is omitted from the English translation (5). A similar variant is attached to the passage in which Tocqueville compares June, 1848 and June 13, 1849: "On the first occasion, the people led more by *appétits* than opinions fought alone" (219/211). The variant substitutes *désirs,* for *appétits,* a term more closely linked to *cupidité,* whereas *appétits* suggests the hunger and need that give rise to desire (310).

17. Tocqueville, *Selected Letters,* 206.

Memoir on Pauperism of 1840 or his 1848 speech in the Assembly against the "right to work" provision of the new Constitution; such texts reveal a typical nineteenth-century mixture of Christian charity and libertarian economics.[18] We have already seen evidence in the *Recollections* itself of a providential view of poverty and a belief in immutable economic laws. Yet all these other writings are also texts that invite a reading in terms of their rhetorical devices and the ambiguities generated by language.

What is at stake in our analysis of the *Recollection's* passages on the workers' motives is not the question of Tocqueville's general beliefs about social justice, but the question of how a system of antitheses may constrain what the text is able to say on this issue. When one reads closely, Tocqueville's text as a whole seems to tilt toward blaming the worker's greed as it was inflamed by socialist ideas; nor does the text show much sympathy for the workers' plight before the June Days or any concern for their treatment in the aftermath. If we consider the code that appears to channel the discourse of the text, one reason for Tocqueville's insistence on the worker's greed and socialist ideas as opposed to their need becomes apparent. If need were seen as a dominant or even equal factor with greed and socialist ideas, then the term *workers* would no longer fall so clearly into the "morally unworthy" column of the code. As a result, the workers' repression and punishment in the June civil war by the worthy forces of property and order would lose a great deal of moral justification. The contending forces would line up no longer as property, order, liberty, and grandeur on one side and socialism, anarchy, equality, and greed on the other; instead, June might have to be seen as a more fundamental human struggle over the just distribution of goods in society, a struggle in which those who actually triumphed would appear to have fought as much to keep their privileges as to preserve liberty. Such a breach in the mode of ordering the elements of the text would have threatened its

18. In 1848, of course, "right to work" meant the opposite of what it does in contemporary conservative discourse. Then it was an important slogan of the Left and referred to a right of guaranteed employment. The phrase was included in the preamble to the draft of the Constitution of 1848 but by fall 1848 when the debates opened, the June Days had thrown the country into reaction. Tocqueville's speech attacked any state effort to interfere with a free economy. The speech may be found in *Oeuvres complètes* (B), 9, 536–52. See also André Jardin, *Alexis de Tocqueville, 1805–1859* (Paris: Hachette, 1984), 394–99.

entire system. Hence, though acknowledging signs of misery and de-privation among the working class, the text must minimize them in order to maintain intact its thematic code.

The hesitations and tensions examined here set in relief both the constraining force of the code as well as the inevitable fissures and counter-thrusts that disturb the surface of discourse. Of course, since Tocqueville also believed in private property as an immutable law of society, the expression of that belief in this case is "overdetermined" by the thematic system channeling the discourse of the text.[19] If he had chosen to directly address the interrelationship of liberty, property, and poverty and to question the reigning economic assumptions of his time, his discourse might have broken out of the matrix that seems to constrain it in the *Recollections*. As it stands, when he decides in March 1848 to throw himself "headlong into the arena" in defense of the "laws which constitute society itself," he appears to be primarily defending property rights (105/85). The mirror of the text certainly shows us, for example, the bitter fear of revolution which overtakes the inheritor of the Chateau de Tocqueville. Does this mean that the text forces us to read with Marx's eyes and see in Tocqueville a man who thinks he defends divine and immutable laws but is really just defending his class interests; and, the most deadly irony of all, that on this deeper level, his interest is identical with that of the greedy bour-geoisie whatever his refinements of value and yearnings for *grandeur*? It is surely a possible reading and one we cannot ignore.[20]

Nevertheless, there *are* the ambivalent references to "need." Their intrusion into the otherwise consistent code of the text is a grainy reminder of facts that roughen the smooth surface of writing and reading and lead us beyond the limits of the text's systematic encoding

19. The best general discussion of Tocqueville's social and economic beliefs remains Seymour Drescher, *Dilemmas of Democracy: Tocqueville and Modernization* (Pitts-burgh: University of Pittsburgh Press, 1968).

20. One is also reminded of an earlier passage in the *Recollections* which referred to the Restoration as a time when the nation "became prosperous and great in becoming free" (86/65) and of the preface to the twelfth edition of *Democracy in America* issued in 1848 after the February insurrection: "It is not a question now of finding out whether we are to have a monarchy or a republic in France; but we still want to know whether it is to be an agitated or a tranquil republic, an orderly or a disorderly republic, pacific or warlike, liberal or oppressive, a republic which threatens the sacred rights of property and of the family, or one which recognizes and honors them." *De la démo-cratie en Amérique*, 1, 1, "Avertissement de la douzième édition", XLIV.

of 1848. Moreover, two other aspects of the text force us to back off slightly from either a strictly structuralist or a strictly class-interest analysis. The first is the text's stylistic handling of the workers as compared to the bourgeoisie. With few exceptions the workers during the June Days are given a relatively serious narrative treatment, with use of detail that sometimes enhances their stature (carefully built barricades, military organization), and this conflicts with the text's more typical portrayal of workers according to the classical conventions of comedy and burlesque. Second, there is a reflective passage where Tocqueville shows himself capable of temporarily rising above his class limitation to the extent of questioning whether his judgement on socialism will remain correct. At the end of his discussion of the socialist character of the February Revolution, he imagines—from the vantage of 1851, it must be admitted, well after the defeat of the workers and the triumph of reaction—that "in the long run the constituent laws of our modern society will be drastically modified." He thinks it impractical to actually destroy them and put others in their place, yet he hesitates: "for . . . as I consider the prodigious diversity of the world, not only in its laws, but in the principles of the laws and the different forms, whatever one says, that the right of property has taken and continues to take on the earth, even today, I am tempted to believe that what one calls necessary institutions are often only those institutions to which one has grown accustomed, and that in matters of social constitution, the field of possibilities is much vaster than men living in each society imagine" (96–7/76). If the text's predominant treatment of workers follows the stereotypes of stage (burlesque), iconography (smock), morality (envy), politics (anarchy), nevertheless, the workers' revolt and struggle are taken seriously and not satirically reduced as are the greedy gyrations of the bourgeoisie. If the issue of justice is never directly addressed by the text, there are still points in the text where human suffering forces itself to the surface, if only in the most general terms. Finally, if socialist ideas are never treated seriously, the fundamental issue socialism raised in 1848 at least momentarily breaks through the code of the text in this reflection on the possible cultural relativity of ideas of property. Each of these incongruities with the thematic matrix and pictorial conventions works to render the code of the text unstable, just as the countercurrent of satire tends to undermine the tragic direction of the plot.

Women

Another illustration of the uncertainty of the text with respect to justice can be drawn from its treatment of women. Consider the ways in which women are present in the text. First, there is the hovering presence of Marie Tocqueville, who read the manuscript and/or to whom it was read aloud. We know this from Tocqueville's marginal notes to himself concerning passages that Marie said should be omitted or shortened (99/53). She is not only his helpmate in the secret task of mirroring the truth of 1848, she also appears in the text itself as the worthy (that is, courageous, supportive) wife in comparison to his brother Edouard's hysterical and helpless type. Her courage and support are mentioned among the factors influencing Tocqueville's decision to run for the Assembly: "I felt moreover, that I was still in the prime of life; I had no children; I had few needs, and above all I had in my home the support, so rare and so precious in a time of revolution, of a devoted wife whose firm and penetrating spirit and naturally elevated soul would keep her equal to any situation and above any reversal" (105/85).[21] When the June Days arrive, the text shows her calmly letting her fatigued husband sleep late even though she has listened to the first sounds of cannon fire since dawn. Later the text lets us know that although she has left for the safety of the suburbs as the fighting gets nearer, she has had the presence of mind before leaving to send her husband a note concerning the porter's rumored boast to kill him.[22]

Compare this treatment of his wife to what the text tells us of his sister-in-law's behavior on February 24, when the fighting was far less serious. Tocqueville's brother Edouard and Edouard's wife Alexandrine and their children showed up on the Tocqueville's doorstep early that morning. "My sister-in-law had lost her head as usual. She already saw her husband dead and her daughters raped." But it is not just this woman's lack of courage and her hysterical behavior which

21. One might think this kind of rhetoric was put in just so Marie could read it, but similar comments are scattered throughout Tocqueville's letters.
22. An even more direct statement comes in Part III of the *Recollections* where Tocqueville mentions how, despite her illness during his trip to study the German revolution, she told him to go on, which he did regretfully, " . . . it is in moments of difficulty or danger that her courage and good sense are a support to me" (198/188).

disgusted Tocqueville, it was above all her lack of public spirit! He continues: "What really made me impatient, however, was that in her lamentations over the fate of her family there was no concern for her country. . . . She was actually after all, very kind and even quite bright, but had contracted her spirit and hardened her heart by confining them narrowly in a sort of pious egoism in which she lived, occupied solely with the good Lord and her husband and her children and especially her health, scarcely paying attention to anyone else; the most respectable woman and the worst citizen one could find" (62/39–40). Edouard de Tocqueville's wife exemplifies many of the characteristics the nineteenth century valued most in its women—piety, devotion to family, and feminine weakness. Of course, these same "feminine" qualities were also the basis of women's perceived inferiority and male contempt for them. Here Tocqueville seems to value intelligence, strength, and courage in women.

Two other political wives appear in the text, Mme de Beaumont and Mme de Lamartine, whose forthright behavior may be contrasted to that of the rich bourgeoise Mme Paulmier, who took to bed just before a dinner party because she was so upset by seeing a scuffle in the street below her window (52/30). Ironically, the only other models of the supportive, courageous spouse are the wives of the workers in the June Days. Tocqueville was struck by the fact that "the women took as much part as the men," preparing and carrying ammunition, "and when it was time to surrender, they were the last to give up" (152/137). If there is a kind of admiration implied here for their courage and an acceptance of their role, it is not surprising since they are working-class women and physical labor in support of male combatants does not contradict the sort of work they normally do. Yet the text cannot avoid a little depreciation of their working-class female motives: "these women carried their housewifely passions into battle; they counted on a victory to put their husbands at ease and raise their children. They loved this war as they would have loved a lottery" (152/137). The tone of this comment reminds one of the description of their daughters' "virile way of wearing their virginal" costume and their "brawny arms," which pelt the Assembly with bouquets during the Festival of Concord in May. There is a condemnation of women who step out of their assigned feminine role, and at the same time a depreciation of the feminine, much as there was a certain contempt shown for the brother Edouard's wife who so completely exemplified femininity. (Of course, working-class women are more susceptible to comic or burlesque treatment.)

There is an equally striking ambiguity in the treatment of the two most prominent exemplars of femininity and masculinity in women, the Duchess of Orleans and George Sand. The duchess is just what a woman should be; even the slight characterization we are given under-lines her appropriate role and dress as wife (widow) and mother. Yet the Duchess of Orleans, though a perfect figure of womanhood, is twice praised in the text for the generally masculine virtue of courage. Tocqueville met George Sand at a literary luncheon on the eve of the June civil war and he admits he was already prejudiced against her. "I detest women who write, especially those who systematically disguise the weaknesses of their sex, instead of interesting us by displaying them in their true colors. In spite of that she charmed me. I found her features rather massive, but her expression wonderful; all her intel-ligence seemed to have retreated into her eyes, abandoning the rest of her face to raw matter. I was most struck at finding her with something of that naturalness of manner characteristic of great spirits" (150/ 134–35). By chance Tocqueville ends up seated next to her and is impressed by her knowledge and analysis of what was going on in the workers' camp. As a result, even though he rejects her feminist and socialist views and her moral behavior, he cannot help admiring her intelligence and naturalness.

What are we to make of women in the text of the *Recollections?* There is an acceptance of the stereotype of women as weak and an anxiety about women who act like men instead of remaining in their assigned feminine role and style. Moreover the women singled out for greatest praise are wives on whom their husbands can count—even if they are passing ammunition to use against the forces of order. On the other hand, the virtues that are clearly most prized in women for this text are courage, public spiritedness, and, at least in the case of Marie Tocqueville and George Sand, acuteness of intellect, virtues that were not at the top of the list in the nineteenth-century stereotype of femi-ninity. From one perspective the ambivalence in the text's treatment of women is no surprise since many of those qualities which Western society still values as ideally feminine are the same ones for which women continue to be despised. From another perspective one might note that Tocqueville can at least admire intellectual accomplishment and political concern on the part of women, whereas Daumier, who was deeply sensitive to injustice and suffering in almost every other area, was blatantly stereotypical and reactionary when it came to women.

In any case, even though the text seems controlled by a set of simple polarities with respect to women, when examined closely the consistency vanishes. Here again we could attempt to resolve the ambiguity by going outside the text to the famous chapters on women in *Democracy in America* or to passages in Tocqueville's letters, but we would find similar ambiguities there. In a letter to Mme Swetchine in 1856, for example, he stresses the importance of inculcating a sense of civic responsibility in women and yet in the same letter he limits the civic role of women to the indirect one of encouraging and supporting husbands to take up their civic duty.[23] Even if we were to arrive at a satisfactory synthesis of these other passages, it is only by virtue of an independent methodological decision that we can subordinate the passages in the *Recollections* to that synthesis.

Greatness/Greed

Perhaps the most serious instability in our table of codes resides in its systematic nature. If particular pairings like those involving workers and women vacillate and at times threaten to switch sides, can the total column be more than a teetering stack? We have considered the ambiguities that emerge when the text's deployment of certain concepts (workers' need/greed, femininity/masculinity in women) are examined closely. Another kind of ambiguity besetting our matrix becomes apparent if we examine the presiding terms of the thematic hierarchy which also furnish the main counters of the plot. We have argued that the greatness/greed (*grandeur/cupidité*) polarity underwrites all the political and social oppositions and infects them with a moral sense, turning the plot of the *Recollections* into a morality play in which the worthy and unworthy struggle over the destiny of France. In order to arrive at this polarity it was necessary to subsume a complex of related significations under each term: greatness encompassing disinterest, high aims, nobility, glory; greed encompassing

23. *Oeuvres complètes* (M), 15, 2, *Correspondance d'Alexis de Tocqueville et de Francisque de Corcelle: Correspondance d'Alexis de Tocqueville et Madame Swetchine* (Paris: Gallimard, 1983), 298–99.

pettiness, baseness, selfishness, the taste for well-being. As part of the text's moral code the two sets should be mutually exclusive in their application to actions, individuals, or classes—and this is usually the case. Yet it is also obvious that only an excessively rigid discursive practice could maintain a totally exclusionary symmetry in the application of so many terms. Thus, Barrot is generally ranged on the side of greatness despite his occasional lapses into self-interest and the bourgeoisie, although given to material comfort and egoism, is treated as temporarily capable of courage and concern for the nation in the moment of crisis. As A. Kibédi Varga has shown, such plays on the tension between the synonymity and antithesis of closely related terms was at the heart of the rhetorical and grammatical practice of description in French classicism.[24] But the absence or even switching of sides by one of the four synonyms for either *grandeur* or *cupidité* can lead to a serious instability in the text's thematic code when it concerns an operative characteristic of one of the crucial agents in the text. This is the case with respect to the greed (*cupidité*) of the workers which by its place in the binary code excludes any trace of genuine moral greatness from their struggle. If we closely examine the terms associated with greed as it is applied to the workers and the bourgeoisie, however, we will find a small difference with respect to the associated term pettiness (*petitesse*) which ends up making a big difference.

The text connects bourgeois greed with pettiness and self-serving, whereas working-class greed is associated with passion, violence, and vulgarity. Of the bourgeoisie we read not only that its "hearts and minds . . . were empty of political beliefs and ardors and there scarcely remained anything but the taste for well-being" (99/78), but also that Tocqueville "saw the surprise, the anger, the fear, the greed (*cupidité*) . . . a pack of dogs one pulls off the prey, their mouths still half-full" (54/32). Bourgeois pettiness and greed are also associated later in

---

24. A. Kibédi Varga, "Synonyme et antithèse," *Poétique* 4 (1973): 307–12. Classical description often played upon the nuances of difference among sets of synonyms in order to create a series of antitheses. Thus in Retz's famous portrait of the Queen, she is said to have "plus d'aigreur que de hauteur, plus de hauter que de grandeur, plus de maniers que de fond, plus d'inapplication a l'argent que de libéralité, plus de libéralité que d'intérêt" (309) Kibédi Varga cites Vaugelas's analogy of the writer's use of synonyms in a description to the painter's use of multiple brush strokes in a portrait. It is the *difference* within synonymity which achieves the effect of representational veracity (311–12).

the text when Thiers and his ilk have returned to politics with their *"petites passions"* for offices (229/224), petty passions that the revolution has only made more acute (226/221) and which Tocqueville now has the aplomb to manipulate by appealing to these politician's "ambition or their greed (*cupidité*)" (237/233). The difference between the *cupidité* of the bourgeoisie and that of the workers is this: whereas the greed of the bourgeoisie is associated with pettiness and goes hand in hand with complacency about the great political issues of the day, the workers' greed is associated with extreme political passions. The text notes that before February there was only "languor, impotence, immobility and boredom" in the upper half of society, whereas in the lower half, the stirrings of a genuine "political life began to show itself in feverish but irregular symptoms" (35/11).[25] When the June revolt finally comes, the text stresses again and again the passionate *cupidité* of the workers: "it was this mixture of *désirs cupides* and false theories which made the insurrection so formidable" (151/136); "the greedy (*cupide*), blind and vulgar passions which sent the people to arms" (159/144); "socialist theories continued to penetrate the spirit of the people in the form of greedy (*cupides*) and envious passions" (178/165). In terms of the text's *own code*, however, these passions of the workers should also be seen in some senses as *grandes*. These are not the "petites passions" of a bourgeoisie hanging on to its petty comforts or scheming to further enrich itself through government posts. The workers want nothing less than social justice and to achieve it they are prepared to risk their lives in order to change the basis of society, an undertaking that is great by the same standards of seriousness, high aims and concern for the nation as a whole which is part of the meaning of *grandeur* and is opposed to the pettiness and selfishness associated with bourgeois greed.[26]

Certainly the workers' drive for equality is also a "greedy," and "envious," passion since it lacks the disinterest in material well-being

25. The lack of passion under the July Monarchy was not a new theme with Tocqueville. See Tocqueville's letter to Ampère of August 1841, where he laments the lack of passion, "we no longer know how to will, to love, to hate." *Oeuvres complètes* (M), 11, 152.

26. One cannot help being reminded of the passage from Tocqueville's 1847 manifesto which he quotes near the beginning of the *Recollections:* "Soon there will be a battle between those who have and those who have not. . . . Then we will again see great public agitations and great parties" (37/13).

requisite to the full meaning of *grandeur* in the text. The workers passionately desire a share of the well-being enjoyed by the bourgeoisie and the aristocracy. Since *grandeur* and *cupidité* must exclude each other in the code of the text, however, the discourse of the *Recollections* cannot formally recognize any degree of moral *grandeur* in the workers' revolt. At most the text can associate their greedy desires with the ridiculous socialist theories that gave them the *illusion* they were fighting a battle for justice. Given the bounds of the textual code, only a few individuals like Tocqueville and his friends are able to act with a disinterest that approaches *grandeur* and there seems no place for workers among men of such elevated sentiments. For one thing, workers' inherent *bassesse* would not permit it; at most, like Eugène, the contented valet, they might be capable of a wholesome and simpleminded acceptance of their place in society. Thus, for all its sophistication about class interests, social mores and political culture, the social and political discourse of the *Recollections* generally remains captive to its underlying moral code. It is only when we closely examine the fine grain of differences within the text that we begin to discern not only the power of this code to shape the text's discourse but also the points at which the code disjoins itself for the attentive reader. In this third example of the code's internal fractures, the small difference we have discovered in the association of *petitesse* and *cupidité* allows us to read the workers' revolt as in part an act of *grandeur*. Despite the powerful symmetry of the text's binary system, it contains within itself the basis for contesting its code.[27]

Truth/Literature

Finally, one should consider an ambiguity in the text's commanding formal polarity of literature and truth. This pair is not only deployed in a moral critique of the events and actors of 1848, but it controls the

---

27. One could, of course, make a more *ad hominem* attack on the code of *Recollections* and point out that its positioning of *grandeur* in the binary system connects it with the outlook of a landed aristocracy (*tant est grand la vitalité de ces vieux corps aristocratiques*) (177/64) which is immune from the kind of desire for equality which afflicts those without property or security. This is precisely the complaint of Sainte-Beuve in 1865, who, of course, had not read the *Recollections* but had noticed similar themes when he reviewed the collected works published by Beaumont in the 1860s. *Nouveaux Lundis,* 10 (Paris: Michel Levy, 1874), 317–18.

text's commitment to the spontaneous mirroring of truth as opposed to the studied use of literary device. But there are occasional moments when the text, by the excessive force of its attack on the literary, makes the reader wonder if there is not a fascination of the forbidden at work. Thus the exaggerated portrait of Lamartine makes him out to be not only totally self-centered and oblivious to the needs of his country but also the pure incarnation of literature in politics, giving no thought at all to truth but only to effect.

The most revealing instance of an excessive attack on the "literary spirit," however, is the text's account of Tocqueville's argument with his close friend, the writer J. J. Ampère on the night of February 24. Ampère was as excitedly optimistic about the events of February 24 as Tocqueville was bitter and depressed. The two fell into a hot argument, Tocqueville battering Ampère with the full weight of the "indignation, pain and anger that had accumulated in my heart." He remembers among other things shouting at his friend: "You understand nothing of what is happening; you judge like some Parisian idler or a poet. You call this the triumph of freedom; it is the final defeat. I tell you, this people you admire so naively has just succeeded in showing it is incapable and unworthy of living in freedom" (89/68). The problem with Ampère, in Tocqueville's view, was that he was inclined "to import the spirit of the salons into literature and that of literature into politics." "What I call the spirit of literature in politics consists in seeing what is ingenuous and new rather than what is true, in preferring what makes for an interesting *tableau* rather than a useful one, in being more sensitive to make the actors play and speak well, independently of the effects of the play as a whole, and, finally, to be convinced more by impressions than by reasons (88/67). Although given to indignation, Tocqueville was notoriously restrained in his relationships. The vehemence of his attack on his friend Ampère and the terms in which it is couched suggest we are touching a crucial issue for the writer himself. If we set what he tells us of the literary spirit in politics against his own rejection of literariness for the *Recollections*, there is an evident tension. The most obvious example of deliberate literariness in the text is the moralizing ending to Part 1, where Barrot, Thiers, Guizot, and Louis-Philippe are shown as receiving their just deserts. This ending is certainly contrived in the sense Tocqueville explicitly set out to avoid. Yet, most of the literary devices used by the text are less obvious and less consciously employed. One goal of my analysis has been to show how rhetorical and literary the *Recollections* is despite its attempt to give us a mirror of truth rather than a work of literature. It is precisely the refusal of Tocqueville's discursive *practice* to honor his own truth versus literature dichotomy which makes the *Recollections* and his other texts still readable today. We read them in part because their insights continue to strike us as "ingenuous and new," because their *tableaux* are not only "useful" but "interesting," because their "impressions" are often as convincing as their "reasons"; in sum, because they are not only truth but also literature.

Yet to the extent the avoidance of literariness means the refusal to use rhetoric in a merely *ornamental* way, Tocqueville has been relatively successful. In the *Recollections,* as in his other writings, rhetoric is as much an instrument for *exploring* the world through discourse as a device for simply expressing a preconceived meaning. Hence, the elements of traditional rhetoric such as comparison and antithesis allow the text to make sense of the world in discourse without reducing it to an unambiguous system that would be of interest only to the analyst of past ideologies. That Tocqueville does not have as much control of his text in the *Recollections* as he did in *Democracy in America* or will in the *The Old Regime and the Revolution* can be taken as a tribute to his relative success in resisting literary intentionality. In this section on ambiguities in the *Recollection's* code I have also explored ways the text escapes *our* intentionality as readers, how it not only breaks out of our genre and plot categories but also defies our efforts to establish a univocal meaning for its code. Yet the ambiguities we have discovered do not nullify our efforts to uncover the constraints that codes of discourse impose on a writer like Tocqueville; they only show them to be constraints rather than inviolable laws. Like all discourse, that of the *Recollections* is constituted by ordering devices that disintegrate in our hands when pressed too hard, yet are essential to the text's intelligibility and uniqueness.

5

VOICE

When a writer of the thirteenth century referred to "the philosopher," he was not inviting his readers to imagine a certain personality who lived in ancient Athens but invoking a tradition of authority and a set of texts. For us, names such as Aristotle or Darwin, Shakespeare or Freud, may refer to a complex of ideas, stand for a cultural period, recall a style of thinking, or invoke the aid of a certain prestige. To say that the individuals who bore these names are historically less important than the constellation of associations and functions attached to their names is not to deny we can learn something about their work from their lives; it means only that to mention a name is not a simple act and we ought to ask what it is we are doing. By "Tocqueville" do we mean a certain kind of political thinking and way of analyzing society; do we mean the set of writings which includes *Democracy in America,* the *Recollections,* and *The Old Regime;* or do we mean that aloof anglophile aristocrat and frustrated parliamentarian who divided his time between the Chateau de Tocqueville and Paris?

A similar complexity emerges when we ask: who is the "I" that addresses us in the *Recollections?* At first glance the text, as a memoir, would appear of necessity to be the monological production of Alexis de Tocqueville in convalescent retreat at his chateau in La Manche or his apartments in Versailles or Sorrento. If we look more closely at the discourse of the *Recollections,* however, the author seems to have distributed his text in several voices. Just as the public meaning of a name is to be found in its functions, so in this partly private and confessional document, who "Tocqueville" is will not be discovered by focusing on extratextual evidence for the singular personality that produced it, but by analyzing the various discursive functions assumed by the "I" who writes.[1]

Over the last seventy years voice or point of view has not only come to be seen by many literary critics as *the* instrument for pursuing the craft of fiction but has also produced a forest of theories, typologies, and terminologies.[2] Even the terms *voice* and *point of view* themselves have been at times rejected, opposed to each other, or redefined beyond recognition. Voice seems to imply that each mode of discourse in a work must be the expression of a particular persona lying behind it, but textual voices are as much an effect of writing as of authorial intent, as much a grammatical as a psychological phenomenon. Similarly, point of view can refer both to an attitudinal/ideological perspective on events and to a physical or psychological standpoint toward events. I have chosen to retain the term *voice* to refer to the general phenomena traditionally signified by both voice and point of view, but I often substitute the phrase "mode of discourse" or "discursive viewpoint" in order to emphasize that we are dealing with strands within the total fabric of discourse.[3]

1. Bakhtin makes a similar point about the non-identity of the writing and the "written" self. "To identify oneself absolutely with oneself, to identify ones "I" with the "I" that I tell is as impossible as to lift oneself up by the hair." Cited in Todorov, *Mikhail Bakhtin: The Dialogical Principle* (Minneapolis: University of Minnesota Press, 1984), 52.

2. There seem to be three major stages in modern point of view theory. The first begins with Henry James's argument for the superiority of "showing" over "telling" and led subsequent theorists to establish prescriptive typologies. The normative nature of these typologies led in turn to a revolt against general typologies from two directions: in America, Wayne Booth argued from the perspective of rhetorical analysis that authorial presence is subtler and more complex than any typology based on showing versus telling could accommodate; in Europe, formalist and structuralist critics, ignoring authorial presence, focused on the development of a narratology within which point of view was reconceptualized as only one enunciative dimension. The third stage, while incorporating the rhetorical and formal-structural approaches, has emphasized narrative as an act of communication which takes place in a particular social-historical context.

3. Gérard Genette has persuasively argued the case for *distinguishing* point of *view* ("who sees?" which he terms "mode"), from *voice* ("who speaks?"). Gérard Genette, *Narrative Discourse* (Ithaca, N.Y.: Cornell University Press, 1980), 185–86, and Gérard Genette, *Nouveau discours* (Paris: Éditions du Seuil, 1983), 28–29. In a first person non-fiction narrative, however, these differences are less important than in a first or third person fictional account. Although I have learned as much from Genette's work as from any other theorist, I have decided to avoid his particular terminology

One contemporary theorist, Boris Uspensky, has developed a matrix for analyzing voice or point of view which systematizes the multiple senses of ordinary usage. Rather than a typology of voices (for example, "first-person retrospective," "editorial omniscience," "I-narrator"), he suggests a criteriology that consists of "planes" of analysis. The planes Uspensky describes are (1) the *psychological,* concerned with the extent and nature of knowledge; (2) the *spatial-temporal,* concerned with perspective and scope; (3) the *ideological,* concerned with evaluative judgments; (4) the *phraseological,* concerned with grammar, tense, style, and so on. In addition one can consider each of these planes in terms of an *external/internal* axis, that is, whether events or characters are seen or described from "within" a certain psychological or ideological perspective or from "outside."[4]

Although formal criteria of the kind Uspensky has developed are more flexible and descriptive in their applicability to specific texts than are the older typologies, this kind of structural approach is incomplete since it does not give sufficient attention to another plane of analysis which, in my opinion, is the crucial one: what one could call *discursive function.* By function I mean simply what has to be accomplished in the act of writing. Whether one looks at narrative discourse with the help of traditional rhetoric or from the perspective of contemporary "speech act" or communication theory, every text can be seen as having to accomplish certain tasks.[5] Some of these tasks are common

---

which is highly useful to specialists but would overburden the general reader. Thus in using "mode of discourse" or "discursive viewpoint" I combine two things which Genette distinguished.

4. Boris Uspensky, *A Poetics of Composition* (Berkeley: University of California Press, 1973), chaps. 1–4. Taken together the spatial-temporal and psychological planes parallel Genette's "mode" (distance and focalization) and the ideological and phraseological planes parallel Genette's "voice."

5. Both Genette and Susan Snaider Lanser have broadly defined these tasks following Jakobsen's description of linguistic functions in the act of communication. For Genette's list see *Narrative Discourse,* 256–58, and *Nouveau discours,* 90. Lanser's categories are (1) *Status* (identity, credibility, skill of narrator), (2) *Contact* (physical and psychological relation to reader), (3) *Stance* (relation to form and content on grammatical, psychological, spatial-temporal and ideological planes). *The Narrative Act* (Princeton, N.J.: Princeton University, 1981), 86–106. Although one could interpret Uspensky's planes as functions (especially *ideology*) they can more usefully be assigned, as Lanser does, to the task of criteria for the function she calls *stance* and

to nearly all forms of discourse, others vary depending on authorial intention, choice of genre, and social-historical context. In addition, each text normally has a set of tasks specific to its own aims. Obviously, the primary task of a narrative text is to narrate, just as the primary task of a legal brief is to persuade through precedent and argument, even though legal briefs may use narrative and narratives use arguments. Other functions of discourse common to most narrative texts include: establishing the writer's status and credibility; creating a certain kind of rapport with the reader; identifying the situation or context for reading the text; offering directions to the reader concerning the organization of the text; summarizing or commenting on key events, themes, arguments, etc.

All these functions can be grouped under two broad categories: first, functions that concern the writer's relation to the reader and to the general character of the text as a whole, and second, functions that concern the writer's relation to the content of the text. I have already discussed the first group of writerly functions in my initial analysis of the *Recollections'* opening paragraphs and we will return to these functions at the end of this chapter. As for the functions that make up the second group, that is, those concerned with the writer's relation to content, I believe it is possible to identify and name each by describing their distinctive spatial-temporal, psychological, ideological, and phraseological stance. Naturally, like all conceptual analyses, the process of distinguishing and naming these strands of discourse must pull apart what the reader experiences simply as a continuous flow. Yet it is only by performing this operation that one can understand the pattern of voices which gives the discourse of the *Recollections* its particular force and interest.

I have already found it necessary from time to time to distinguish in the text the perspective of the Tocqueville who is writing in 1850–51 from that of the Tocqueville who was on the scene in 1848–49. Despite the short lapse of time involved, there are manifest differences

which I am treating as "recollection" and so on. What she treats as *contact* and *status* I have called the *writerly function*. Finally, one cannot help noticing that many of these functions were already covered by the categories of traditional rhetoric within *disposition*.

between the two perspectives in information as well as in feeling and attitude. It is one thing to be in the midst of a revolution not knowing how it will come out, another to be sitting at one's writing desk in Sorrento looking back. In a text like the *Recollections,* the crucial question with respect to voice, therefore, is how this difference between the narrator and the protagonist will be handled. As Gérard Genette has pointed out, there is no more reason for an autobiographical narrative to view events from the limited perspective of its hero than from that of its narrator. On the contrary, one would normally expect the narrator to describe things from his or her more knowledgeable perspective.[6] Hence, for the *Recollections* to tell the story of 1848 from the point of view of the protagonist (the Tocqueville of 1848) is the result of a deliberate stylistic choice, a choice that Tocqueville announces in the opening paragraphs as one of the ruling limitations on his account. Yet it has been equally apparent throughout my exposition of the text that the narrator also has much to say about events from the perspective of 1850–51. Hence, it is clear that there are at least two voices in the *Recollections,* one of which I call the voice of *recollection* since it seeks to faithfully reproduce the experience of Tocqueville in 1848, the other I call *commentary* since it typically intervenes to comment from the perspective of 1850 on the material generated by the recollective voice.

This division of the text into recollection and commentary would hardly be noteworthy were it not that the perspective of the narrator-commentator itself turns out on closer analysis not to be a simple one, but divided among at least four different functions each with distinguishing marks on one or more of the planes outlined above. In summary, these functions are: *commentary proper, wisdom, impersonal narration,* and *reading instructions.* Naturally, there are overlapping instances and ambiguous cases, but there are also a sufficient number of clear examples of each kind of discourse to make a summary analysis possible. In each case I will describe the general characteristics of the voice in question, using Uspensky's matrix of criteria to enable us to see similarities and differences more clearly.

Finally, there is a *writerly* function that concerns the situation of the *Recollections'* composition, the status of Tocqueville as a writer, and his relation to the reader. This function is not only to be distinguished

6. Genette, *Narrative Discourse,* 198–200, and *Nouveau discours,* 67–73.

from the others in its occasionally explicit manifestation in certain passages, but also for the way it underwrites the other functions, producing a specific kind of *authorial presence*. For that reason I will delineate the other voices first and turn at the end of the discussion to the question of the writer's presence in the text.

Recollection

Recollecting discourse, quite simply, *is* the secret mirror, the supposedly spontaneous nonliterary discourse of "truth" which performs the central discursive function of eyewitness narration. Here one can see even more clearly the significance of the *Recollections'* opening meditation on the secret mirror. Although memory is of necessity an activity of the present (in this case 1850–51), in the opening passages of the *Recollections* it is treated as if it were a pure medium, a flawless (because secret) mirror reflecting the perceptions, thoughts, feelings, and actions of the Tocqueville of 1848. Nevertheless, the "images" in this metaphorical mirror of memory must become language and that is the function of recollective discourse. Since it is the Tocqueville of 1850–51 who writes, however, the writing itself must provide the reader with clues about what is written from the point of view of Tocqueville the participant in 1848 and what is written from the perspective of Tocqueville the writer of 1850.

Although writing is spontaneously able to embody remembered events and experiences as if told from the point of view of the past and readers are easily able to enter the atmosphere of this recreated past, giving an account of *how* writers and readers are able to do this is not as easy. Grammatical tense alone, for example, is not a certain marker of temporal perspective since past experiences can be narrated in the present tense and readers can decode past-tense narratives as engendering a fictional present. Even in a nonfiction text like the *Recollections,* it is less tense per se than shifts in tense or the combination of tense with other markers which signals a shift from the perspective of the writer's present to that of the experienced past.

Although externally viewed, everything remembered by a writer is in the "now" of the act of writing, what is intentionally grasped in the writer's consciousness and embodied in the text is the "now" of the past. Readers, for their part, though they know (if one asked them) that the text is a product of the writer's "now," normally do not attend to the writer's "now" but to the text's world of the past which has its own "now." I speak of a past "now" rather than simply of "then" in order to stress the way language can lead readers into a time frame, in this case into a past "now point" from which the reader will understand everything that is recounted as before, after or cotemporal with this past moment.[7] When Tocqueville writes, "I remember that two days before the revolution of February, finding myself at a grand ball at the Turkish ambassador's, I ran into Duvergier de Hauranne," it is not the "now" of the act of "I remember" (for example, 1850), but the "now" of February 23, 1848, to which the reader attends. It is a "now" because we are quite prepared for this paragraph of the text to order its tenses around events before, simultaneous with, or subsequent to the past "now" established by the opening line. The general function of the recollective mode of discourse in the *Recollections* is to provide the linguistic means whereby the reader may be drawn into this past of 1848–49.

Yet even in passages clearly in the recollective mode, the "now" of the writer can make itself suddenly felt, often in subtle ways. Consider these sentences which describe the morning of February 25, the day after the flight of Louis-Philippe: "I found the streets peaceful and half deserted, as one ordinarily finds them in Paris on Sunday morning, when the rich sleep and the poor rest. One encountered from time to time, along the walls, the victors of the day before, but most were returning home without bothering passersby. In the few shops that were still open, one could see bourgeois, who appeared frightened but above all astonished, like spectators who, arriving at the denouement, still seek the true meaning of the play" (90–91/69–70). This example seems unambiguously in the recollective mode; we are situated there and then, walking the streets with Tocqueville in 1848. Yet we cannot help but ask if every phrase in this section really reflects just what the Tocqueville of 1848 saw and thought. We have no trouble crediting the first part of the sentence "In the few shops that were still open one could see bourgeois, who appeared frightened but above all aston-

7. Ann Banfield uses "NOW" as a technical term in her grammar of narrative and representation. Ann Banfield, *Unspeakable Sentences: Narration and Representation in the Language of Fiction* (London: Routledge and Kegan Paul, 1982), 163–65. The notion of a "now point" in the past can be found among thinkers as diverse as Russell and Husserl.

ished" to Tocqueville in 1848; but what about the remainder "like spectators who, arriving at the denouement, still seek the meaning of the play"? Did Tocqueville really think this simile in 1848, or is it not a literary embellishment we owe to Tocqueville the writer of 1850? Should it be seen as a cotemporal pause (recollection) or a brief retrospective digression (commentary)? There is no way to be certain and in the normal course of reading, the question would probably not arise. But the ambiguity is worth noting since it underlines how difficult it was for Tocqueville to establish and maintain the recollective mode of discourse by remaining resolutely in the perspective of 1848 and allowing the secret mirror to do its work.[8]

In order to describe in a more general way how the act of writing achieves this differentiation of recollection from commentary, wisdom, and impersonal narration, I will consider recollective discourse in terms of the four planes of analysis outlined above. On the *spatial-temporal* plane, recollective discourse normally presents events from the perspective of Tocqueville in 1848, from where he sat in the Assembly and from the limited view and knowledge of events he had as he walked the streets of Paris acting into a future yet unknown. *Psychologically,* such passages are from "within" the Tocqueville of 1848–49, evoking not only what he saw but also his thoughts and feelings, especially his fears and hopes for the future of the Republic, and for his own role in events. *Ideologically,* the recollecting discourse is not far from the assumptions underlying passages of explicit commentary, yet certain differences between the two can be sensed especially when it comes to judgments on events or persons. In the passages of recollection the judgments on personalities or policies are usually more spontaneous and harsher than in those of commentary, where there is often a softening brought on by subsequent experience. For example, from the perspective of 1850, Tocqueville tells us that Lamartine's task was more difficult and his actions more appropriate than Tocqueville the participant had realized in 1848 (129–30/111–

---

8. Banfield has argued with respect to fiction that such metaphors may still be read as part of the narrative itself (or of represented speech) and need not be attributed to the narrator or treated as authorial intrusion. But with a nonfiction work we can more legitimately ask whether a recollected perception, thought or feeling is accurately recalled and whether it is represented in a manner consistent with the probable experience and language of the protagonist (something we can check from other sources than the text in question).

112). In our chapter on the pictorial and thematic codes, we have already examined the ideological ambivalence ingredient in Tocqueville's outlook on workers. In general one can say that it is in the recollective passages where Tocqueville's spontaneous stereotypes are most evident.

But there is another, more subtle aspect of ideology, which we could call, following Frederic Jameson, the ideology of form.[9] The choice of the pure eyewitness approach, the invocation of the secret mirror and of spontaneity as opposed to literary composition, in itself implies that one may thereby achieve not only honesty but truth. Yet the most powerful ideological seduction is to appear to have no ideology, which in this case is part of the function of the rhetoric-of-antirhetoric ingredient in the secret mirror.

It is the characteristics of the *phraseological* plane which are most interesting with respect to the way they distinguish the discourse of recollection from other modes. Tocqueville's voice of recollection is primarily a descriptive, representational discourse, most of the time "telling" but occasionally "showing" by giving us a narrative chain embedded with bits of dialogue and vivid description. There are also what we could call grammatical "markers" that signal a shift in the text from one discursive perspective to another. In the case of recollective discourse these signposts take two forms, one an introductory phrase in the first person invoking a mental state, the other a shift to the French simple past tense (aorist). Markers of the first kind are phrases such as: I remember that (*Je me souviens que*); I recall that (*Je me rapelle que*); I found that (*Je trouvais que*); I noticed that (*Je remarquai que*). The last example, by the way, is also in the aorist providing a double marker. As obvious and trivial as some of these marking devices may seem when we make them explicit, they can automatically shift the discursive viewpoint without our consciously taking note of them. They are quiet signals that we have crossed a border and thus they play a crucial role in determining the way the text shapes our response.

As beginning students of French learn to their regret, the French language is not only equipped with different sets of tense endings for

9. Fredric Jameson, *Marxism and Form* (Princeton: Princeton University Press, 1971), 402–3.

incomplete past actions (the imperfect: *elle allait,* she was going or used to go) and completed past actions (the perfect or *passé composé: elle est allée,* she went), but also has a second set of endings for this same completed past (aorist or *passé simple: elle alla,* she went). Although the aorist or simple past was once regularly used in spoken discourse where it seems to have designated a more distant past than the *passé composé,* its near disappearance from spoken usage has led to the widespread view that it functions less as a tense than as a conventional sign for literary narrative, whether of the novel or history. As Roland Barthes put it, "withdrawn from spoken French, the simple past, cornerstone of the Narrative, always signals an art; it is part of the ritual of Belles-Lettres."[10]

There is an often cited essay of Emile Benveniste, however, which has argued for a deeper linguistic significance to the aorist. Benveniste suggests that the two systems of past tenses should be seen not merely as French conventions for written (aorist) as opposed to spoken (perfect) language, but as two complete systems of utterance (*énonciation*) which he terms "history" and "discourse," respectively. Discourse, for Benveniste, is characterized by its constant, though implicit, reference to the speaker, to an "I" addressing a "you," whether the communication is oral or written, and it can employ any tense *except* the system: aorist, imperfect, pluperfect. The chief distinguishing mark of the "historical" mode of enunciation, on the other hand, is the aorist and the exclusion of "every 'autobiographical' linguistic form" so that it appears "events seem to narrate themselves."[11]

Yet as Louis Marin suggests, just as Benveniste's "historical" enunciation "brings about the *simulation of an absence,*" autobiographical writing seems to reverse this process by combining the first person with aorist narrative to bring about a simulation of presence even in passages whose normal effect on the reader should, according to Ben-

---

10. Roland Barthes, *Le Degré zéro de l'écriture* (Paris: Éditions du Seuil, 1953), 25–26; *Writing Degree Zero* (New York: Hill and Wang, 1967), 30. Barthes also suggests that the aorist serves the additional function of distancing and objectifying the past, which he sees as a function designed to assure the bourgeoisie of the stability of its world and to allow it to universalize its values in the act of representation, *Writing Degree Zero,* 31–32.

11. Benveniste, *Problèmes de linguistique générale* (Paris: Gallimard, 1966), 239–42.

veniste, be that of "events narrating themselves."[12] Thus there is an oppositional grammatical effect in first-person historical narratives since they seem to combine the supposedly exclusive forms of personal "discourse" and anonymous "history." In a historical memoir like the *Recollections,* therefore, the title and opening passages, which invoke readerly expectations appropriate to the memoir genre, combined with the omnipresence of the "I," set up a constant *tension* whenever we encounter aorist passages, since the aorist leads us to expect an anonymous narrative. This is one reason why aorist passages do not draw the reader's attention directly to the "I" of the writer but down into the "now" of the past. Consider the following passage, which describes Tocqueville's actions immediately after Guizot's announcement of his own dismissal. Tocqueville has just walked out of the Assembly in the company of Dufaure:

> Je le quittai bientôt et me rendit chez M. de Beaumont; là, je trouvai tous les coeurs réjouis. J'étais loin de partager cette joie et, me trouvant avec des gens devant qui je pouvais parler en liberté, j'en donne les raisons. (55)

> I soon left him and went to Beaumont's; there, I found everyone rejoicing. I was far from sharing that joy and, finding myself with people before whom I could speak freely, I gave my reasons. (34)

Except for the use of the first person, this passage is consistently in Benveniste's "historical" mode of enunciation, combining the aorist with the imperfect. Thus, the "I" does not draw the reader's attention to Tocqueville the writer in 1850 but by its conjunction with the aorist draws the reader down into the "now" of the represented past where that other Tocqueville (of 1848) lives and speaks as "I."

Consideration of a more complex passage of recollective discourse, however, will show that the recollective mode has even greater flex-

---

12. Louis Marin, "The Autobiographical Interruption: About Stendhal's *Life of Henry Brulard,*" *Modern Language Notes* 93 (1978): 597–603. For similar critiques see Jean Starobinski, "The Style of Autobiography," in *Autobiography: Essays Theoretical and Critical,* ed. James Olney (Princeton, N.J.: Princeton University, 1980), 73–83; Banfield, *Unspeakable Sentences,* 149–67. A more general analysis of the Benveniste polarity can be found in Colin McCabe, *Tracking the Signifier* (Minneapolis: University of Minnesota Press, 1985) 82–92.

ibility that this duality of the "I" when it comes to the representation of time. In the following statement, Tocqueville is commenting on Dufaure's argument that the constitution should provide for a single chamber to better face a strong, popularly elected chief executive.

> Je me souviens que je lui répondis qu'en effet cela pourrait se rencontrer, mais que ce qui était sûr dès à present, c'est que deux grands pouvoirs naturellement jaloux l'un de l'autre et placés dans un tête-à-tête éternel (ce fut mon mot), sans pouvoir jamais recourir à l'arbitrage d'un trois-ième pouvoir, serait aussitôt en mauvais procédé ou en guerre et y resteraient constamment jusqu'à ce que l'un eût détruit l'autre. (185)

> I remember that I replied to him that it could be the case but what was certain at present, was that two great powers naturally jealous of each other and placed in an eternal tête-à-tête (that was my term), without ever being able to have recourse to the arbitration of a third power, would at once be on bad terms if not at war with each other and would remain so until one had destroyed the other. (174)

Here the mixture of the present, imperfect and aorist tenses is moti-vated by the fact that the act of recollecting/writing takes place in the present but the spatial perspective of the recollection itself is that of the past, that is that of the Tocqueville who sat on the Constitutional Commission in the spring of 1848. Moreover, the statement from 1848 which is recollected in this passage has within itself a reference to its own present and to its own future, to a future, moreover, which had come to pass by the time of the act of writing (the conflict of the Assembly with Louis-Napoleon) and whose outcome, which lies in the future of the act of writing in 1850 (the Napoleonic coup), is known to the reader but not the writer.

Thus the temporal possibilities of the "recollective" discourse are extremely complex and permit what at first glance appears to be a straightforward expression of memory, to carry several levels of signif-icance. In the passage we are considering there is (1) a level of factual recall (aorist), that is, what Tocqueville happened to reply to Dufaure in the spring of 1848; (2) a level of actualization of this recall (present) in 1850, that is, the implicit assertion that Tocqueville's prediction of a death struggle between the executive and legislative (in the future of the past recalled) was coming true in the present of 1850; (3) a level of "reference" to the outcome of this prediction (future), that is, the reader's knowledge of the December 2, 1851, coup in which Louis-Napoleon did, in fact, destroy the Assembly. The reference to the specifically realized future of the text cannot, of course, be an authorial intention, but is an artifact of any knowledgeable reading. Here is one of the points where the theory of point of view will often differ for historical works as compared to fictional ones. Normally, readers can no more know how the events of a purely fictional world "came out" in the future outside the text than they can know how many children were born to Lady Macbeth (the historical novel constituting an important boundary case). Thus our consideration of recollective discourse on the phraseological plane has shown how it can contain not only the viewpoint of Tocqueville in 1848 but can at the same time reflect the psychological and ideological viewpoint of Tocqueville in 1850 and, because it is a historical text, remind the knowledgeable reader of the outcome of processes ongoing at the time it was written but unknown to the writer.[13]

Commentary

Although the discourse of commentary is normally directed toward the content of recollection, it stands on its own in the text as the second most frequent strand of discourse. The Tocqueville of 1850–51 has much to say about the events of the previous three years and we know from his other works that commentary and analysis are his preferred mode of writing. Indeed, part of the personal achievement of the *Recollections* is that Tocqueville was able to write a recollective narrative at all. If the recollecting voice is the spontaneous reflection of the secret mirror, the voice of commentary functions as the voice of social

---

13. Doritt Cohn has called attention to a similar temporal flexibility in the use of narrated monologue in both third-person and first-person fiction; *Transparent Minds: Narrative Modes for Presenting Consciousness in Fiction* (Princeton: Princeton University Press, 1978), 126 and 167. There is no question in this passage from Tocqueville of a monologue, however, but only a narrated or reported speech; the complex temporal effects are the result of the combination of the typical autobiographical form (aorist and first person), the narrative situation (narrating self plus experiencing self), and the text's referential character (evoking the reader's knowledge of subsequent events).

analysis and reflective political history. The discourse of commentary is *spatiotemporally* omnipresent with respect to the events of 1848–49 and *psychologically* external to those who participated in the events (including the Tocqueville of 1848), attempting to make sense out of them in terms of where things had arrived by 1850. As we have already noted, passages of commentary sometimes also display a greater *ideological* tolerance than those of recollection, for example, his evaluation of Lamartine or his reflection on the possibility that beliefs about property arrangements are socially conditioned. Although there is sometimes a modulation of the ideological stance owing to the reflective situation of the writer, and perhaps also to the fact that the proletarian threat had by then been defeated, in general the same stereotypes and thematic polarities hold for the discourse of commentary as for that of recollection. Considered in terms of the ideology of form, the discourse of commentary reflects Tocqueville's conscious political and moral commitments. Although at times the ironic and satiric seem about to overwhelm both the recollected participant and the writer-commentator, and a sigh of resignation occasionally escapes the convalescent of Sorrento, the mode of commentary exists to draw specific political and moral lessons from the events of 1848. On the *phraseological* level, commenting discourse is characteristically analytical and evaluative and tends not only toward a more abstract vocabulary but toward the balanced periods typical of Tocqueville's rhetoric in his other works. The characteristic marker of commentary is a generalizing vocabulary often accompanied by a shift from the aorist to the present tense.

In order to see how the commentary mode works we need to consider an example where the text switches from one mode of discourse to another. The passage in the pastoral chapter describing Tocqueville's return to the ancestral chateau clearly moves from recollection to commentary, marked by a shift from past to present tense and from specific representations to a generalizing discourse. The first part of the passage is in the aorist and draws the reader into the "now" point of April, 1848: "I arrived unexpectedly. The empty rooms. . . ." (J'arrivai sans être attendu. Ces salles vides. . . .) (113/94). Then, after drawing us by means of the aorist and the enumeration of vivid detail into the concrete "now" of this past and through it into a memory extending back to childhood, the paragraph suddenly shifts to the present tense and the present time of the writer.

J'admire comme chez l'homme l'imagination est plus colorée et plus saisissante que le réel. Je venais de voir tomber la monarchie; j'ai assisté depuis aux scènes les plus terribles et les plus sanglantes; eh bien! je le déclare, aucun de ces grands tableaux ne m'avait causé et ne me causa une émotion aussi poignante et aussi profonde, que celle éprouvée par moi, ce jour-là, à la vue de l'antique demeure de mes pères et au souvenir des jours paisibles et des heures que j'y avais passés sans connaître leur prix. Je puis dire que ce fut là et ce jour-là que je compris le mieux toute l'amertume des révolutions. (113–114)

I marvel at how much more colorful and compelling man's imagination is than reality. I had just seen the monarchy fall; since then I have witnessed the most terrible and bloody scenes; well! I tell you, none of these tableaux caused then or later an emotion as poignant or profound as I experienced that day at the sight of the ancient home of my fathers and the memory of the peaceful days and happy hours that I passed there without knowing their price. I can say that it was there and on that day I really understood the full bitterness of revolutions." (94–95)

Here Tocqueville the writer-commentator gathers together the past "now" of April 1848 ("experienced by me on that day") along with the immediate antecedent of that past ("the monarchy fall") and its June outcome ("terrible and bloody scenes") and finally, the more distant past of childhood ("the peaceful days . . . of my fathers"). This summary of four levels of past experience follows a transitional generalization about the imagination in which the "I" suddenly becomes that of Tocqueville the writer commenting in 1850 on his past experience. Without this shift to the present tense, the transitional sentence "I marvel at the way man's imagination is more colorful and compelling than the real" would be read as a thought of Tocqueville in 1848. This shift from the past to the present and from detail to generalization clearly marks a shift from the discourse of recollection to that of commentary and emphasizes the distance between the narrating self and the experiencing self, a distance perfectly epitomized in the final sentence of the paragraph which functions rhetorically as a summary of the entire episode. For this final sentence emphatically marks its moment of utterance as the present of 1850. "I can say that . . ." (*Je puis dire que . . .*), yet what he experienced, that is, the moment when he "understood the full bitterness of revolutions," is just as emphatically located in a specific aoristic past, "it was there and that day" (*Ce fut là et ce-jour là*).

Sometimes, however, passages that comment on the action or situations narrated in the recollective mode use the typical tense of recollective narration, the aorist, thus creating an ambiguous situation for the reader unless some other mark of recollection or commentary comes along to help. Near the end of Part 3, Chapter 9, for example, the text shifts from several pages of aorist eyewitness description of the June Days to a long passage that comments (still in the aorist) on the reasons for the victory over the workers. "We triumphed, however, over this formidable insurrection; moreover what saved us was just what made it so terrible. . . . If the revolt had had a character less radical and seemed less fierce, it is probable that most of the bourgeoisie would have stayed home; France would not have rushed to our aid" (158/144). Two things about this passage tend to make one read it as written from the viewpoint of commentary despite the preponderance of the aorist. First, the psychological and ideological perspective seems too considered and the enumeration of counterfactuals is too complete for the perspective of someone involved in the action, for example, France had not yet "rushed to the aid" of the forces of order at the point in the narrative where this comment occurs. Second, the phrase "We triumphed, however . . ." (*Nous triomphâmes, pourtant . . .*) itself already puts us at the end of the war and tends to shift the reader to the viewpoint of Tocqueville in the winter of 1850–51.

Thus, the division of a text into discursive functions is not a matter of finding some simple marks of identification which unambiguously announce every shift in perspective. Occasionally, the temporal differences are redundantly marked: "My opinion then, however, and it has remained the same since, was that the leading demagogues did not intend to destroy the Assembly but only sought at this point to make use of it through intimidation" (131/114). But most of the shifts back and forth between the viewpoint of recollection and commentary are more subtle than this and occasionally are impossible to sort out. I do not find this an embarrassment to my analysis since the aim is not to reduce the text to a heap of labeled fragments, but to identify the set of devices that generate our experience of the text's characteristic style. Certainly I have shown so far that the operation of writing with respect to viewpoint is far more intricate than any simple division into the voices of narrator and actor can grasp.

Wisdom

The mode of discourse I have referred to as wisdom is closely related to that of commentary, sharing similarities on several planes. I call it wisdom because it is typically the enunciation of a general rule or principle or a universal moral/political lesson. There are three types of wisdom in the *Recollections*. Closest to commentary are generalizations about Parisian or French character since they are place specific although they do extend beyond the 1848–49 revolution, for example, "It is the street urchins of Paris, ordinarily, who start insurrections and they usually do it gaily, like schoolboys off on a holiday" (51/29). Sometimes these sayings are embedded in a sentence which is otherwise part of a recollective passage: "And, as the French in their political passions are as rationalist as they are unreasonable, these popular assemblies [the clubs] spent all their time fabricating principles which could later justify acts of violence" (131/114).

A second type of wisdom consists of broad generalizations about social or political behavior. The longest and most important passage of this kind is the discussion in Part 2 of the role of causes and accidents in history which begins: "I hate, for my part, those absolute systems which make all the events of history depend on great first causes" (84/62). Most other generalizations of this sort appear in passing, sometimes as part of a sentence written in another discursive mode. For example, in a paragraph written in the recollective mode describing the state of affairs as Tocqueville found it on returning to Paris in late May 1849, just after the election of 150 Montagnards had so terrified the majority, he writes of the party of order: "it was going to form more than two-thirds of the new Assembly; however, I found it prey to a terror so profound that I could only compare it to that which followed February, so true it is that in politics one must reason as in war and never forget that the effect of events depends less on what they are in themselves than on the impression they make" (199/188).

The final type of wisdom is a mode of discourse still more universal but with a moral and/or metaphysical turn. Such I believe is the sense of the famous wind and cord passage which draws the "lesson" of the Banquet Affair.

Il faut avoir vécu longtemps au milieu des partis et dans le tourbillon même où ils se meuvent pour comprendre à quel point les hommes s'y

poussent mutuellement hors de leurs propres desseins et comme la des-
tinée de ce monde marche par l'effet, mais souvent au rebours des désirs
de tous ceux qui la produisent, semblable au cerf-volant qui chemine par
l'action opposée du vent et de la corde. (50)

One has to have spent years in the whirlwind of party politics to realize
how far men drive each other from their intended aims and how the
destiny of the world marches by the effect, but often contrary to the
desires of those who produce that effect, like the kite which flies by the
opposed action of the wind and the cord. (28)

Each type of wisdom discourse shows a progressive expansion of
spatial-temporal scope beyond that of commentary. Whereas commentary concerns the interpretation of specific events or situations in
1848 from the perspective of 1850, wisdom sayings refer to the French
character in general, to larger political and sociological patterns, or
finally, to a universal moral or political lesson. *Psychologically,* commentary is external to recollective discourse and enjoys the fuller
information of 1850 and 1851, whereas wisdom discourse is external
even to the viewpoint of commentary and looks at things from the
most encompassing perspective.

Ideologically, commentary reflects Tocqueville's political judgments as of 1850, whereas the discourse of wisdom seeks to be supra-
personal and ideologically nonpartisan. In terms of the ideology of
form, wisdom discourse is an attempt to look on politics philosophi-
cally and to rise from such a contemplative stance to the level of
universal moral reflection. This concern to contemplate "man in his
nature," which was enunciated at the very beginning of the *Recollections,* reflects a step back from the immediate political commitments of
the discourse of commentary. It is an effort to join that tradition of
French moralists who speak to the ages and thereby turn our attention
from the concrete demands of the historical situation.

It is on the *phraseological* or stylistic plane, however, that the
distinction of wisdom discourse from commentary is most apparent.
Commentary can take a variety of forms but is generally analytical or
descriptive whereas the discourse of wisdom tends to be compact,
balanced, and aphoristic. Wisdom also has its characteristic markers,
little phrases which indicate its universalizing scope, for example: "I
have always found that" (*J'ai toujours trouvé qu[e]*) (164/150); "how

often have I not seen around me" (*Combien n'avais-je pas vu près de moi*) (111/92); "Moreover, I have always held it a maxim that" (*J'ai d'ailleurs, toujours eu pour maxime que*) (220/214). In general most passages of wisdom discourse typically occur within sections of recollection, sometimes aiding the flow of recollected narrative by providing a generalization which helps us understand the connection of events and at other times drawing an inference or a lesson from a singular happening (201/191).[14]

Reading Instructions and Impersonal Narration

The two other types of discourse I have mentioned, impersonal narration and reading instructions, play a much smaller role in the text than the forms we have just discussed. The discourse of reading instructions gives directions concerning subject-matter limitations and style and, from time to time, interjects a statement that orients readers to the ordering of the text. In my opening chapter I analyzed the most important of the passages written in this mode: the third paragraph of the *Recollections* which states the eyewitness and temporal limitations on the text's scope. The other instances are easily identified. A number of the later interventions are reminders of the intentions and limits laid down at the beginning or excuses for temporarily violating them (that is, the few occasions he uses secondhand testimony).

Reading directions are located in the same *space-time* as that of the discourse of commentary but unlike comment, are *ideologically* "neutral," seeking only to guard the intended virtues of writing, for example, sincerity, truth, consistency, eyewitness reporting. One could, of course, argue that such virtues themselves cannot be ideologically neutral since they are in the service of the ideology pervading the other modes and that even to pretend that sincerity, truth, and consistency are virtues in the midst of a deadly class struggle can be an attempt to

14. Embedded wisdom commentary is, of course, a typical device of the nineteenth-century novel. George P. Landow has usefully distinguished such wisdom statements from the prophetic discourse of the "sage." Although Tocqueville often predicted or warned, most of his writing belongs in the tradition of wisdom typical of the *moralistes* rather than that of the prophetic sage as described by Landow. *Elegant Jeremiahs: The Sage from Carlyle to Mailer* (Ithaca, N.Y.: Cornell University Press, 1986), 22–29, 158–62.

hide the class-bound nature of one's commitment behind lofty moral-izing. *Psychologically,* the discourse of textual direction is external to all the other discourses; *phraseologically,* it is brief and addresses the reader directly concerning the form and ordering of the text rather than its content. A few citations will quickly convey its modus:

> The next day, I was given some curious details concerning this scene, which I would report here if I had not resolved to speak only of what I saw. (141/124–25)

> I am going to violate the rule I imposed on myself never to speak on the basis of another's. . . . (157/142)

> I did not wish to interrupt the story of our interior miseries in order to speak of the embarrassments which we met externally . . . I return now. (234/230)

The least frequently encountered mode of discourse in the *Recollec-tions* is *impersonal narration.* As its name suggests, it is a viewpoint which seeks to have no point of view. It alone perfectly fits what Beneviste describes by "history" as opposed to "discourse." *Spatially and temporally* it speaks from no place and no time in particular, neither from the 1848 of the participant nor the 1850 of the commen-tator and moralist. *Psychologically,* as its name implies, it is external to anyone and it speaks in a tone as *ideologically* flat as possible, pre-tending to be neutral.[15] *Phraseologically,* it employs the most undistin-guished syntax; it is the prosaics of prose. If it has any "markers," they are of the type "as everyone knows" and the use of the aorist. One would not expect to find much writing of this type in a document as personal as the *Recollections.* We can pick out a sentence here and there, an occasional paragraph, but the discourse of recollection or commentary almost immediately reappears: "One will remember that at the opening of the session of 1848, King Louis-Philippe" (47/24). The only passages of any length that are written in the neutral style are

15. As Roland Barthes has shown, however, the pretention of such historical dis-course to dispassion and anonymity are part of an ideology of the "real." See in Barthes's 1967 essay "Le Discours de l'histoire," reprinted in *Le Bruissement de la langue* (Paris: Éditions du Seuil, 1984), 153–66, in English as *The Rustle of Language* (New York: Hill and Wang, 1986), 127–40.

a few paragraphs in Chapter 4 of Part 3 which give us background information on European affairs (238–40/235–37) (244–45/241–43). Impersonal narration plays such a small role in the *Recollections* that it would hardly be worth mentioning except that the presence of this mode of historical representation, typical of many nineteenth-century narratives, throws in relief the specificity of the other modes of discourse.

Style

The characteristic rhythm of voices in the *Recollections,* which could be called its style, is determined by the way these five modes of discourse are orchestrated. The bulk of the text is in the recollective mode with extensive passages of commentary introducing, summarizing, or connecting the longer sections of recollection. The brief formulations in the mode of discourse I have called wisdom also connect statements within the discourse of recollection or commentary or draw a lesson from them. Despite their distance in viewpoint, these brief reflections or aphorisms seem a natural part of the flow of recollective prose. Partly because Tocqueville did not set out to construct a literary work, his writing did not immediately achieve a characteristic pattern of voices in the *Recollections*. In fact, if we look at the mix of the various modes of discourse as it develops we can see that it took Tocqueville a while to arrive at the particular rhythm which constitutes the *Recollections'* style.

One of the reasons Tocqueville had trouble finding the right style for the *Recollections* is that his customary way of writing was the short expository essay or chapter, not the sustained narrative. A careful examination of the opening sections of the *Recollections* reveals Tocqueville's gradual discovery of the appropriate balance of discursive modes for this text. The *Recollections* begins by announcing its intention of holding up a secret mirror to 1848 and one could justifiably expect the passages which immediately follow to be a spontaneous first-person narrative, that is, recollection. Instead the reader is offered a general portrait of the period from 1830 to 1848, and when an occasional passage from the recollective standpoint does break in, the function is always illustrative rather than representational. The same is true of the recollective passages in the account of the Banquet Affair which contains all the elements of a classical rhetorical essay.

The theme of this "essay" is that opponents in politics end up pushing each other to extreme positions far beyond what either desires. The story elements, first-person recollections and portraits again serve as illustrations of this theme rather than as representations of the course of events. After an *exordium* announcing its theme (44/21), this "essay" proceeds immediately with the rhetorical *confirmation* by presenting in turn examples (in the form of the portraits we examined) from the dynastic opposition and then from the government in order to show how each party obstinately and carelessly pursued their course oblivious of the revolution they would ignite. The last stage in an essay following traditional rhetorical form would be the *peroration* or conclusion, and at the end of this gallery of examples is, in fact, a one-sentence recapitulation in the instruction mode: "Here I need to reestablish a little the historical sequence, in order to more conveniently attach to it the thread of my recollection" (47/24). Clearly, something has gone wrong. It seems that the text has got ahead of itself, and the writer, by this intervention, shows us he realizes he has left part of the story untold. The text then starts over on the Banquet Affair, yet still not in the recollective mode but in the voice of impersonal narration: "One will recall that at the opening of the session of 1848, King Louis-Philippe." This recapitulation of the debate over the right of assembly finally gives this little essay on the Banquets what traditional rhetoric called *narration* (the facts and circumstances) which here functions as a supplement to the preceding arguments of the *confirmation*, providing additional examples of the way excess on each side pushed the other to yet further excess. The essay is now ready for a true *peroration,* which begins with a direct rhetorical appeal from writer to reader: "And see how human affairs are pushed ahead on the rebound!" This inaugurates a paragraph in the commentary mode which summarizes the rebound positions of the three leading parties and concludes with the already cited elegiac wisdom passage about the wind and the cord (50/27–28).

For its first thirty or so pages, then, the *Recollections* is only recollective to the extent of illustrating passages of commentary, and its account of the affair of the Banquets has taken the specific form of a traditional rhetorical essay using remembered incidents as examples. If the *Recollections* had continued in this vein it would have ended up closer to the style of *Democracy in America.* But the rest of Part 1 is quite different. Immediately following the wind and cord paragraph, the text turns to a genuinely recollective mode of discourse drawing us into the concrete "now" of the past and with more or less brief interruption stays in that mode to the end of Part 1 (51/29). From here on we are in the street or the Assembly with the Tocqueville of 1848 sharing his perceptions and feelings, the point of view is resolutely "there and then," we learn of events as he learned of them, piecemeal through friends or rumors. Even events that would be of great significance to any narrative of 1848 (the massacre on the boulevard des Capucines) are not described if they were not witnessed; we learn of them only by hearsay as the Tocqueville of 1848 did. To be sure, there are many passages of commentary as well as several short interventions in the wisdom mode; but genuinely recollective prose dominates the discourse from this point on. The secret mirror is working.

Tocqueville temporarily laid the *Recollections* aside at the end of July 1850 and did not take it up again until November of that year when he and Marie and their servants were installed at Sorrento. Then it is as if he must once again struggle toward recollective discourse. Part 2 opens with a long commentary passage on the causes of the February Revolution and, though the text abruptly returns to the recollective mode in its account of Tocqueville's bitter thoughts and feelings on the day the king fled, the next chapter soon becomes a long commentary on the socialist nature of the revolt. It is only with Chapter 4 of Part 2, the pastoral account of Tocqueville's election trip to La Manche, that the recollective mode takes over and again sets the dominant tone of the writing from this point down to the end.

Given the commentary-dominated pattern of voices that was established at the beginning of Part 1 and reasserted itself early in Part 2, the reader would expect at the end of the text some return of commentary or, failing that, a writerly address that will tell us why commentary is absent. But even the little phrase terminating the final paragraph is firmly in the space-time of recollection: "the cabinet was about to fall" (263/262). As we suggested earlier, if Tocqueville had taken up his text again, as a writer he would have faced an almost insoluble difficulty. Our study of its discursive pattern shows why. The rhythm of discursive modes which orders the surface of the text and constitutes its distinctive style would surely have to be broken. Specifically, the commentary mode, after Louis-Napoleon's coup, Tocqueville's arrest, and the military repression, could hardly have taken the same form on the temporal, psychological, and ideological planes. Nor is it likely that the overall pattern of voices could have continued; one imagines it would have been difficult for commentary not to become dominant and for the perspective of December 2 not to bleed subtly into the voice of recollection. By ending without its projected "final" chapter, or any account of the coup, however, the text breaks off in the midst of its recollections and the secret mirror of recollection is operative to the end with no closing words of wisdom to tell us what the story has meant.[16]

Presence

I began with the thesis that instead of looking for a person behind the "I" of the text I would examine the discourse itself to see what traces of voice and viewpoint might be at work. Instead of a sovereign author commanding his narrative and interpreting its events to us, I found a complex texture of discursive viewpoints. Does this mean that Alexis de Tocqueville has simply dissolved into his own act of writing, that he has become no more than a character or a type in his own narrative? If I have not attended to him as author, to an image of a flesh-and-blood Tocqueville which one might project on the basis of outside biographical information, it is because I wanted to understand the working of the discourse itself. Given such a focus, my handling of what lies "outside" or "behind" the text must be approached with circumspection. Because I set out to examine the surface of the writing

16. We know from notes written on Tocqueville's way back from Sorrento in April 1851 that he intended to make the cabinet's handling of the Roman revolution and the restoration of papal control in Rome his final chapter. "Tell it from one end to the other, and take it up to our departure from events, with a little epilogue which will make known how it happened that after they overturned us, because we did not show enough vigor, they gave up everything, not only in Rome, but in all of Italy (286–87/288–89). There is some evidence from notes among his papers that Tocqueville may have begun to gather material in order to write the projected chapter on the Roman affair. However, this would have involved publicly embarrassing his friend Corcelle, who was the French representative in Rome and did not carry out Tocqueville's instructions, as well as criticizing the Pope. Perhaps equally influential in disuading Tocqueville was the fact that he would have needed to consult documents at the Ministry of Foreign Affairs and thus to request a favor of Louis-Napoleon's government. (I am grateful to André Jardin for pointing out these considerations, in a discussion in May 1985). See also Maurice Degros "Les *Souvenirs*, Tocqueville et la question romaine," in *Alexis de Tocqueville, Livre du Centenaire, 1859–1959* (Paris: C.N.R.S., 1960), 157–70.

as it passes before the reader, to have kept an image of the author and his intentions constantly before me, would have transformed the text from evidence of the act of writing into the expression of a life.

No doubt there is a sense in which each of the types of discourse I have identified can be interpreted as a persona or mask of the author. As recollector, Tocqueville is the "attentive observer" who seeks to give us a scrupulously honest report of what he saw and thought, the secret mirror personified. As commentator, Tocqueville is the statesman/scientist whose generalizations and political prescience are offered as indispensable advice for his countrymen of France and Europe. As purveyor of wisdom, Tocqueville is a moralist in the French tradition of Montaigne, La Bruyère, and Voltaire, offering reflections on human motives and actions. One could even see the purpose of the text as an opportunity for the display of these personae, making the text ultimately a vehicle for moral wisdom in the broadest sense. (Neutral narrative is, of course, defined by the absence of persona and the reading instructions serve purely a housekeeping function.) Yet even if we think of the three primary discursive modes of recollection, commentary, and wisdom as reflections of authorial personae, we do not encounter a single presence but a series of masks.

What I have said thus far, however, does not do full justice to the reader's experience of the text. There *is* a presence in this text; not that of a sovereign author but of a writer, who seeks a particular relationship with his readers and with the history of 1848 as he remembered it. The trace of an author's activity as writer of a text is discerned in the language and disposition of the text itself. This writerly function has already been encountered in the analysis of the opening paragraphs of the *Recollections*. Those paragraphs are not a housekeeping matter like the remarks on textual omissions, but an inauguration. By the invocation of the secret mirror along with the disavowal of literary intent, the passages begin to establish a bond of intimacy with the reader. There is a kind of spoken or at least epistolary quality to those paragraphs; we do hear a "voice" in the more literal sense. "Momentarily removed from the theatre of public life and unable to engage in any continuous study due to the precarious state of my health, I am reduced in the midst of my solitude, to consider myself for a moment or rather to contemplate the contemporary events around me in which I was either an actor or a witness" (29/13). What gives these opening paragraphs their immediacy is the sense that we are overhearing a meditation. The writer is giving himself the conditions for the text at the same time he is revealing these rules to us. The presence in the text is the presence of *this* writer—not simply the image of a Tocqueville we already know or can reconstruct from evidence outside the text, but the presence in these opening lines of a voice seductively inviting us to read.[17]

As the text develops, another more indirect sense of writerly presence is generated by the tensions between the textual "I" and the aorist tense in the discourse of recollection. Since language has no *visual* means for distinguishing the past "I" from the narrating and/or commenting "I" (other than shifting to the third person), the grammatical and visual identity of "I" implies an existential identity of the past and present Tocqueville and creates a penumbral effect of writerly presence even in those passages of the text which are in the recollective mode. In each of the other modes of discourse the writer is also indirectly present under the discursive masks.

The Tocqueville who writes this text was and was not the recollector, the commentator, the man of wisdom. He speaks everywhere in the text yet seldom in his "own" voice. Only in the opening paragraphs and again in the cover notes, which he inscribed on the packets of pages making up each of the three parts ("written at Tocqueville, July, 1850"), and perhaps also in those moments of confession and self-examination, or those rare rhetorical confidences to the reader ("See how . . . !," "Well! I declare to you . . ."), do we directly encounter the writer, speaking *solely in his role as writer of the text.* In these latter moments the writer emerges from the protective personae of a particular mode of discourse, but usually only in a phrase, a fragment of intimate address. This is not Rousseau baring his soul at every turn, congratulating or flagellating himself; Tocqueville as writer is reticent, diffident, neither more nor less interested in himself than in those around him.

Thus, the "I" of the *Recollections* is dispersed in a series of discursive modes yet is also present everywhere in the text as the "I" of the writer. Normally, when the writer speaks it is from some specific position, from behind a mask. It is as if there are roles in writing as in

17. On the general theme of textual "seduction" see Ross Chambers, *Story and Situation: Narrative Seduction and the Power of Fiction* (Minneapolis: University of Minnesota, 1984).

life, as if the self behind or within the text were as elusive as the authentic self of everyday existence. We often want to be more than our roles and so it is with the texts we read; we seek in them a personality, a centered self, an authorizing power. And it eludes us. We find traces everywhere but the traces always seem to be under one disguise or another. Nevertheless, we sense a presence, an elusive presence of the writer simulated by discourse itself, an echo effect of grammar.[18]

Finally, the writer of this text is present in the way the text itself breaks off; "and the cabinet was about to fall." He is present there, of course, by the absence of a final discourse of any kind. If Tocqueville does not speak to us at the end of the text in the discourse of wisdom and commentary, telling us what his text has meant or, at least, offering us an appropriate clue, neither does the intimate address characteristic of the text's opening paragraphs return to explain why he did not "finish" his account of 1848. Faced with the vacancy left by the end of the discourse, we find ourselves listening for the sound of a voice. We focus on this absence for a moment, wondering why it breaks off so abruptly. We get no response from the text; it is done. The presence of Tocqueville the writer, commenting on what followed October 29, 1849, can indeed be found, but only in other texts and other voices.

18. Banfield has criticized the widely held "dual voice" theory which sees the presence of the narrator always accompanying either narration or represented speech and thought. *Unspeakable Sentences*, 183–89. Others have countered that her view cannot do justice to the continuity of narration in a whole text. Cohn, *Transparent Minds*, 294. Part of the sense of presence which I have tried to describe is the result not only of the use of the same word "I" for both the writer of 1850 and the actor of 1848 but of the combination of this grammatical artifact with the knowledge that the Tocqueville of 1848 is a "real" person, one whose actions and words can be verified from other sources.

6

REFERENCE

If a reading of the *Recollections* as text is to illuminate the methodological issues intrinsic to a rhetoric and poetics of history, relationships must be considered which I have bracketed thus far. One relationship is that of the text to the events of 1848; the other is that of the text to its author. In this chapter, devoted to the truth of the *Recollections,* I am concerned in the first section with how well the *Recollections'* story of 1848 represents the chronicle of events as established independently of the text.[1] The second and third sections examine the more general aspect of the relation between rhetoric and reference by comparing the *Recollections'* embodiment of events in narrative discourse with the discursive devices used in a work of analytical history, Marx's *Class Struggles in France,* and in a historical novel, Flaubert's *Sentimental Education.*

The Chronicle of 1848

The major methodological hindrance to comparing the *Recollections'* account with the facts of 1848 is, of course, the question of how

1. I am using a conventional "correspondence" view of truth only as the starting point for reflection on the issue of how history as a kind of writing is related to the "object" it "represents." Since a full scale statement of a position on historiographical reference, let alone of the correspondence view of truth, is beyond the scope of our inquiry, I will have to be content with staking out a general perspective rather than defending it in detail.

we get to these facts in their pristine reality. By now even the most antispeculative historian has learned that there is no such thing as a "bare" fact, an atom of truth lying about to be combined with other particles in the reconstruction of past reality. We always come to a past that has already been narratively and analytically organized for us by tradition and scholarship, and we come armed with a set of questions that have the power to reorganize the received views and to constitute certain remnants of the past into relevant evidence. If we choose, for example, to examine the provincial police records of 1848–51, it is because we have some question—implicitly a hypothesis—concerning the role of surveillance and police power in the provinces and its connection with the repression of the Left, or as evidence for the emergence of the centralized bureaucratic state, or as part of the phenomenon of a "disciplinary society," and so on. The point is not that "there are no facts, only interpretations" (Nietzsche), but that there are nothing but "facts," millions of them, and one of the functions of initial questions or hypotheses in history is to transform these fragments into evidence for the issue at hand. This does not mean that the past is a heap of random particles awaiting some magnetizing question to draw it into a shape; rather, it is normally already ordered into periods and events (Renaissance, rise of capitalism, the Dreyfus Affair, the Revolution of 1848), into social-cultural units (civilizations, geographic regions, economies, nations, classes, constitutions, ideas), and into problems (development, decline, conflict, legitimization, causation). Each of these traditional ordering concepts and their combination opens up a domain of possible evidence within which and against which subsequent historians pose hypotheses for investigation—or proposals for new period or unit concepts or problems. Wherever a substantially new set of questions or concepts is developed, areas of evidence hitherto ignored or relegated to the background are brought into focus.[2]

Applied to the issue of whether one can legitimately compare the

2. The general position I have outlined here is broadly similar to that developed by Louis O. Mink in a series of articles beginning with "The Autonomy of Historical Understanding," *History and Theory* 5 (1966), 27–47. These articles, along with two previously unpublished essays, have been brought together by Brian Fay, Eugene O. Golob, and Richard T. Vann in Louis O. Mink, *Historical Understanding* (Ithaca, N.Y.: Cornell University Press, 1987). See also Richard T. Vann's discussion in "Louis Mink's Linguistic Turn," *History and Theory* 14 (1987): 1–14.

Recollections' story of 1848 to a general chronicle of events, the above understanding of factuality suggests a more complex relationship of text and referent than is often assumed. If there are no facts in the abstract, then there would appear to be no chronicle in the abstract, no single list of events that forms a neutral source against which various narratives or interpretations may be judged.[3] Rather than a presupposed foundation, a chronology would seem to be an abstraction from an experiential manifold which is itself already informed by a complex interplay of traditional problems, unit assumptions, and narrative forms. Nevertheless, the absence of such a neutral ground does not force us to abandon questions of factuality and accuracy with respect to 1848. If it is true that no facts can appear in the absence of an interpretive framework, it is equally true that there are no interpretive frameworks that do not at least implicitly define a domain of factuality. Once we have framed a set of initial questions against the background of traditional temporal and unit concepts, we have also defined a *scale* and *type* of relevant evidence by which to test our assertions.[4] Any other investigator should be able to enter our problem set and conceptual assumptions and test our assertions by the standards of evidence implicit in it.

With respect to the factual chronicle of 1848, therefore, the first question one needs to ask is: Chronicle of what? What sorts of facts and what scale of events are implied by the concept *Revolution of 1848*? One way to approach this question is to compare the chronologies printed at the beginning of various studies of the 1848 revolution in France. Although these peculiar discursive forms are constructed as aide-mémoires for the reader and do not necessarily reflect the distribution of content in the body of the subsequent text, they are

3. I am using "chronicle" here in the sense of an ideal construct, "the bare chronology of occurrence," a concept which has played an important role in contemporary philosophy of history from Croce to Danto. For an important reflection on the nature of "chronicle" as a traditional literary genre used for representing historical events see Hayden White, "The Value of Narrativity in the Representation of Reality," *Critical Inquiry* 7 (1980): 5–27, reprinted in *The Content of the Form: Narrative Discourse and Historical Representation* (Baltimore, Md.: Johns Hopkins University Press, 1987), 1–25.

4. On scale in historical time there are interesting observations in Siegfried Kracauer, *History: The Last Things before the Last* (New York: Oxford University Press, 1969), 139–63, and in Claude Lévi-Strauss, *The Savage Mind* (Chicago: University of Chicago Press, 1966), 258–63. See also L. E. Shiner, "Some Structures of Historiographical Time," *Southern Journal of Philosophy* 11 (1973): 317–28.

an interesting index of traditional ways of conceiving history *as if* it had a neutral factual skeleton. Roger Price's *The French Second Republic: A Social History,* for example, offers a chronology running from February 23, 1848, "Revolution in Paris," to December 2, 1852, "Proclamation of Napoleon III as Emperor of the French," and containing only seventeen dates and twenty events. Maurice Agulhon's *The Republican Experiment: 1848–1852,* which ends its chronology a year later, December 2, 1852, "Beginning of the Second Empire," starts back on January 2, 1848, with "Michelet's course of lectures is suspended" and in between includes over one hundred fifty dates and two hundred events.[5] Equally striking differences emerge when we compare the chronologies printed at the head of more specialized studies. The text of John M. Merriman's *Agony of the Republic: Repression of the Left* is preceded by a chronology that begins with 1846–47, "severe agricultural crisis," and ends like Price's with December 2, 1852, "France becomes an empire" but Merriman's table includes some eighty dates and one hundred events, many of the latter, as one might expect, specifically concerned with legislative and police action aimed at political repression.[6] Peter Amann's chronology in his *Revolution and Mass Democracy: The Paris Club Movement in 1848,* on the other hand, covers only the period February 24, 1848, to June 26, 1848, the day the workers' rebellion was defeated. He offers a three-column table of around ninety dates and events covering "Government Action Affecting the Clubs," "Popular Demonstrations," and "Significant News from Abroad."[7]

Several things emerge from comparing these and other chronologies of 1848 in France. First, any chronology must choose a beginning and an end. In this case, a major issue concerning the unit "Revolution of 1848" is whether to focus on the period February 22 to June 26 (the Banquets to the June Days) or to begin with the economic crisis of 1847 and end with either the Napoleonic coup or the proclamation of

5. Roger Price, *The French Second Republic* (Ithaca: Cornell University Press, 1972), vii; Maurice Agulhon, *The Republican Experiment: 1848–1852* (Cambridge: Cambridge University Press, 1983), ix–xiv.

6. John M. Merriman, *The Agony of the Republic: The Repression of the Left in Revolutionary France, 1848–1851* (New Haven, Conn.: Yale University Press, 1978), xxxi–xxxvi.

7. Peter H. Amann, *Revolution and Mass Democracy: The Paris Club Movement of 1848* (Princeton, N.J.: Princeton University Press, 1975), xx–xxvii.

the Empire. Second, the *number* of dates one allows between beginning and end sets up a kind of *scale;* a ten-item chronology will define a different level of occurrence than a hundred-item chronology. As part of a social history, Price's cursory list is a short reminder of well-known dates and its brevity no doubt reflects the social historian's interest in more general forces rather than "events," which can be dated. A third defining criterion for what is included is the *type* of occurrence or fact as determined by the problem(s) being investigated, as is obvious in the cases of Merriman and Amann. Finally, *evaluative criteria* are present both in the items selected and in the mode of discourse chosen for the statements in the chronicle. Generally, the discursive convention for chronologies dictates simple declarative statements employing a bland, atropic vocabulary, but anyone constructing a chronology must decide on appropriate descriptive adjectives for each item.

Despite the differences among the chronologies of 1848 when judged by these criteria, there is considerable overlap. What is the source of this commonality? The general chronicle common to all chronologies of 1848 can emerge only by virtue of the existence of some implicit schema contained in the traditional problem set which defines the received meaning of "Revolution of 1848" as a political and social phenomenon extending from 1847 to 1852. This "Revolution of 1848" is a phenomenon built up by over a hundred thirty years of historiographical work; it has achieved not only a certain configuration and a variety of interpretations, but a traditional set of problems. Any chronology of 1848 will be informed by the type and scale assumptions sedimented by this past historical work as well as by new questions and challenges to the traditional configuration. This explains why we can refer our histories or interpretations of 1848 to the "chronicle of 1848" without having to regard that chronicle as the "foundation" of our interpretations in some absolute sense. *The chronicle of 1848 is a variable referent, an instrument rather than a source.* Once we see Tocqueville embarked on a discourse concerning the Revolution of 1848, we refer his text to a certain type and scale of occurrence; his text's inclusions and omissions can then be compared to the now traditional (but variable) chronicle of 1848, which involves a similar scale and type of political and social occurrence. Hence, we may not only legitimately ask whether the *Recollections* is accurate, tendentious, or ignores relevant occurrences, but also consider "facts" of a similar type which Tocqueville may not have even been in a position to know but for which we now have monographical studies based on archival evidence, diaries, posthumous memoirs, reconstructed statistics, iconographic remains.

Since Tocqueville wrote as a participant, it would hardly make sense to demonstrate how much more we can know on the basis of years of research in archival sources and the reconstruction of the statistical base. What *can* be instructive for understanding the relation of writing and history, however, is to compare some aspects of the political chronicle of February 1848–October 1849 as presented in the *Recollections* with the chronicle of the same period as it has emerged in the tradition of political and social history of the past hundred thirty years and is still being modified today.

Beginning, Middle, and End

In the discussion of the *Recollections'* narrative structure I examined some of the effects on readers of Tocqueville's letting his book end in October 1849 and of omitting the year June 1848 to June 1849. Now I am in a position to examine the referential relevance of the text's omission of that year between the end of the June civil war and Tocqueville's entry into the Barrot cabinet of 1849. By omitting this year, the *Recollections* escapes direct and detailed confrontation with the repressive aftermath of June 1848 and the early development of the Reaction. The reader hears nothing of the massacre of workers after the fighting ended or of the summary trials of the eleven thousand who were arrested, with some four thousand five hundred of them sentenced to death, forced labor, or deportation. Although the text takes the time in its account of the third day of fighting in June to recall Tocqueville's reflection on "the frightening rapidity . . . with which the taste for violence and disdain for human life spread in these miserable times" (175/162), there is no indication, even in the notes for the missing year's events, that Tocqueville gave any thought to depicting or mentioning the real massacre that followed the victory of the "forces of order" or to the summary trials and deportations.

The text's omission of June 1848–June 1849 from its "middle" also results in only the most cursory references to the actual progress and mechanisms of the Reaction and to Tocqueville's support for it. Although the text does briefly mention the repressive measures taken after June 13, 1849, and Tocqueville's active advocacy of them, this is taken care of in a single page. What the text never makes the reader fully aware of is the extent to which the full force of the centralized bureaucracy, especially of the prefects and the provincial police, was applied from early on in an effort to crush the "red party." Whether it is the massacre of prisoners in June or the perfection of the legal and institutional apparatus of repression, the completed text is either silent or eschews particulars for the high ground of general moral principle ("just resentments of the nation").

One reason contemporary historians are in a position to notice these substantive lacunae in the *Recollections* is the important research over the past decade into the phenomenon of the counterrevolution of 1848–51. It is not simply that Agulhon, Merriman, Forstenzer, and others have examined the process and mechanisms of the repression of the Left, but that their work represents an explicit break with a general picture of the course of the 1848 revolution derived from Tocqueville and Marx. As Forstenzer points out, Tocqueville treats the social question as "settled" by the defeat of June and blames the threatened collapse of the Republic on an "intraelite power struggle," thus relegating the counterrevolutionary side of events to the status of a minor problem.[8] The demise of the Second Republic cannot be explained, Merriman remarks, without emphasizing "the repression which intervened to check 'the great political mobilization of 1848.'"[9] More generally, Agulhon has argued that the usual configuration of the chronicle of 1848 has obscured the "political education" of the French people that was taking place and the role of the repression in attempting to block this.[10]

These works of revision excellently illustrate the way the definition of a type and scale of factuality implicit in a particular interpretation opens a domain of evidence which can then be used against that interpretation. Tocqueville's social approach to history, emphasizing the long-term importance of general social conditions, states of mind,

8. Thomas R. Forstenzer, *French Provincial Police and the Fall of the Second Republic: Social Fear and Counterrevolution* (Princeton, N.J.: Princeton University Press, 1981), 10.
9. Merriman, *Agony of the Republic,* xx.
10. Maurice Agulhon, *The Republican Experiment.* On the general problem of the reaction see the essays in Roger Price, ed., *Revolution and Reaction* (New York: Barnes & Noble, 1975).

and voluntary organizations and his awareness of the political and social ferment among the "lower" orders of society, should have made his text take note of the fact of "political mobilization" in 1848 and the question of whether it was to be channeled or simply crushed.[11] The current historiographical exploration of the extent and means of repressing political participation in 1848–51 calls attention to a related aspect of the period after 1849 which the *Recollections* also ignores—the "struggle for the countryside."[12] The *Recollections* sees only the peasant known to aristocratic and bourgeois myth—"last to rise and last to sit down." Although Tocqueville came from a predominantly rural department and lived off the rent of his land, one would never guess from reading the *Recollections* that much of the countryside and many of the small communes of France were in political ferment.[13]

Given the commitment of the text to truthfulness, the lack of attention to an organized repression of which Tocqueville not only approved but actively supported is cause for reflection. In one sense of the word *truth*, of course, the *Recollections* seems to be truthful, that is, it is "honest," insofar as it accurately reflects in its mirror what Tocqueville saw and thought and did. Tocqueville's values, class position, and experience up to 1848 hardly prepared him to act or react otherwise. His *text* is another matter. Cut loose from its author, it stands before us to be judged not only by the limitations of its author's ideology, but also by the standards of evidence implicit in the text itself. The per-

11. In his letters during the early weeks of the revolution he sees the need of notables like himself to lead the people in the "right" direction, that is, toward order and the preservation of property rights. Roger Boesche, ed., Alexis de Tocqueville, *Selected Letters on Politics and Society* (Berkeley: University of California Press, 1985), 203–5. Tocqueville did object to the electoral law of May 31, 1850, which had the effect of disenfranchising nearly three million voters, mostly urban workers. But his objection was less to restricting the franchise than to the immediate political effect of depriving the second Republic of "the moral power of universal suffrage" (289/291).

12. The theme of the political struggle for the countryside has been the topic of a number of influential studies, for example, Maurice Agulhon's *La République au village: Les populations du Var de la Révolution à la Seconde République* (Paris: Plon, 1970).

13. No doubt La Manche was in one of the most conservative regions of France as one can see on any map of political agitation and radicalism, but Marx, who only spent a few months in Paris in 1849, has more to say about the political attitudes of the peasants in the *Class Struggles* than Tocqueville in the *Recollections*. Merriman, *Agony of the Republic*, xvi–xviii and xxix.

sonal tone of this text should not deceive us; like all Tocqueville's writing it has large ambitions and exacting standards; it interweaves its recollections with commentary and wisdom intended to be superior in insight to the supposedly more partisan views of those like Guizot and Thiers (83/61). We are required by the text's *own* standards to ask why the obvious is absent or matters of central importance are ignored or glossed over in a paragraph. Although these questions cannot be answered from within the text alone, the results of the earlier analysis of the text's discursive strategy can help identify the techniques that contribute to minimizing the repression. On the one hand, the text's pictorial and thematic codes treat workers or peasants only in the most moralistic and stereotypical fashion. On the other, the text's episodic and montage effects operate even more powerfully than this ideological bias since the chronological presentation of a series of moral-political *tableaux* keeps unwary readers (unless they are historical specialists) from even raising the question of an organized repression. Thus, a comparison of the text with the general chronicle of 1848 not only allows one to determine important lacunae and ideological distortions in its "representation of reality"—something one would expect of any historical text—but a literary analysis can reveal the *discursive devices* by which historical texts produce such effects. Thus, the text's skirting of the more sinister aspects of the Reaction, like its ambiguity concerning workers and women, grandeur and greed, is generated not only by a particular way of thinking and perceiving, but also by a particular set of discursive practices.

The Class Struggles in France

So far in this chapter I have restricted my investigation of rhetoric and reference to an analysis based on the domain of evidence opened up by the *Recollections'* own social-political approach to historical phenomena. Turning to the texts Karl Marx wrote on 1848, however, one encounters a discourse that involves a conceptual framework and problem set that in part generate a different kind of evidence. Here, the important question will not be the omission of major aspects of the traditional political chronicle of 1848, but the less tractable question of how to judge the respective value of two historical discourses when their type and scale assumptions differ fundamentally. A comparison of the *Recollections* with Marx's texts also has another advantage; though Marx produces a narrative that lends itself to plot and voice analysis, his works on 1848 anticipate the kind of contemporary social history that gives the study of problems priority over telling a story.

Since numerous studies compare the political theories of Marx and Tocqueville and the content of their respective interpretations of 1848, I will focus instead on the discursive strategy of Marx in his two major texts on 1848.[14] I have chosen to concentrate on *The Class Struggles in France* since it is the work of Marx on 1848 which most nearly parallels the *Recollections* in coverage, and to supplement my analysis of it with a brief consideration of *The Eighteenth Brumaire of Louis Napoleon*.[15]

Plot

Class Struggles is at once the elaboration of a thesis and a satiric narration. It is also an essay in recuperation since it seeks to explain why the June 1848 revolt in France failed and at the same time to show that it did not really fail since it was part of a longer-term revolutionary process still at work. What was overcome in the various setbacks to the proletariat in 1848–49 was not the revolution itself but only certain "pre-revolutionary appendages" which were "the product of social relationships which had not yet developed to the point of sharp class antagonisms." The revolutionaries, Marx claimed, could only be

14. Among the best known discussions is that of Raymond Aron in *History, Truth and Liberty* (Chicago: University of Chicago Press, 1985), 165–95. There is an older but still useful discussion of Marx and Tocqueville directed specifically to the *Recollections* in Edward T. Gargan's *Alexis de Tocqueville: The Critical Years, 1848–1851* (Washington, D.C.: Catholic University Press, 1955).

15. The three articles which make up the main body of the text known as *The Class Struggles in France: 1848 to 1850* were written by Marx in London in the spring of 1850 and published in numbers 1, 2 and, 3 of his and Engels' *Neue Rheinisch Zeitung, Politisch-ökonomische Revue* from March to May 1850. These articles, along with what now constitutes the fourth chapter (consisting of two excerpts from an article that appeared in the November issue of the same journal), were published together in book form by Engels in 1895. The English citations for the *Class Struggles* and *The Eighteenth Brumaire* are from Karl Marx, *Surveys from Exile*, ed. David Fernbach (New York: Random House, 1974) and will be given by page numbers in parenthesis in my text. For the textual history see Fernbach, 9 and 35.

freed from such "illusions, ideas and projects . . . by a series of *defeats*." "In a word: revolutionary progress cleared a path for itself not by its immediate, tragi-comic achievements, but by creating a powerful and united counter-revolution; only in combat with this opponent did the insurrectionary party mature into a real party of revolution. To demonstrate this is the task of the following pages" (35). The story line of *Class Struggles* is easily summarized. The February Revolution appeared to be the "beautiful revolution" because it was the time of fraternity between the proletariat and the republican elements of the bourgeoisie united against the "financial aristocracy" that had ruled behind the screen of monarchy since 1830. Although the republican bourgeoisie was forced to grant the workers a number of social concessions, the election of a huge conservative majority to the new Assembly in April actually confirmed the exclusively bourgeois character of the Republic by "propelling all fractions of the exploiting class at one go to the heights of state power and thus tearing off their deceitful masks" (56). When the Assembly revoked the few concessions that had been made to the workers, it had no choice but to start another revolution, this time the "ugly revolution" of June, "a fight for the preservation or destruction of the *bourgeois* order. The veil which shrouded the republic was torn asunder" (58–59).

Thus far, with the exception of its greater emphasis on class interests, Marx's story of 1848 has a shape similar to that of other contemporary observers, including Tocqueville. But Marx's story takes a unique turn once the proletariat is off the stage. Through its victory by proxy, Marx argues, the big bourgeoisie had confirmed its control of society behind the political forms of the Republic, and the greedy party of order instituted policies that began to financially ruin the middle and petty bourgeoisie. As a result many members of these classes were gradually being forced into an alliance with the proletariat in late 1849 and early 1850. The third chapter ends with an excitedly optimistic analysis of the resulting successes of the "red party" in the elections of March 10, 1850, treating these victories as a harbinger of another revolution.

10 March was a revolution. Behind the ballot slips lay the paving stones . . . [The bourgeois] republic had only *one* merit: *it was the forcing house of the revolution* . . .

10 March 1850 bears the inscription: *Après moi le déluge!* (125)

Ending with these lines, the series of three articles tells the story of a triumph emerging from tragedy, of the crushed, premature revolt of June 1848 about to become a victorious revolution in which the proletariat will lead the lower strata of the bourgeoisie and the peasants. Indeed this "ending" was already foreshadowed by the closing lines of the first article/chapter of *Class Struggles* where it is said:

> Only since it has been dipped in the blood of the June insurgents has the tricolour become the flag of the European revolution—the red flag!
> And we cry, *The Revolution is dead!—Long Live the Revolution!* (62)

This is the fundamental pattern of comedy, though we are not accustomed on stage (and scarcely in fiction) to having the reconciliation be merely imminent and all the action seemingly taken up by suffering and struggle. The mask or veil of tragic suffering (June Days) hides the truth of comedic reconciliation, not as something *present* under the veil, as hidden actuality, but as something *future*, as possibility. The tragic plot completes itself in the text; the comic plot completes itself beyond the text. Marx's approach transforms the genre of narrative history into a new genre we might call "scientific apocalypse." "Science" stands for Marx's interpretive framework, which opens up a new type and scale of fact and the possibility of various interpretations based on it. "Apocalypse" stands for the proclamation that the moment is at hand and the call to be ready for action.[16]

Voice

At first glance it might seem that a set of analytical essays by a single author is even less likely to manifest a variety of "voices" than a

16. A few months after he completed the text formed by these first three articles, Marx wrote an essay on European developments from April to mid-August of 1850, part of which Engels published in *The Class Struggles* as Chapter 4. Here we find a completely different tone. This article chides "the people" for "annulling" the revolutionary situation of 10 March 1850 by provoking a new election in late April (131). The remainder of the essay, and its longest section, is devoted to a satirical analysis of the clash between Bonaparte and the royalist majority in the Assembly. The tone of this entire fourth section is one of caution, if not weariness, rather than anticipation. By adding the material of this later article with its complaint that "the date for decision was postponed again," Engels has made Marx's text turn back on itself. Given the way the final text of *The Class Struggles* was put together by Engels, one should not press this fourth "chapter" too hard in an investigation of Marx's emplotment of 1848 for purposes of narrative comparison.

memoir, but I believe we can identify a pattern of four voices in *Class Struggles.* The dominant voice is clearly that of *unmasking discourse.* Although the unmasking passages do not make up the largest quantity of the text, they do set its tone. They mark the overall discourse as one of revelation, a disclosure of the real social-economic forces at work behind particular historical appearances of the present, for example, the class function of the *Garde Mobile,* the class interests represented by the National Assembly, how the June Days was really the first battle in the modern class war. Unmasking discourse is easily recognized since it plays on the polarities of appearance and reality, form and substance, veil and truth, phrase and matter, parody and original. Phraseologically, it is balanced and compressed, employing such obvious markers as "costume," "mask," "secret," "concealment."

Satiric narrative, the discursive mode that makes up the bulk of the text, depends on its proximity to unmasking discourse for its effects. Passages of unmasking discourse are brief and make frequent use of appearance/reality comparisons, whereas satiric discourse is lighter and more prolix, tending toward comparisons that bring out incongruities or enormities, frequently expanding into exuberant invective. Although one cannot as easily point to specific "markers" for this mode of discourse, there is a characteristic use of the theatre metaphor and a preference for the device of reversal or chiasmus. From the opening mention of the "tragi-comic achievements" of the February Revolution, almost every major event of the next two years is somewhere referred to in theatrical terms. February is said to have forced all classes of French society to "quit the boxes, the pit, the gallery and to act for themselves on the revolutionary stage!" (43). The proletariat is "temporarily removed from the stage" by the June civil war and its story replaced by the "comedy of intrigue" between Louis-Napoleon and the Assembly (83), which the Montagne took "tragically" when it staged the "procession" of June 13, 1849, which resulted not in a "bloody tragedy" like June 1848, but in "a lamentable prison-filling melodrama" (94). Equally characteristic of Marx's satirical writing in *Class Struggles* is the frequent use of ironic reversal and the chiasmus, giving the whole a feeling of dialectic wit: "The republic had announced itself to the peasants with the *tax collector;* they announced themselves to the republic with the *emperor.*" Where Tocqueville favored the rhetorical figure of the antithesis, in satiric narrative Marx is the master of the chiasmus which can link multiple sets of terms in ironic parallel.

The third discursive mode, *analytical generalization,* is the specifically "scientific" discourse in Marx's text. As one might expect, on the ideological plane it tries to be above or outside any particular point of view or interest as a totalizing discourse which speaks with a voice devoid of pathos focused on the *long durée.* If one were to look for "markers" here they would be terms of universality or necessity on the one hand and neologism and technical vocabulary on the other. In its purest form the passages of analytic generality are few, but stand out unmistakably from the satiric narrative and unmasking discourse, for example: "While this general prosperity lasts, enabling the productive forces of bourgeois society to develop to the full extent possible within the bourgeois system, there can be no question of a real revolution" (131).

At the opposite discursive pole from analytic generality and even rarer in the text are the *performatives,* for example, *"The revolution is dead!—Long live the revolution!"* These urgent calls to action serve not only as a call to arms paralleling that of the end of the *Communist Manifesto* of 1848, they are positioned in the text at the end of the first and third articles/chapters in such a way that they pick up and complete the three major discursive modes of the text. There is, therefore, an internal logic to the discourse of *Class Struggles* according to which *analytic generality* forms the basis for unmasking discourse which in turn controls the *satiric narrative,* ending with the *performatives* cited above. Yet these four discursive modes are not actually deployed in this purely deductive sequence, that is, from generalizing to unmasking to satiric to performative. Instead, the text takes up matters chronologically in deference to the narrative skeleton of history and marshals its discursive voices in a complex pattern where the moments of analytic generality that are meant to control the deeper meaning of the text appear to emerge spontaneously from its unmasking and satiric moments.

Marx and Tocqueville

A number of parallels and contrasts between the overall Marxian and Tocquevillian discursive strategies are immediately apparent. There is a tendency in both *Class Struggles* and the *Recollections* for satiric prose and theatrical metaphor to undermine each text's more serious intentions. There are equally striking parallels in their discursive rhythms. Similar internal functions are played by Tocqueville's recollective discourse and Marx's satiric narrative, by Tocqueville's commentary discourse and Marx's unmasking discourse, by Tocqueville's wisdom discourse (of the political insight type) and Marx's analytical generality, by Tocqueville's wisdom discourse (of the moral reflection type) and Marx's performatives.

Yet the differences are equally striking. In the *Recollections* the recollective discourse has an independence from commentary owing to the desire and effort to achieve spontaneity and sincerity in writing, and there is no effort to achieve a deductive integration derived from theoretical ideas contained in the wisdom mode. With *Class Struggles* the reverse is the case. Although the actual deployment is not deductively linear, the discourse is logically controlled by the theoretical ideas developed in the analytical passages. Thus, the smoother rhetorical surface of Tocqueville's text is deceptive when compared to the somewhat jerky and abrupt transitions of Marx's text. Marx is struggling with 1848 in a dual effort both to generate and to apply a theory of historical development. Tocqueville, however, is more settled in his central moral/political convictions but less deductive in his approach to political analysis.

Tocqueville and Marx are well known for their contributions to the modification of the traditional historical schemata. Both tended to see the historical process in terms of the *long durée*—even an event so temporally focused as the revolution of 1848—and both saw the outward changes in political leadership or political form (monarchy versus republic) as less essential than underlying social changes. The most direct indication in the *Recollections* of the interpretive framework that informs Tocqueville's writing about history is the brief enumeration of "causes" and "accidents" leading to the February Revolution. Four of Tocqueville's six "causes" concern general *social and cultural factors:* "the passion for material pleasures . . . the democratic disease of envy silently at work"; "economic and political theories . . . which tended to encourage the belief that human misery was due to the laws and not to providence"; "the contempt felt for the ruling class"; "the mobility of everything—institutions, ideas, mores and men—in a society on the move, which had lived through seven great revolutions in sixty years" (85/62–63). One item concerns *administrative structure:* "the centralization thanks to which control of Paris . . . was all that was needed to complete a revolution" (85/63).

Most important of all for comparison with Marx, however, is the first item on the list which appears to grasp a *technological and economic factor:* "The industrial revolution, which for thirty years had been making Paris the leading manufacturing city in France . . . which had brought in a flood of laborers now out of work" (85/62). Yet we would be wrong to think that Tocqueville's mention of the industrial revolution indicated a serious opening up of the domain of technological and economic phenomena since the only significance Tocqueville draws from it is the resulting large population of workers in Paris who happened to be unemployed in 1848. A similar demur must be entered at Tocqueville's recognition of the June struggle as a class war. Although he saw the workers' aim as not so much to change "the form of government, as to alter the organization of society," the concept of class Tocqueville employs here does not open up the same range of evidence as Marx's. For Tocqueville the "classes" of French society are still those defined by social and cultural differences that were the familiar object of general knowledge. The "people" proper, "those who work with their hands," have simply been infected with the "democratic disease of envy" and a jumble of radical social theories. They are still "the people" of traditional perception even if they have come to be regarded by Tocqueville and others as *"les classes dangereuses."*

With Marx, of course, many of the social and cultural phenomena that Tocqueville sees as more enduring and effective than governmental forms are found to be just as superficial as political forms when compared to class interests based on the organization of production. It is easy to argue, therefore, that the Marxian expansion of the interpretive framework for ordering the historical field is more inclusive than Tocqueville's—it can encompass not only the type of fact Tocqueville's approach generates but also a range of factuality which Tocqueville's perspective ignores. Yet the comparison is not quite so simple since Marx not only employs a wider interpretive schema but seeks to develop from this expansion a total theory of history which places all phenomena above the base in a status of dependency, and thus runs the danger of narrowing the framework itself. Marx's particular interpretation of 1848 fails to do justice to the very facts of political structure and political culture which are the points of strength in Tocqueville's approach. This can be seen even better if I supplement the discussion of *Class Struggles* with a brief consideration of certain rhetorical aspects of *The Eighteenth Brumaire of Louis Napoleon.*

Reference

The Eighteenth Brumaire

If the events of April and May 1850 had already forced Marx to tell a different story in his fourth article of *Class Struggles*, the Napoleonic coup of December 2, 1851, blatantly nullified his previous political expectations. By spring 1852, when Tocqueville had retired to write his chapters on the reasons for the success of the first eighteenth Brumaire, Marx set about unmasking the basis for the second. In doing so he retells the entire story of 1848, but this time one feels it is not so much an essay in recuperation as an act of revenge against history itself.[17] The rebuff that the Napoleonic coup gave Marx's political prognostications in *Class Struggles* neither discouraged him nor forced a deep reassessment of his theory but imparted a combative energy that generated some of his finest satiric demolitions. For our purposes there are two important points of comparison between the *Eighteenth Brumaire* and the *Recollections*.

First, both texts make heavy use of the theatre image. We have already seen how extensively Marx employed theatre metaphors in the satiric reductions of *Class Struggles* and the frequency with which Tocqueville chides the revolutionaries in 1848 for their theatricality. In the *Eighteenth Brumaire* Marx not only takes note of the theatrical character of 1848 ("the revolution of 1848 knew no better than to parody at some points 1789 and at others ... 1793–95") but also turns it into a generalization about all revolutions and even about the historical process itself in his often quoted opening: "Men make their own history, but not of their own free will ... they timidly conjure up the spirits of the past to help them; they borrow the names, slogans

---

17. LaCapra has underscored the tremendous energy of Marx's satiric invective, a rhetorical achievement whose apotropaic significance is linked to the threat which the successful Napoleonic coup presented to Marx's developing theory. One cannot help asking if December 2, 1851, does not become the occasion of so much savage invective and parodic excess precisely because it struck the Marxian interpretation at its most vulnerable point, that is, the denigration of political form to total dependency and the unremitting scorn for liberal institutions. Had events themselves not raised the possibility that political institutions and habits are more than a veil for class interests based on productive modes, that they are also instruments of genuine social change? As LaCapra points out, the very excess of Marx's language tends to undermine the determinism that treats the inherited ideals and images by which men make their history as delusion. Dominick LaCapra, *Rethinking Intellectual History: Texts, Contexts, Language* (Ithaca, N.Y.: Cornell University Press, 1983), 228–29. See also Jean Paul Riqueleme, "*The Eighteenth Brumaire* of Karl Marx as Symbolic Action," *History and Theory* 19 (1980): 58–72.

and costumes" (146). The way each text situates and develops the theatre analogy is characteristic of differing ways of construing the discourse of historical process. Tocqueville's observation is a sociological generalization concerning national character, enunciated in the mode of irony and ultimately in the service of a satiric reduction. Although Marx's text makes an even more brutal satirical employment of the theatrical metaphor, he goes on to draw a sociological and historical generalization of the widest scope. Yet, to the extent he formulates it as an explanatory principle, Marx makes it the more vulnerable to counter example. What in Tocqueville is at once suggestive, tentative, and derisory becomes in Marx a mixture of scientific hypothesis and carnival denigration. Whatever the errors and follies of the French, the discourse of the *Recollections* treats them as redeemable. The discourse of the *Eighteenth Brumaire* moves on a different plane, where human behavior in society is controlled by deeper forces of which consciousness is captive. Tocquevillian discourse is still part of a classical rhetoric of persuasion rooted in the belief in a moral providence that sets the larger bounds to human action but leaves us free within that circle to choose our direction. Marx is struggling to generate a new discourse on a background of morally anonymous forces which, nevertheless, allows a call to human action to hasten the day.

Second, if one compares the textual treatment of the workers in the *Recollections* and the *Eighteenth Brumaire*, some startling results will emerge. Marx, in his preface to *Eighteenth Brumaire*, scored Victor Hugo's satirical *Napoleon the Little* for inadvertently undermining its own intention by giving so much space to Louis-Napoleon that Hugo's book made it appear as if a single man had changed the destiny of a nation (144). Despite the passages of analytic generality in *Eighteenth Brumaire*, it is ironic that the energy of Marx's unmasking discourse not only overwhelms all historical obstacles in its totalizing sweep, but also generates a text in which the activity of the proletariat is obscured and Napoleon's struggle with the bourgeoisie holds the foreground. This had already happened to a considerable extent in *Class Struggles*, where the proletariat appears infrequently and the actual fight in June is laconically described in two sentences. In *Class Struggles* the few other passages on the French working class underscore its naïveté in seeking its interests alongside the bourgeoisie and its inability to assume the role of a genuine proletariat. The remaining eighty percent of

Class Struggles is taken up with the unmasking and satirizing of the bourgeoisie and its struggle with Napoleon; in *Eighteenth Brumaire* the proportion on Napoleon and the bourgeoisie is even higher. Although the June insurrection is called "the most colossal event in the history of European civil wars," the proletariat's defeat not only means it "passed into the *background* of the revolutionary stage," it virtually disappears from the remainder of Marx's text. Instead, the ingenious "Crapulinski" and his bourgeois and aristocratic opponents become the focus of the story. As Jeffrey Mehlman has suggested, in Marx's narrative the tragedy of the proletariat is swallowed in a farce played out between the dominant classes and a supposed mediocrity who manages to dupe them all and bring about a comic repetition of 1799.[18]

Yet one might see a similar effect of narrative structure undermining authorial values in the *Recollections*, where those values are the opposite of Marx's. Tocqueville, whose attitude toward the condition of the working class was thoroughly paternalistic, and who regarded their revolt as an expression of "greedy desires" enflamed by ridiculous theories, nevertheless produced a work that makes the social civil war of the June Days the crucial turning point in the narrative. Although as attuned to the theatrical and ironic dimensions of 1848 as Marx, Tocqueville's work has a tone of tragic seriousness which grants the proletariat its central role in a drama of liberty and equality, *grandeur* and *cupidité*. Most telling of all, Tocqueville not only refused in his person to accept the coup and the new regime but kept it out of his book. His real "completion" of the story of 1848 and riposte to the coup of 1851 was *The Old Regime and the Revolution,* which has the effect of diminishing even the revolutionary claim made on behalf of the first Napoleon.

The examination of the interpretive frameworks implicit in the rhetorical strategies of Marx's and Tocqueville's texts has shown how intimately the rhetorical and referential aspects within each text are bound together. It will profit the investigation of the relation of rhetoric and reference to consider now the import of a work of literary fiction dealing with 1848.

---

18. Jeffrey Mehlmann, *Revolution and Repetition: Marx, Hugo, Balzac* (Berkeley: University of California Press, 1977), 19.

Sentimental Education

One can lay out a typology of at least five ways of viewing the presence of history in *Sentimental Education,* each of which can appeal to a body of evidence in the text and in Flaubert's correspondence.[19] Part of the complexity and difficulty of Flaubert's novel is that it does so many things with history at once: (1) tells us something about 1848, (2) depicts the moral atmosphere of a generation, (3) denigrates the idea of "making History" through political action, (4) explores the tension between political history and private life, and (5) deconstructs both the Balzacian *Bildungsroman* and the traditional historical novel.[20] The one *structural feature* of the novel's use of

19. I will be using the translation of Robert Baldich, except where a more literal rendering is needed: Gustave Flaubert, *Sentimental Education* (Harmondsworth: Penguin Books, 1964), 7. The French text, whose page numbers will be given first, is *L'Éducation sentimentale* (Paris: Classiques Garnier, 1969). There is an extensive literature on the problem of fiction and history in *Sentimental Education,* among which the most helpful are Peter Brooks's essay in *Reading for the Plot: Design and Intention in Narrative* (New York: Knopf, 1984); Victor Brombert's chapter in *The Novels of Flaubert* (Princeton, N.J.: Princeton University Press, 1960); Jonathan Culler's *Flaubert: The Uses of Uncertainty* (Ithaca, N.Y.: Cornell University Press, 1974); Claudine Gothot-Mersch, ed., *La Production du sens chez Flaubert* (Paris: Union Générale d'Éditions, 1975), cited in following notes as *La Production du sens;* Anne Green, *Flaubert and the Historical Novel* (Cambridge: Cambridge University Press, 1982); Maurice Agulhon, Philippe Berthier, et al., *Histoire et langage dans "L'Éducation sentimentale"* (Paris: S.E.D.E.S., 1981), cited as *Histoire et langage.*

20. (1) Flaubert engaged in an assiduous research program concerning 1848, reading dozens of books, scouring newspapers, requesting first hand accounts from friends, visiting major sites and painstakingly adjusting his story to fit the facts. Jean Vidalenc, "Gustave Flaubert, historien de la révolution de 1848," *Europe: Revue littéraire mensuelle* (1969): 51–71. (2) "I want to write the moral history, or rather the sentimental history, of the men of my generation"; letter to Mlle. Leroyer de Chantepie, October 1864, cited in Brombert, *Novels of Flaubert,* 156. (3) Flaubert not only believed in the cylical and mechanical nature of History but gave this devastating summation of French history, " '89 demolished the Monarchy and the nobility, '48 the bourgeoisie and '51 the people. There is *nothing* left but an imbecile . . . rabble. We have all sunk to the same level of vulgar mediocrity"; cited in Jean-Pierre Duquette, *Flaubert, ou L'architecture du vide* (Montreal: Presses du Université de Montréal, 1972), 81. (4) Flaubert writes in his notebooks for *L'Éducation sentimentale:* "Show that Sentimentalism (its development since 1830) followed politics and reproduces its phases"; cited in Joseph Jurt, "Die Wertung der Geschichte in Flauberts 'Éducation Sentimentale,' " *Romanistische Zeitschrift für Literaturgeschichte* 7 (1983): 147. (5) The deconstruction of the *Bildungsroman* is the general thesis of Culler's book on Flaubert. Brooks

history which almost all critics acknowledge is the dramatic coincidence of fictive/private events with crucial historical/public events. From this perspective *Sentimental Education* is less about a specific historical event or period or even about history in general, than about the *relation* of history and life, showing how each interferes with the other; private life makes us miss our rendezvous with history and history corrodes or destroys personal relationships. In order to draw the most benefit from a comparison of the treatment of 1848 in *Sentimental Education* with its treatment in the *Recollections,* I will consider the three most important moments when private (fictive) and public (historical) coincide within the plot of the novel.

(1) The novel opens in 1840 with the young Frédéric returning to Nogent by steamboat and getting his first sight of Mme Arnoux, who appears to him like an "apparition" from a romantic novel in the famous scene of the "saved shawl." The next eight years occupy over half of Flaubert's novel and we see Frédéric back in Paris ostensibly to pursue his law degree along with his friend Deslauriers, but really to pursue his sentimental education and specifically Mme Arnoux, a pursuit that at last reaches a turning point in February 1848. With the near connivance of Mme Arnoux's husband, who prefers to spend his time with his mistress, Rosanette, Frédéric cajoles Mme Arnoux into joining him in Paris for an outing and then lays plans to seduce her by temporarily renting and furnishing a room on the street where they are to meet (300/275). As it turns out, Mme Arnoux does not show; but to complicate matters even more Frédéric has picked a street adjacent to the site of the February 22 Reform Banquet and demonstration, which was to set off the Revolution. Not only does he fail to answer his companion's summons to join them in the planned demonstration at this site, he even hides from view when he sees some of them being arrested, lest he miss Mme Arnoux. The next day as he wanders the streets in his chagrin and anger at Mme Arnoux and watches the commotion of the city as it prepares for battle, he happens to pass Rosanette's window and impulsively decides that since he cannot have

---

approaches the novel from a similar intertextual perspective but also sees it as making a negative statement about the value of historical action and historical narrative as such. Brooks, *Reading for the Plot,* 203–9.

the woman he wants, he will try to have Rosanette instead. Frédéric and Rosanette spend the afternoon watching people in the street from her window and then go out for a long, exquisite dinner. Returning on foot, they pass within hearing of the shooting on the boulevard des Capucines, the "massacre" of demonstrators that was a principle catalyst of the rebellion. Frédéric laconically remarks, as they hear the gun fire, "Oh, they're killing a few bourgeois," and Flaubert permits himself one of the rare authorial commentaries in the novel: "For there are situations in which the kindest of men is so detached from his fellows that he would watch the whole human race perish without batting an eye" (307/283). Then Frédéric, "in order to degrade Mme Arnoux more completely in his mind," takes Rosanette to the room he had prepared for his ideal love. On the morning after, Frédéric's curiosity leads him into the streets and he becomes a witness to some of the revolutionary fighting and joins in the invasion of the Tuileries Palace by "the people." When he gets back to Rosanette, she is furious at having been abandoned in the midst of revolutionary turmoil, but Frédéric reassures her and we are told "he kissed her; and she declared for the Republic—as had already Monsignor the Archbishop of Paris, and as would soon with marvelous haste, the Judiciary, the Council of State, the Institute, the Marshals of France, general Changarnier, M. Falloux" (317/293).

What is the significance of Flaubert's conjoining the beginning of the February Revolution with Frédéric's failure to consummate his love for Mme Arnoux and his despairing act of profanation in substituting Rosanette? It can be read on several levels. At the most literal level it underlines Frédéric's apolitical nature and his total lack of civic responsibility or even personal solidarity with his comrades. On a more general level, however, the juxtaposition of the fictive and historical performs an ironic devaluation of the revolution and politics as such. Even the narrator's judgment on Frédéric's indifference could be seen as a kind of diversion of the reader's attention; though the explicit message of the narrator condemns political indifference, the narrative itself by foregrounding an evening of spectacle, luxury, amusement, and eroticism ironically denigrates the political events of the background. But one can also read the juxtaposition in terms of an explicit symbolic exchange between the sentimental and the political. The connection could be taken allegorically as the bourgeoisie (Frédéric) joining the working class (Rosanette) in an act of profanation (Revolution). An equally plausible connection of the private and public in terms of the trajectory of the plot as a whole, however, would be to see Frédéric's failure to consummate his love for the ideal woman and his turning to the courtesan as a foreshadowing of the ultimate failure of the Republic to realize its ideal of liberty. Beginning under the sign of profanation the Revolution will end in the Napoleonic coup, which will coincide with Frédéric's loss of both Mme Arnoux and Rosanette and much else besides.[21]

(2) *Sentimental Education* treats the coming of the February Revolution almost as a comic accident, and as the revolution develops from February to June no side is spared ridicule. Flaubert has reserved for the June civil war, however, his second major juxtaposition of love and revolution; he has Frédéric, on the eve of the June battle, take Rosanette on a romantic trip to Fontainbleau. The text describes their erotic idyll among the reminders of Diane de Poitiers and Henry II and other monarchs and men of letters with only an occasional interference of current history: "Newly arrived travelers told them that a terrible battle was filling Paris with blood. Rosanette and her lover were not surprised. Then everyone left and the hotel became peaceful, the gas light went out and they fell asleep to the murmur of the fountain in the courtyard" (345/322). The next day as they are wandering in the forest of Fontainbleau, and Frédéric is reflecting not on the greats of past history but on the huge trees and on the rocks thrown up by the geologic force of the ages, they hear in the distance the drums beating the general call to arms in a village, and Frédéric thinks it "trivial beside their love and eternal nature" (349/325). Many commentators have seen in the juxtaposition of the Fontainbleau idyll and the June civil war in Paris one of the masterstrokes of Flaubert's novel. But like the similar conjunction of Frédéric's erotic adventure with the beginning of the February Revolution, it is not clear just what is symbolized. Is it a direct allegory—for example, the giant trees grappling with each other as the bourgeoisie and proletariat fight hand to hand—or is it an ironic allegory of contrast, the bourgeois Frédéric on an erotic idyll with the working-class Rosanette, while the bourgeois and proletariat classes are locked in a death struggle? Or is the contrast a more general

21. This is the interpretation given by Victor Brombert in "*L'Éducation sentimentale:* Articulations et polyvalence," *La Production du sens,* 55–58. A similar interpretation is found in Jurt, "Die Wertung der Geschichte," 148–50.

one, as Brombert suggests, between the pettiness of the Parisian political battle and the grandeur and agelessness of the great trees and geological formations, an opposition of History and Nature?[22] One could also argue that since readers have had plenty of set battle scenes in novels, another one would not have conveyed the violence and cruelty of the battle any more effectively than its presence by absence in the striking contrast of what the informed reader knows of the savage battle in Paris with the peacefulness of Fountainbleau where, after shrugging off news of the Paris fighting, Frédéric and Rosanette fall asleep to the "murmur of the fountain in the courtyard."

(3) But before the June Days can be reduced to nullity in the face of this romanticized geo-history of Fountainbleau, a newspaper arrives with the name of Frédéric's worker friend Dussardier listed among the wounded and Frédéric, suddenly feeling guilty for his bourgeois egoism, rushes back to Paris on the last day of fighting. Frédéric finally finds the wounded Dussardier, who has fought on the side of the Republic and against the workers, but Dussardier is tormented by doubt as to whether he did the right thing, given the unkept promises that had been made to his comrades. No such scruple, we are told, troubled another of Frédéric's friends, the socialist Sénécal, who fought with the workers and is now imprisoned with nine hundred others in the basement of the Tuileries at the edge of the Seine; the wounded who die there are left to rot among the living whose cries of execration or pleas for pity and food are ignored. One National Guardsman, old man Roque, from Frédéric's hometown of Nogent, is so furious at the damage done his *pied à terre* in Paris that he cannot stand the prisoner's cries any longer and fires into the mass of them, killing a youth and silencing the rest. If the reader has begun to think Flaubert had it in for the Revolution and "the people," this incident signals the moment for the other side to begin to bear the full force of Flaubertian irony and moral indignation.

The text now moves toward its denouement with one after another of Frédéric's former republican and reformist friends selling out: Hussonnet, the bohemian writer, begins to turn out a reactionary sheet; Rosanette declares for the Reaction as quickly as she did for the Republic; Deslauriers, who had rushed to become a provincial com-

22. Brombert, *The Novels of Flaubert*, 177–80. See also *La Production du sens*, 61–62, and Brooks, *Reading for Plot*, 200–203.

missioner under Ledru-Rollin, now breathes hatred of the workers and
becomes secretary to Dambreuse the banker; Vatnaz gives up femi-
nism when she comes into a little money; Pellerin, the artist, is now as
eager to paint what the Right wants as he was to find an elevating
image of the Republic; and even the arch socialist Sénécal ominously
"declared for Authority" (394/369). And Frédéric? Not only does he
decide to throw in his lot with M. Dambreuse and the conservative
group around him (Rue de Poitiers connection), but he aspires to
become Mme Dambreuse's lover, not because he has any real passion
for her but as a challenge to his ego and a route to advancement.

The narrative picks up speed as it moves to resolve various aspects of
the plot—though it will do so, as Peter Brooks remarks, less by a
process of integration than by one of dissolution and liquidation. With
M. Dambreuse' death, Frédéric is now ready to marry Mme Dambreuse (all the while keeping Rosanette) when in a last impulsive act he
borrows money from Mme Dambreuse in order to preserve Jacques
Arnoux from bankruptcy and thus keep Mme Arnoux within reach. In
the complications that ensue Frédéric ends up brutally rejecting
Rosanette, Mme Arnoux leaves Paris anyway, and Frédéric breaks
with Mme Dambreuse. Although Flaubert has this catastrophic ending
of Frédéric's affective life and hope of wealth coincide with the December 2, 1851, coup of Louis-Napoleon, Frédéric is too depressed over
his personal disaster to think about politics.

Nevertheless, the novel has not forgotten history. When the despairing Frédéric does go out on the street the day after the coup, Flaubert
has him ask a worker if there will be fighting and gets the reply, "We're
not such fools as to get ourselves killed for the rich!" A bourgeois
retorts, "Filthy Socialists! If only they could be wiped out this time!"
(435/410). Filled with disgust for the city where he has suffered so
much and which is now full of hatred and stupidity, Frédéric flees Paris
for his hometown of Nogent, dreaming during his train ride of the
simple and charming Louise Roque who had loved him with such
abandon and whom he spurned for his more ambitious erotic schemes
in Paris. He arrives in Nogent on a Sunday only to see Louise emerge
from the town church in a wedding gown and on the arm of his best
friend, the ambitious Deslauriers. Stunned, Frédéric jumps back on the
next train for Paris and arrives in the rain to find Napoleon's cavalry
galloping through the streets and the population in terror; his worker
friend Dussardier, the only one in the novel who has not sold out, is

also in the streets on this Sunday and refuses to budge when a squad of police approach; Dussardier shouts "Vive la République!" and is killed immediately—by none other than his old friend Sénécal, the former revolutionary socialist now turned police agent.

Frédéric's private dream of ideal love and his profane desires and ambitions have finally come to naught at the same time as France's pursuit of liberty and equality collapses in the Napoleonic coup. As for fraternity, the novel has Frédéric's best friend Deslauriers betray him on almost the same page that the petty bourgeois socialist, Sénécal, brutally cuts down his former comrade, the worker, Dussardier. There seems to be little uncertainty as to the meaning of these ironic juxtapositions of public and private failure—only the most cynical or uninvolved reader can resist a reaction of shock and disgust.

These last acts of betrayal are followed in the text by a great silence, a gap of seventeen years (much admired by Proust), which is lifted only by two brief closing chapters. The first contains the famous scene in which Frédéric and Mme Arnoux meet for one last time and freely speak their love for each other; yet it is a love in the past and will never be consummated. The second recounts Frederic's reunion with Deslauriers whom Frédéric implicitly forgives for his various betrayals (443/417). The famous last image of the novel, of course, is their remembering a youthful trip to a bordello in Nogent (an incident vaguely alluded to in the novel's second chapter) and the final lines of the novel have Frédéric and Deslauriers each saying "That was the best we ever had!" As many critics have noted this apparently cynical ending to a novel of sentimental education is not only a commentary on Romantic passion, but picks up the many other references in the work to prostitution and selling oneself.[23] Although there is a thread of tenderness and loyalty in Frédéric's love for Mme Arnoux, like the romanticized humanitarian sentiments of 1848, it is finally an illusion and can never be physically consummated.

Here, it seems, is the most specific connection of sentimental education and political education in the novel, the point where the story of Frédéric's and Deslaurier's failed dreams recapitulates the failed social and political dreams of 1848. And it reveals that political education itself is also a matter of sentimental education, a formation of the feelings. Yet the coincidence of major turns in Frédéric's sentimental

23. Brombert has developed the theme of prostitution in *The Novels of Flaubert*, 128–38.

education with significant political moments is not a rigid one and the
critic should beware of pressing these incidents too hard for symbolic
content. Flaubert makes his reader work hard to find the meaning not
only of individual episodes but of the pattern of the whole, and we
have seen how the reader often comes up frustrated at the decidability
of the most crucial nodes in the text. As Brooks and Culler have
shown, Flaubert also manipulates the free indirect style in such a way
that in many passages which give historical information or commentary we cannot be certain who is speaking—one of the characters, the
narrator, or the "voice of science."[24] The overall effect of this uncertainty, however, is to keep the reader at an ironic distance from the
history of 1848. Not that the novel treats the ideals of the revolution as
totally ridiculous; what is ridiculous, it seems to be saying, is the
attempt to realize them. The only solace is in memory and its narration—for this is what Frédéric and Mme Arnoux, Frédéric and Deslauriers do in the final scenes: they remember and recount the past to
each other. In this sense the remark about the adolescent trip to the
brothel is not cynical at all. The best we have, Flaubert seems to be
saying, is memory transformed into narrative.

Memory transformed into narrative is, of course, also a way of
describing the memoir. Considering the *Recollections* in the light of
Sentimental Education can put in relief certain aspects of the *Recollections'* discourse which are strikingly parallel to the devices of historical
fiction. In an earlier chapter I briefly compared the *Recollections,
Sentimental Education,* and Duveau's *1848* with respect to selection
and duration and observed that the *Recollections* as memoir stood
midway between fiction and history in its freedom of selection and
temporal adjustment vis-à-vis the chronicle of events. To those general
structural similarities between historical novel and memoir, may now
be added that the memoir, like the historical novel, has as its central
problem the relation of private and public with the obvious difference
that the conditions or events of the private realm reported in the
memoir bear an implicit claim to factuality. Correspondingly, the
discourse of the memoir shares with that of the historical novel its
potentiality for being written from the point of view of the historical
participant rather than the perspective of an omniscient narrator typical of scientific history. Of course, when scientific history takes a

24. Brooks, *Reading for the Plot,* 199; Culler, *Flaubert: The Uses of Uncertainty,*
117–18.

narrative form, it too is subject to such constraints of narrative discourse as selection and duration, the relation of the private (character) and public, and even to the constraints of point of view and voice however narrowly some historians may conceive them.

Yet, for all these formal similarities among historical novel, memoir and history, there is a sense in which, for our normal reading practice, the traditional historical novel remains purely a novel and belongs entirely to the realm of fiction. Consider the following passage from *Sentimental Education*, describing the day after Louis-Philippe's flight and the declaration of the Republic.

As business was at a standstill, anxiety and curiosity brought everybody out into the streets. The general casualness of dress blurred the distinction between the various social classes, hatred was concealed, high hopes were expressed, and the mob was in a gentle mood. Pride in a hard-won right was written on every face. There was a carnival gaiety in the air, a sort of campfire mood; nothing could have been more enchanting than Paris in those first days.

Frédéric gave the Marshall his arm, and they strolled through the streets together. She enthused over rosettes decorating every buttonhole, the flags hanging from every window, and the bills of every color posted up on the walls; and here and there she tossed a few coins into a collection-box for the wounded, placed on a chair in the middle of the road. Then she would stop to look at caricatures depicting Louis-Philippe as a pastrycook, an acrobat, a dog or a leech. But Caussidière's men with their swords and sashes frightened her a little. (317–18/293)

Duveau, Agulhon, and other historians have not hesitated in their esteem for the acuteness of Flaubert's evocation of the atmosphere of the city during the first days of the Revolution. Yet it is typical of *Sentimental Education* that general descriptions of public history are rare and when they do occur they are skillfully woven into the fabric of the private history of Frédéric and his friends. Recent studies of Flaubert's drafts have shown how he progressively erased or blurred references to specific historical figures, dates and occurrences in order to evoke only the general atmosphere and mentality of 1848.[25] On the other hand, the small details are often quite precise, the descriptions of carriages and clothes or the enumeration of the things Frédéric and

25. Anne Herschberg-Pierrot, "Le travail des stereotypes dans les brouillons de la 'Prise des Tuileries,'" *Histoire et language*, 43–53.

Rosanette saw in the streets and shop windows the day after the February Revolution. In the passage just cited the first paragraph could be lifted out and incorporated into a narrative history with little alteration; the second clearly belongs in a novel. Yet for the average reader both paragraphs flow together as part of a *single* discourse. Once the fictional pact has been entered into, everything in *Sentimental Education* lies under the sign of fictionality. Thus, there is a sense in which the Paris of 1848 in *Sentimental Education,* no matter how scrupulously reconstructed for the sake of verisimilitude, is as fictional as the invented characters who inhabit it and they are as "real" as the streets they walk on or the carriages in which they ride. No doubt there is also a sense in which the Paris of 1848 reconstructed by the historian is also a "fiction"; it is "made" with the help of the constructive imagination. Duveau, for example, creates three fictitious types—"the hosier," "the cabinetmaker," and "the mechanic"—whom he follows through 1848 in order to dramatize class interests and conflicts.[26] Nevertheless, we expect *everything* in Duveau's descriptions, including these nameless characters, to be under the sign of factuality, potentially warrantable by evidence. As readers we normally treat a work of history as part of the literature of fact no matter how many errors it may contain, and we treat a traditional historical novel as part of the literature of fiction even when everything within it is warrantable, since the actual is absorbed into the possible.

Thus our response to a historical novel like *Sentimental Education* appears curiously ambivalent. On the one hand, we read it as fictional through and through, as generating a "world" in which the real is transformed into the imaginary. On the other hand, we cannot help but think of this fictional world in relation to the "real" world of 1848, that is, the world attested by documents and artifacts and reconstructed in the various historical narratives or analyses we have read. Yet, as Paul Ricoeur has suggested, it may be precisely the fictionality of a novel's alternative world which makes it useful for our transactions with the documented world. Flaubert's fictional world of 1848 invites us to "refigure" our previous historical understanding of the world of 1848.[27] Thus, there are good grounds for comparing the

26. George Duveau, *1848: The Making of a Revolution* (New York: Random House, 1966), 18–19.
27. Ricoeur's thesis of the intersection of the fictional and historical in the refiguration of time receives its definitive summation in *Temps et récit, III, Le Temps raconté*

Recollections and *Sentimental Education* with respect to the question
reference, especially since my concern here is not so much with the
accuracy of details as with the ways discourse and reference are linked
in writing about history. I want to consider four aspects of each text:
first, a comparison of the place of sentiment in politics; second, the
treatment of the Reaction; third, narrative voice; and finally, the
question of plot.

Sentiment

Both the *Recollections* and *Sentimental Education* happen to give
the reader three scenes from the February Revolution in detail: in the
Recollections we have the satiric description of the February 24 deba-
cle in the Assembly, the invasion of the Assembly on May 15, and the
Festival of Concord on May 21; in *Sentimental Education* we have an
ironic portrayal of the fighting on February 24, the carnivalesque
invasion of the Tuileries, and the merciless satire of political association in the passage on the *Club de l'intelligence*. In each case revolutionary sentiments are satirized, ridiculed, and treated as literary or
theatrical imitations. Flaubert scores the illusory, romantic character
of his bourgeois antihero, Frédéric, whose political sentiments, if more
ephemeral than his erotic desires, are equally derivative and futile. It is
striking that Tocqueville's·satire of the bourgeoisie and "the people"
at revolution also focuses on the authenticity of sentiment. In the midst
of the tumultuous Assembly meeting of February 24, invaded by a
shouting mob armed with swords, bayonets, and rifles, Tocqueville
was struck by its false, imitative character and the invaders' lack of
genuine revolutionary feeling—"they imitated [their fathers] gestures
and their poses as seen at the theatre, since they could not imitate their
enthusiasm or feel their furor" (75/53). This failure of political senti-

<hr>

(Paris: Éditions du Seuil, 1985), 264–79. No doubt, this "refiguration" is one reason
we tend to value historical novels for the truth of their portrayal of general conditions
and consider gross errors or the manipulation of well known facts to mar such works
on the grounds of verisimilitude. Lukacs argued that the historical novel is not a
separate genre or subgenre but simply a novel with a specific problem, i.e., the use of
individuals and segments of reality to evoke the social totality in the process of
development, *The Historical Novel* (Lincoln: University of Nebraska Press, 1983),
127.

ment, of course, is a general deficiency of the bourgeoisie for Tocqueville. They have become a class without political passions or any sense
of grandeur since their sole desire is to preserve their comfortable life:
"and there hardly remained anything . . . but the taste for well being, a
sentiment very tenacious and exclusive but very soft, which accommo-
dates itself to any form of government which will allow it satisfaction"
(99/78). Compare Flaubert's description of the men around M.
Dambreuse who "had served at least four governments and would
have sold France or the human race in order to guarantee their fortune,
spare themselves a moment's uneasiness or embarrassment" (264/
240). Even when the *Recollections* allows its actors more elevated
desires than comfort or gain, their feelings are likely to reflect only the
sentimentalism of the "literary spirit in politics." Yet there is one point
in the *Recollections* where more elevated sentiments do emerge. The
June civil war is a *kairos* momentarily eliciting the higher feelings of
patriotism and solidarity from bourgeois, aristocrat, and peasant
alike. Whereas in *Sentimental Education* all feelings are sooner or later
revealed to be counterfeit or reversible, in the *Recollections* true sentiments can ultimately be distinguished from derivative or feigned ones.

Reaction

Both works drown the claims of the Revolution, "the people," the
bourgeoisie, and socialism in irony, satire, ridicule, and comic mise-
en-scène. Flaubert, of course, goes much further than Tocqueville on
every score, widening his flood of abuse to embrace any group or
individual with a desire for power or reform, or even a belief that
political action is worth the effort. It would be a mistake, however, to
conclude that the demolitions of *Sentimental Education* are only in
the service of an apolitical nihilism. Even if excessive, Flaubert's abuse
falls on all parties alike, whereas Tocqueville's text largely spares the
Reaction. The *Recollections* pays no attention to the massacres at the
end of the June Days (whereas Flaubert dramatizes one particularly
disgusting incident in the shooting of prisoners by old man Roque),
nor would one gather from the *Recollections'* brief description of the
Reaction how early it began or how bitterly determined and violent it
was. The *Recollections* shows Tocqueville participating in it and willing to justify it as necessary because of the "abuse of freedom," and
justifying his own proposals for further restrictions on the press and

limiting assembly on the grounds others would have done worse. *Sentimental Education,* on the other hand, treats the Reaction with scorn and satire equal to anything it dishes out to socialists and "the people." In fact, its contempt for the latter is more for stupidity and ugliness, whereas the reactionaries are shown as driven solely by greed and savagery. In a passage which seems to come unambiguously from the narrator, we are told that after the June Days, the fury of those who had not fought also needed an outlet so "they exacted vengeance on the papers, the Clubs, the gatherings, the doctrines, on everything that had exasperated them for three months; and despite the victory, equality . . . displayed itself triumphantly, an equality of brute beasts, an equal level of bloody degradation; the fanaticism of the selfish matched the frenzy of the needy, the aristocrat experienced the fury of the mob, and the white hat was no less savage than the red" (358/334). If *Sentimental Education* ends up seeming so apolitical, it is in part because it contains an implicit moral vision that condemns oppression, brutality, and killing no matter what the justification.

Read in the light of *Sentimental Education,* the *Recollections* appears even more clearly the work of a partisan who rejoiced in the "deliverance of the nation from oppression by the workers of Paris" (242/165) and who was still working a year later to defeat the socialist party wherever it reared its ugly head. It was only after the Napoleonic coup had put him definitively on the sidelines that Tocqueville became again a liberal critic on the "outside" who, like Flaubert, could scorn the role which a bogus fear of socialism played in sustaining the Napoleonic dictatorship. If one puts the underlying moral code of each narrative side by side, Flaubert's apolitical moral judgement on violence in the name of political ideals does not appear so inferior to the moral code of Tocqueville that can legitimate violence and repression in the pursuit of grandeur.[28]

28. Tocqueville was in no sense a pacifist nor did he shrink from the idea of using violent repression in the interest of order or grandeur. He was an enthusiastic champion of the conquest of Algeria and of its military pacification. If he was untainted by racism of any kind, as his letters to Gobineau prove, he also believed in the superiority of Western civilization and wanted France to have her share of empire. See André Jardin, *Alexis de Tocqueville, 1805–1859* (Paris: Hachette, 1984), 302–27.

Voice

At first glance it might seem hazardous to attempt a comparison of discourse in a first-person memoir and a novel, especially a novel by Flaubert, hailed as a pioneer of indirect free style and master manipulator of point of view. But our discovery of multiple voices or modes of discourse in the *Recollections* suggests a legitimate comparison of the use of narrative voice in the two texts. Following Peter Brooks, I indicated that Flaubert often seems to deliberately muddy the narrative waters, to employ shifts in voice which are so imperceptible and/or ambiguous that we cannot tell "who" is speaking. This labor could be in service of Flaubert's famous impassivity, the effort to let the narrative unroll as if from the perspective of an indifferent deity. "When will one make history as one ought to make the novel," Flaubert asks in one of his letters, "without love or hatred for any character? When will one write facts from the point of view of a cosmic joke (*une blague supérieure*), that is as the good Lord sees them, from on high?"[29] Of course, by the twentieth century, we have long since learned how to write history from such a "higher" vantage point, but Flaubert's practice in *Sentimental Education* reflects anything but cosmic neutrality—his merciless pillorying of every class, his demotion of every effort to achieve personal or political ideals, may be impartial as to its target, but it hardly seems the height of human impassiveness to set up the trope of Irony as the ultimate cosmic power. Yet Peter Brooks suggests that the central principle governing the discourse of *Sentimental Education* is less that of impassivity than that of interference: people are always in the wrong place at the wrong time, friendship exists in the mode of betrayal, desire in the mode of failure or of disappointment when achieved, the political and personal constantly subvert each other. Flaubert's ambiguous use of the indirect free style also makes interference and chiasmus "come to inhabit the text in its very verbal texture," with the result that the "uncertainty and inconsistency that arise from interfering voices and ideological systems characterize the whole presentation of 1848."[30]

By contrast, voice in the *Recollections*, despite its variety, seems

29. Letter of October 8, 1852, cited in Green, *Flaubert and the Historical Novel*, 23.
30. Brooks, *Reading for the Plot*, 193–99.

utterly perspicacious. For not only does the narrator divide his discourse into a recollective voice embodying the experienced past and a commenting voice of the time of writing with its subdiscourses of wisdom, but the attentive reader seldom has difficulty in distinguishing them, especially since each voice has its characteristic grammatical markers. The result is that, despite occasional ambiguities, the reader can usually tell whether a sentiment or conviction belongs to Tocqueville the actor of 1848 or to Tocqueville the writer of 1850. The larger uncertainties in the text derive more from the instability of its binary code or from satiric countercurrents to narrative sequence than from disturbances in narrative voice itself.

It is this relative clarity in the distribution of narrative voices which is partly responsible for the effect of authorial "presence" in the *Recollections,* just as the interference and instability of voices in *Sentimental Education* are largely responsible for our sense of the narrator's "absence." Similarly, the *Recollections'* discourse seems transparent to the world it invokes when compared with the deliberately labored syntax of *Sentimental Education.* The elusiveness of the novel's narrator, "his," "her," "its" failure to declare itself, combined with such stylistic devices as syntactic delay, descriptions that seem to exist for themselves, a metonymical microstructure where things connect by contiguity—such devices of deliberate clumsiness keep the reader at a distance, and underline the linguistic character of this constructed world.[31] Here, it seems, is the truth in Brooks's and Culler's contention that *Sentimental Education* is less about 1848 or History in general than it is *about narrative,* about the way life *becomes* novel and history.

Nothing of this modernist self-consciousness can be found in the *Recollections,* which operates as if the impediment to transparency were entirely a matter of honesty and diligence. Armed with the device of the secret mirror, supplied with a will to truthfully recounting memory and with the shield of secrecy against the subversive effects of the ego, Tocqueville writes with the assurance that his discourse will not only be transparent to the world but that its rhetorical forms will be transparent to the reader, who can rationally decide whether or not to assent to its appeal. In Flaubert's discourse there is no longer the

31. Culler, *Flaubert: The Uses of Uncertainty,* 202–7.

same confidence in the transparency of either writing or reading; instead, rhetoric in general and the Balzacian "historical" discourse in particular have become suspect. The reader is put off, kept at a distance, forced to ask if this is a narrative at all, if life itself can become a narrative, if it can be made into something like a Balzacian novel or a coherent history.

Plot

In my earlier chapter on plot I noted that both the *Recollections* and *Sentimental Education* employ an intermittent presentation that tends to prevent episodes from flowing together in narrative continuity. The differing narrative mechanisms by which each work generates this intermittent structure, however, result in opposite plot effects. As Michal Peled Ginsburg has shown, the narrative in *Sentimental Education* moves metonymically, with one encounter touching off another by contagion rather than by similarity. Moreover, characters can metonymically substitute for one another in a process that empties all characters and actions of a centered meaning.[32] In the *Recollections*, on the other hand, the separate episodes tend to become *tableaux* deriving their meaning metaphorically from the binary moral code, which is made explicit through the voice of commentary. The closest parallels to the major *tableaux* of the *Recollections* in *Sentimental Education* are those scenes where exemplary events from the political history of 1848 and the turns in the private story of the characters intersect. Yet owing to the "metonymical sliding" and substitution of which Ginsburg speaks, these intersections of the public and private can, as we have seen, support multiple and sometimes contradictory thematic interpretations.

Dominick LaCapra has gone even further in analyzing the failure of meaning in these private/public episodes, speaking of the tendency in the novel for the private and the political to "merge or even collapse" into each other. He concludes that *Sentimental Education* shows "the potentially catastrophic absence of viable articulations that would allow for both limited mediation and engaging supplementary interac-

---

32. Michal Peled Ginsburg, *Flaubert Writing: A Study in Narrative Strategies* (Stanford, Calif.: Stanford University Press, 1986), 132–53.

tion between distinguishable entities."[33] The *Recollections,* on the other hand, seeks not only to maintain the integrity of the public and private spheres (disinterest) but also to mediate narratively between them through Tocqueville's personal commitment to establishing a Republic of "regular liberty." Although we may find in the *Recollections* elements of a one-sided, antidemocratic liberalism, the text's treatment of Tocqueville's political actions is consistent with the general mediating role envisaged for himself and his fellow notables in the era of democracy.[34] Hence, even though the *Recollections* ends with a "fall," its moral code not only distingushes truth from literature, and greatness from greed, but also implies that political action guided by right sentiment is the best we have. Even Flaubert's novel, although it seems to denigrate every dream of greatness whether of love or of power and to teach the futility of historical action, still puts the question of the relation of the private and the political unmistakably before the reader. Reading *Sentimental Education* and the *Recollections* together suggests that the truth envisaged by the historical memoir and the historical novel is not merely an abstract truth about reference, but a practical truth about historical responsibility.

33. This quotation is from LaCapra's essay "Collapsing Spheres in Flaubert's *The Sentimental Education,*" in his *History, Politics, and the Novel* (Ithaca, N.Y.: Cornell University Press, 1987), 92. I am grateful to Dominick LaCapra for allowing me to read this chapter in advance of its publication.

34. LaCapra points out in the essay just mentioned that antidemocratic or elitist liberalism is the one political ideology of 1848 which has no specific embodiment in *Sentimental Education*—unless we choose to see Dambreuse as a parody of Tocqueville. This absence is less surprising, he suggests, when we remember that it is close to Flaubert's own political beliefs as reflected in his letters, though the novel itself, while in some ways reinforcing this view by its one-sided treatment of socialism, can also be seen as undermining even this political perspective. Ibid., 86–90.

7

AUTHORSHIP

In the previous chapter I lifted the brackets around the issue of referential cogency; in this chapter I lift them from the phenomenon of authorship. There is no question that a knowledge of Tocqueville's biography and the intellectual and literary influences he experienced has been of great—even indispensable—value to our textual study. Those particular aspects of authorship, however, are not be the direct object of attention in this chapter. Rather, I consider authorship only with respect to some ways an analysis of the *Recollections* can illuminate Tocqueville's other texts. Even here the aim is not to produce a new synthesis of Tocqueville's "thought" but to gain a new perspective on his central texts by reading them in the light of this marginal one. Three results of the preceding study of the *Recollections'* discourse can be particularly suggestive: the binary moral/political code, the pattern of voices or discursive viewpoints, and the tension between rhetoric ("vertical" devices of tableau and code) and narrative ("horizontal" devices of structure and shape).

Democracy in America

Most readers of *Democracy in America* have noticed that the text is organized around a series of oppositions whose leading terms are aristocracy/democracy and liberty/equality. The discourse of *Democracy in America* is an exercise in the rhetorical commonplace of definition, accomplished through a series of comparisons in which each typological pole is potentially open to explication through a further comparison. The concept of democracy is defined vis-à-vis aristocracy as the condition of and passion for equality, but this democracy itself is further divided into a *socially* conceived democracy where equality is the supreme passion as compared to a *politically* conceived democracy where liberty is as highly prized as equality. One can follow the unfolding of these comparative distinctions in several directions within the text as Tocqueville attempts to persuade us to rethink the fundamental terms in which we conceive modern political life.[1] By examining a typical chapter of *Democracy in America* that appears to be purely about the political concepts liberty versus equality, I will show that Tocqueville's comparative political discourse is underwritten by a moral code close to that of the *Recollections*. The chapter selected is Chapter 1 of Volume 2, Part 2, "Why Democratic Nations Show a More Ardent and Enduring Love for Equality than Liberty" (2, 101–4/503–6).[2]

After a brief rhetorical *exordium,* the argument develops hierarchically, descending from the most abstract idea of a complete equality coinciding with complete liberty, through the notion of an equality that is the dominant fact and experience of the democratic

1. Anyone approaching the text of *Democracy in America* today will be in the debt of James Schleifer's *The Making of "Democracy in America"* (Chapel Hill: University of North Carolina Press, 1980). Yet when Schleifer comes to the question of discourse, he sees it as a matter of tone and surface effects. Tocqueville's compulsion for revision, we are told, "arose from more than stylistic considerations" and "even more fundamental than his striving for literary excellence is the characteristic style of logic or pattern of thought," which makes use of comparison and distinction (279). Schleifer has correctly put his finger on key devices of the Tocquevillian text, but these devices are not those of "logic" as opposed to "style," but commonplaces of traditional rhetoric. Remarks similar to Schleifer's can be found in Jean-Claude Lamberti's *Tocqueville et les deux démocraties* (Paris: Presses Universitaires de France, 1983), 28, where he speaks of the democracy-aristocracy contrast as "not a mere rhetorical procedure." But rhetoric is never "merely" rhetorical unless it is reduced to the sole dimension of eloquence. One recent interpreter of Tocqueville who recognizes the importance of understanding his works rhetorically is Michael Hereth, *Alexis de Tocqueville: Threats to Freedom in Democracy* (Durham: Duke University Press, 1986), 91–111.

2. Alexis de Tocqueville, *Oeuvres complètes* (M), *De la démocratie en Amérique,* vol. 1, 1 & 2 (Paris: Gallimard, 1961); English translation by George Lawrence, *Democracy in America* (Garden City: Doubleday, 1969). Numbers in parenthesis give the volume and page of the French edition first, the English translation second. I have occasionally modified Lawrence's excellent translation in the interest of terminological consistency.

age, then through three social-psychological arguments each of which suggests that equality is more immediately enjoyed and understood than freedom, to culminate in two historical allusions to the ancien régime and the revolution of 1789. At the heart of this argument are the three social-psychological reasons "which at *all* times lead men to prefer equality to liberty" (2, 102/504). First, that political liberty is easily lost or destroyed but social equality once attained would be very difficult to reverse. Second, that the dangers of freedom when carried to excess are readily apparent, but "only perceptive and clearsighted men" can see the distant dangers of equality, dangers that only "gradually insinuate themselves into the body social" (2, 103/505). Third, the pleasures of equality are not only immediate but are felt by everyone in their daily life and "to taste them one needs only to live," whereas political liberty comes only with sacrifice and effort and "occasionally gives a sublime pleasure to a few" (2, 103/505). Examined by themselves, I believe, none of the arguments in this chapter is very convincing; in fact, each seems to rest on premises that at best are contestable and at worst too general to prove anything. Taken together, however, they build toward an effect of plausibility for those elite readers who think of themselves as among the "perceptive and clearsighted men" referred to in the text. This reasoning is not simply an argumentative fault in *Democracy in America* but paradoxically a source of its interest as a text; rhetoric is not the art of persuading everybody at once but of tailoring one's arguments to the audience at hand.[3]

There is something else going on in this essay besides offering general "reasons" for the democratic age's love of equality over liberty; rhetorically its language morally denigrates equality and exalts liberty. The one is described as cheap, easy, immediate, making its petty enjoyments constantly available to all; the other is referred to as costly and fragile, its benefits coming in the long run and offering its lofty pleasures only from time to time and to a few. This more indirect message is, of course, a variation on one of *Democracy in America*'s most prevalent comparative devices: playing off the characteristics of

3. Lamberti has pointed out that Tocqueville carefully kept his criticisms of the middle class out of *Democracy in America* both because he wanted to persuade them and because he needed their support to get elected. Lamberti, *Tocqueville*, 82–83 and 261.

aristocratic societies against those of democratic ones. Elsewhere in *Democracy*, the drive for equality is associated with the vulgar passion for material well-being, with individualism and with the general mediocrity of democratic society. Freedom, on the other hand, is associated with those virtues which are compatible with the aristocratic values of "glory" and "independence." If the aristocrats and bourgeois "notables" for whom *Democracy in America*'s rhetoric seems destined were to be persuaded of the gravity of the task of guiding democracy, they must be made not only to appreciate the inevitability and dangers of equality, but to be impressed with the sublimity, difficulty, and sacrifice required for the preservation of liberty.[4]

Read in the light of our analysis of the thematic code of the *Recollections*, elements in *Democracy in America* which are often overlooked in the typical political reading stand out in relief. In *Democracy in America* as well as in the *Recollections* is an underlying moral code that gives the discourse much of its affective appeal. In the chapter we have been examining, equality is associated with petty enjoyments or possessions (*petites jouissances*) and liberty with lofty satisfactions (*sublimes plaisirs*). If greed and greatness do not appear in name in this chapter and appear only occasionally elsewhere, their synonyms are everywhere in *Democracy in America*. The *Recollections'* polarity of *grandeur* versus *cupidité* can especially be felt in the text's ambivalence toward the "taste for material comfort" (*goût du bien-être*), which Tocqueville treats as the dominant motive force of American society. In America the passion for material well-being fixes on relatively petty comforts (*ces objets sont petits, mais l'âme s'y attache*), which are so absorbing that people tend to lose sight of those "more precious goods which constitute the glory and *grandeur* of the human species" (2, 138/534). Tocqueville goes on to point out, however, that Americans are very anxious in the midst of their material prosperity and he attributes this to the fact that social and economic equality produces a competitive drive to attain more and more (2, 143/538). He also argues that this obsession with getting ahead can endanger the political participation essential to maintaining democratic liberties, since

4. Lamberti has analyzed this chapter from the perspective of its place in the development of Tocqueville's thought, showing the way it already reflects the shift away from a pure opposition of equality and liberty to a more nuanced examination of the role of revolution. Lamberti, *Tocqueville*, 72.

people will be tempted to turn government over to any one or any group that will preserve order and allow the free pursuit of material gain (2, 147/540). The one thing that can momentarily tear Americans away from the *"petites passions"* that agitate their lives is religion since worship turns them toward an ideal world where all is *"grand, pur, éternel"* (2, 149/543). The typical American "appears one moment to be animated by the most selfish greed, and the next by the most lively patriotism." (*Il paraît tantôt animé de la cupidité la plus égoiste et tantôt du patriotisme le plus vif.*) (2, 148/541)

Thus, although *Democracy in America* emphasizes the largely positive effect of the passion for material comfort on politics due to the moderating influence of religion, like the *Recollections*, the *goût du bien-être* is associated with *petitesse, égoïsme,* and *cupidité* in opposition to *désintéressement, élévation,* and *grandeur.* No doubt Tocqueville takes a much harsher view of *"égoïsme"* and the *"goût du bien-être"* in the *Recollelctions* than in *Democracy in America* where they are incorporated in "individualism." One reason, of course, is that in the *Recollections* he is dealing with a society lacking many of the conditions that in America tended to offset the ill effects of materialism on civic responsibility. Another important difference is that France's revolutionary history had left it by 1848 a society socially and economically divided. It would take us too far afield to explore in detail the relative weight throughout *Democracy in America* of this moral code vis-à-vis the text's better-known political polarities. Nevertheless, even this brief discussion shows the important rhetorical role played in *Democracy in America* by a set of moral polarities similar to those which underwrite the *Recollections.*

There would seem no place in *Democracy in America,* however, for the kind of tension between rhetoric and narrative found in the *Recollections.* Although there is a brief section in the introduction to *Democracy in America* describing the seven-hundred-year march of western civilization toward greater and greater equality, by the end of this little story Tocqueville is speaking of democracy as a "social state imposed by Providence" (1, 5/12). Since this continuing and irresistible march of equality of conditions is said to have reached its "extreme limits" in America (1, 1/9), rhetoric and narrative can never interfere with each other in *Democracy in America.* Rhetoric simply *follows* narrative in the text since the opening narrative of the irresistible march of equality is the ever present premise of *Democracy in*

America's rhetorical arguments. Because democracy is treated as an already accomplished fact in America, it need not be narratively explained but only rhetorically explored so as to distinguish libertarian democracy, which appeals to our higher moral instincts from the purely egalitarian democracy, which appeals to our petty and base desires. Lacking the ongoing tension between rhetorical and narrative modes, *Democracy in America* also has a less complex and marked set of voices than the *Recollections* or *The Old Regime*. To find the full range of Tocqueville's discursive practice in one of his major works, we need to turn our attention to *The Old Regime and the Revolution*.

The Old Regime and the Revolution

In 1850, forced by fatigue and illness to retreat to Sorrento, Tocqueville not only took up the second part of the *Recollections* but began to ask himself if the best contribution he could make to his time and to posterity was not through writing rather than active political life. Tocqueville's career reflections can be followed in letters to his friend and distant relation Louis de Kergorlay, where Tocqueville offers not only the earliest plans for what was to become *The Old Regime and the Revolution* but also a direct comment on the conflict between rhetoric and narrativity. Tocqueville reminds Kergorlay that he had been thinking for some years of writing another book, on *"un grand sujet de littérature politique,"* dealing with contemporary Europe. He is also convinced that such a discussion would have to be attached to a historical narrative. "I need to find a solid and continuous base of facts for my ideas. I can only procure one by writing history; by attaching myself to a period whose narrative will provide the occasion to depict the men and affairs of our century, and allow me to make of these separate paintings a single picture (*de faire de toutes ces peintures détachées un tableau*)."[5] It is not surprising that the notion of *tableau* should appear here since Tocqueville is writing Part II of the *Recollections* at this time, but equally striking is his recognition that although narrative is neither his main interest nor his forte, he cannot do without it. Tocqueville sees the problem from the point of view of the writer of narrative history. "The principal merit of the historian is to

5. Alexis de Tocqueville, *Oeuvres complètes* (M), XIII, 230–31.

know how to weave the fabric of facts, and I do not know if I can handle the art. What I have succeeded in doing best so far, is to judge facts rather than recount them; such an ability can only be exercised in history proper from time to time and in a secondary fashion, lest one violate the genre and burden the narrative."[6] As I pointed out in the chapter on voice, Tocqueville experienced a similar difficulty with recollective narrative discourse as he began Part 2 of the *Recollections* just a month before he wrote this letter to Kergorlay.

In the light of these problems with narrative, the opening line of the *The Old Regime and the Revolution* in 1856 takes on a new weight: "The book I publish at this moment is not a history of the Revolution . . . but a study of that Revolution" (69/vii).[7] In *The Old Regime* Tocqueville turned his narrative handicap into an advantage and produced one of those rare works whose thesis not only has to be disposed of one way or another by subsequent researchers, but whose analytic and discursive strategy remains equally instructive. As François Furet has put it: "If Tocqueville is a unique case in the historiography of the Revolution, it is because his book forces us to decompose the object 'French Revolution' and to reconceptualize it."[8] Fernand Braudel, on the other hand, sees Tocqueville's historiographical achievement in more general terms as an anticipation of the *Annales* school. The "center of gravity of his thought is drawn towards a history which is deep, slow moving, as opposed to a history of events."[9] Both characterizations are needed to do justice to the genre exemplified by *The Old Regime* in which a conceptual critique of an accepted historical object and a comparative analysis of long term social and political trends are integrated into a singular *tableau* of a past society.

If the ordering metaphor of the *Recollections* is the dramatic *tableau*, the ordering metaphor of *The Old Regime* is the painterly *tableau*. The text frequently refers to itself as a kind of painting (159/197,

6. Ibid., 232.

7. Alexis de Tocqueville, *Oeuvres complètes* (M) Vol. II, 1, *L'Ancien Régime et la révolution* (Paris: Gallimard, 1953); *The Old Regime and the Revolution* (Garden City: Doubleday, 1955). References to the French edition will be given first followed by the page number of the American edition. I have for the most part found it necessary to make my own translations since Stuart Gilbert's translation is so free at points as to approach paraphrase.

8. François Furet, *Penser la Révolution française* (Paris: Gallimard, 1978), 33.

9. Fernand Brandel, "Préface," in Alexis de Tocqueville, *Souvenirs* (Paris: Gallimard, 1978), 16.

193/138) and to the results as a picture or portrait (147/81, 156/94). The final, summary chapter, for example, begins: "In concluding, I want to assemble several of the characteristics which I have already painted separately, and, from this old regime whose portrait I have just made, see the Revolution emerge as if of itself" (244/203). Whereas the dramatic *tableaux* of the *Recollections* capture a series of exemplary incidents and moral types reminiscent sometimes of the *peinture moral* of Greuze and at others of the *tableau de Paris* tradition, *The Old Regime* assembles a series of separate delineations of social conditions and political institutions into a large canvas reminiscent of what art historians call "history painting" (for example, Poussin, David). Yet the dramatic *tableau* and "history painting" are not so far apart since both select morally significant and typical moments. In fact, one could see Tocqueville as ironically exemplifying the very "democratic" idiom he regretted in certain remarks he made about painting in *Democracy in America*, where he contrasted the elevated style of Raphael who sought to "make man something better than man" with the democratic realism of David and his school who gave us "an exact representation of man" and of everyday life (57/468). If I insist on the importance of the *tableau*/painting metaphor, it is because in a painting the elements composing it are neither systematically subordinated nor sequentially ordered. One leaves *The Old Regime* aware that arguments and observations drawn from various levels of abstraction and domains of inquiry have been composed in such a way as to produce a general picture which serves as the confirmation of its thesis that the Revolution merely accelerated and completed processes that had been going on for generations and that the crucial features of postrevolutionary society were already there, hidden behind the screen of anachronistic privilege. Such a thesis obviously calls for something like a *tableau*, a picture of the old society which will reveal the essentially democratic and modern reality behind the feudal appearances.

Moral Code

The function of this *tableau*, however, is not merely representational but also rhetorical. It is part of *The Old Regime's* more general aim of persuading its readers to take up the cause of liberty in the spirit of their ancestors of 1789 "when love of equality and love of liberty filled their hearts; when they wanted to found not only democratic institutions but free ones; not only to destroy privileges but to recognize and consecrate rights; a time of youth, of enthusiasm, of pride, of generous and sincere passions, a time which, despite its errors, men will remember forever" (72/x–xi). In writing of the old society Tocqueville always had in mind the new one; he did not want to simply discern what it died of but how the unfortunate Napoleonic outcome might have been avoided. "My aim was to create a *tableau* which was strictly accurate, and at the same time, instructive." Hence, whenever he has found in the past those "male virtues" like "independence, the taste for *grandeur,* faith in oneself and a cause" he has put them in relief and has similarly emphasized those vices of the old society which linger on in the new (73/12). This passage reveals a polarized discourse of moral/political edification familiar to us from the *Recollections* since the appearance of greatness soon evokes the theme of greed, specifically the obsession with money. The most common passions of democratic societies in his time, Tocqueville writes, are those of gain, riches and material well-being, passions that have penetrated all classes and eventually will "enervate and degrade the entire nation" (74/xiii). As its introduction makes clear, *The Old Regime* will also be a rhetorical essay using the commonplace of comparison to show that the exercise of liberty is the only thing that can turn people away from pettiness and greed toward higher values and service of their nation.

Only liberty can . . . draw citizens out of their isolation and constrain them to approach each other, to warm them and reunite them by the necessity of reaching an understanding, to persuade and please each other in the conduct of their common affairs. Only liberty is capable of tearing them away from the worship of money and the little worries of their everyday private affairs and to make them see their country above and beside them; only liberty can, from time to time, substitute for the love of well being higher and more energetic passions, and furnish for ambition objects greater than the acquisition of riches, and create the light which permits one to see and judge the vices and virtues of men. (75/xiv)

Not only are the greatness/greed and liberty/equality polarities to be found in *The Old Regime* but many others from the *Recollections,* for example, disinterest/egoism, order/anarchy, aristocracy/bourgeoisie, centralization/local autonomy. Of course, in *The Old Regime* their relative importance is altered: centralization/local autonomy and lib-

erty/equality dominate whereas aristocracy/bourgeoisie and the synonyms of grandeur/greed appear less prominently. Some pairs from
the earlier work (contented versus ambitious domestics, feminine
versus masculine women) obviously play no role at all whereas several
new oppositions more germane to the book's subject take their place.
Among the new polarities are *aristocracy* (a body of citizens who
govern) versus *caste* (whose sole identifying mark is birth) (147–
52/181–88), *independence* (pride in self-reliance and a taste for *grandeur*) versus *individualism* (isolation in private interest) (158/96, 170–
73/111–15) and *obedience* (to legal and moral authority) versus *servi-
tude* (to a *de facto* ruler who can bestow favors) (175–76/118–20). It
seems clear, however, that these new polarities are equally part of a
binary moral code paralleling that of the *Recollections*.

The Old Regime is also like the *Recollections* in the power of its
code to keep Tocqueville from seeing or even seeking evidence which
might force him to alter his binary operators. This is particularly the
case with the concept of "aristocracy," which also plays a crucial role
in *Democracy in America* and the *Recollections*. From the beginning
to the end of his career as a writer, Tocqueville exhibits a nostalgia for
the old days when the French nobility was a "true aristocracy," the
proud, independent defenders of local liberties, the governors and
judges of their domains who lived in intimate contact with "their"
peasants and with the bourgeoisie of the towns, aiding the poor and
unfortunate, and so on. Furet has shown how wide of the mark
Tocqueville was in his description of the nobility's actual financial and
social situation in the eighteenth century, how little Tocqueville
seemed interested in investigating the actual divisions within the nobility, and how he particularly misconstrued the position of the re-
cently ennobled. Furet argues, therefore, that the truth of Tocqueville's
picture of the eighteenth century is vitiated at a key point by his
insistence on seeing the old nobility (his own class) as the bearer of a
tradition of liberty and independence which they betrayed.[10] This is
indeed the same idealized portrait of the aristocracy we met in the
Recollections.

10. Furet, *Penser la Révolution*, 195–201. As Furet points out there are also important differences between *Democracy in America* and the *Old Regime* with respect to
the concepts of democracy, aristocracy, et al. These differences are specifically the
result of Tocqueville's experience of 1848 and make his reflections in the *Old Regime*
laden with pessimism (190–95).

Knowing the falsity of the caste/aristocracy polarity as a representation of the actual condition of the French nobility in the eighteenth century, however, enables one to see more clearly the *rhetorical* function of the comparisons in which "aristocracy" figures, from Volume I of *Democracy in America* through the *Recollections* to *The Old Regime*. First, Tocqueville's way of using it shows that his interest in social classes was not simply in their role as social institutions but in the moral values and ideas they embody. Second, Tocqueville's heavy reliance on the devices of comparison and antithesis has contributed to his theoretical oversimplification of the concept of aristocracy. The logic of these polarities requires that each side be restricted to a few symmetrical dimensions; one cannot become too interested in one pole of a comparison or antithesis for itself without losing the advantage of setting typical parallel properties in relief. Finally, the meaning of "aristocracy" fluctuates depending on the rhetorical situation. When the *Recollections* suggests that participation by the aristocracy along with the bourgeoisie and the people is a requisite of stable government in France, aristocracy has to mean a traditional class defined by birth and not just an elite of morality and talent. In *Democracy in America,* on the other hand, aristocracy means not only a regime of hereditary privilege but the value of audacity and excellence as compared to the mediocrity produced by democratic leveling (1, 255–56/145). The only "aristocracy" a society like America might produce would be the bastard "aristocracy of riches" in which successful greed would proclaim itself the criterion of greatness (2, 166/557). Thus both the aristocracy/democracy and aristocracy/caste polarities are part of a rhetorical strategy to persuade Tocqueville's elite readers that France more than ever needs an "aristocracy" in the sense of men and women who will embody the values of liberty, independence, and *grandeur* as opposed to either the snobbish aloofness of a noble "caste" or the greedy "democratic" obsession with material comfort.

Voice

In Chapter 5 I described a set of characteristics which defined "recollection" as the dominant mode of discourse in the *Recollections*. Is there an equally distinctive voice which colors the rhetorical strategy of *The Old Regime*? At first glance it might seem that a *tableau* of the old society would need only descriptive and analytic prose of the most general type. But the discourse of *The Old Regime* does have a distinctive character: it is strongly *revisionist*. The received view of the Revolution as a decisive break, a view based on surface appearances and well-known events and writings, is contrasted to what Tocqueville has personally discovered, especially through reading anonymous governmental reports. This discourse of "revision" or "disclosure" takes a number of forms but on the phraseological plane it is most often characterized by either a simple opposition to the received view or is marked by the use of a first-person voice to introduce the sources that have shown Tocqueville what is going on beneath the surface (100/23, 101/24, 102/25). An important but less frequent marker contrasts the role of individuals or of specific ideas, laws, or events to the more powerful effect of long-term social practices and habits of mind (70/viii, 127/58, 180/123). In this category belongs Tocqueville's famous comment on classes: "One may cite against me individual cases: I speak of classes, they alone should concern history" (179/122). Distributed throughout the text, comments of this type continually mark the discourse not only as one that revises established views about the Revolution, but as a discourse that seeks to revise our assumptions about the operative forces in history. Perhaps the most striking revisory remarks in the text are those which refer to the breakdown of the various structures of the feudal order as themselves "revolutions," for example, the peasant's acquisition of land (129/60), the separation of nobility and bourgeoisie (150/86), Louis XVI's reforms (242/201).

The other voice which gives the discourse of *The Old Regime* its characteristic texture is parallel to the second major voice of the *Recollections: commentary.* The commentary passages, as in the *Recollections,* are characterized by the time/space of the present, psychologically identified with personal perspective of the author, and ideologically with the "cause of Liberty." Phraseologically, they are usually a few sentences or a brief paragraph offering a pointed comparison of conditions under the old regime with those of the present Napoleonic regime, for example, "the greatest difference in the matter is this, in those days the government sold positions, today it gives them away; in order to get them we no longer offer our money; we do better, we sell ourselves" (155/92, 121–50).[11] But the most eloquent pas-

---

11. Compare *Sentimental Education* on M. Dambreuse who "acclaimed every regime ... truckling to power so fervently he would have paid to sell himself" (73) (Harmondsworth: Penguin Books, 1964).

sages of commentary are those in which Tocqueville directly "instructs" his readers on the theme of liberty, sometimes ending with a statement in the *wisdom* mode. After observing how the sixty years since 1789 have seen so many vain attempts at free government followed by revolution that people have given up on freedom to accept "equality under a master," he writes: "I have often asked where the source is of this passion for political liberty which, in all times, has made men achieve the greatest things humanity has accomplished" (217/168). It cannot be simply a people's resentment of bad government, says Tocqueville, nor can it reside in the satisfactions of the material comforts freedom can bring. "What, in all times, has so strongly attached men's hearts to it, are its own attractions, its own charm, independent of its benefits; it is the pleasure of being able to speak, act and breathe freely, under the government of God and the law. Who seeks in freedom other than itself, is meant to be a slave" (217/168–69). Thus, *The Old Regime* not only intends to disclose the hidden truth about the Revolution by its revisory discourse but to move its readers to accept the moral and political "lesson" of that truth by the discourse of commentary and wisdom that itself re-visions the Second Empire. Louis-Napoleon's regime is not only treated as a pale imitation of the First Empire, but reduced to a mere episode in the epochal struggle between centralization and local autonomy, equality and liberty, greed and grandeur.

Yet the eloquent celebrations of liberty found in so many of the passages of commentary seem almost quixotic when set against the powerful current of the text's own revisory discourse. The implication of the central argument in *The Old Regime* is that since the institutions, practices, and desires that made French society what it had become by 1856 are less the product of conscious intention than of a long social evolution, the prospects for liberty appear dim indeed. This pessimism is everywhere in the book and produces some of its most sadly beautiful passages. We are told, for example, that once the Revolution had overthrown the monarchy, there emerged "a power more extensive, more detailed, more absolute than that of any of our Kings. The whole enterprise appeared extraordinarily bold and unheard of since people thought only of what they saw and not what they had seen . . . his government dead, his administration continued to live, and, every time since, when we have tried to defeat absolute power, we have been forced to place the head of Liberty on the body of a slave" (248/209). Tocqueville goes on in this vein for another three paragraphs—the penultimate paragraphs of the book. There is more going on here than the sort of rhetorical peroration that paints the condition to be remedied in the blackest terms, the better to alarm the reader. On the contrary, the pessimism is the necessary outcome of the text's revisory discourse. The writer who in *Democracy in America* condemned historians of the democratic age for discouraging individual effort has himself produced a work that more effectively depreciates personal intentions and action than any nineteenth-century determinist, since he does not attribute historical change to a few sweeping general causes, but to the slow working of a complex of political and social relations, institutional practices, and socially conditioned habits and desires. Despite this, Tocqueville still passionately believed in making an effort on behalf of liberty, and closes with an appeal to his reader's most noble instincts, hoping to convince us to take up the tragic burden of liberty.

Rhetoric and Narrative

As mentioned above, *The Old Regime* makes clear from the beginning that it will be less a history (narrative) than a study (analysis) of the Revolution. Nevertheless, that "study" intends to show how and why the Revolution emerges from the ancien régime as if by itself. Thus there *is* a narrative line underlying *The Old Regime,* the story of a transformation of an initial situation into a consequent one, from *l'ancien régime* to *la Révolution.* Yet this transformation is an almost immobile movement, a transition in which the end state is revealed to have already been contained in the initial state. The final chapter, for example, opens with the statement that the traits that have been depicted separately will be gathered together so that we may "see the Revolution emerge as if of itself from this old regime whose portrait I have just painted" (244/203). Yet is it not a rule of narrative construction that what emerges in the end be somehow contained or implied in the beginning? Otherwise we have only surprise, contingency, accident, a series of happenings but no story. Yet it is also a rule of narrative that the end state be genuinely different from the beginning. Otherwise we would have only stasis and repetition but no story. The peculiarity of *The Old Regime* as a work of history is not simply that its vertical or integrative code tends to dominate its horizontal or distributive development (as in the *Recollections*), but that the identity of the old society and the new is pushed to the point of obliterating the kind of difference without which there can be no narrative.[12]

But we may be looking in the wrong place for the narrative transformation in *The Old Regime and the Revolution*. After all, the crux of the conventional model of minimal narrative is the location and management of the transformation. In contemporary historiography two main approaches have been explored and analyzed. The traditional way of operating the transition is to fill out the narrative, connecting it step by step so that the transition is stretched out and merges with beginning and end in a "continuous fabric" of the kind Tocqueville doubted his ability to weave. The other way is to join beginning and end analytically by explanatory connectors derived from the social sciences. Part of the ambiguity the reader experiences with *The Old Regime* results from the text's superimposition of the two approaches. On the one hand the text appears primarily analytical and descriptive, developing a portrait of the ancien régime which will allow us to see its near identity with the society that emerged from the Revolution. On the other hand the ancien régime itself is described as undergoing a series of transitions that take place so slowly, and operate in such subtle ways, that the changes were imperceptible to those who experienced them and left no one prepared for the cataclysmic events of 1789–94. As a result, those four traumatic years that are the normal focus of traditional narrative histories of the Revolution are reduced by Tocqueville's text to the function of merely accelerating the long-term "revolution" occurring during the ancien régime itself. On the narrative level, therefore, the text's revisory discourse is in service of a

12. In a fascinating study of *The Old Regime*'s historical discourse Linda Orr has shown how the very success of Tocqueville's deconstruction of the Revolution leads his text into a series of ambiguities. Orr points out that the crucial figure "*sortie comme d'elle-même*" ("emerges as/of/from itself") which is used to describe the arrival of the Revolution (244/203) is also used earlier of the centralization which is also for Tocqueville the substance and sign of the Revolution (85/90 and 129/60). As Orr remarks after attempting to unpack the possible senses and directions of this figure, *comme de lui-même*, "finally all one can say is that something emerges from something like itself, but not itself and runs toward something like itself, but not itself, in fact perhaps in opposition to itself. It is no wonder then that (optical) rhetorical illusions of reversed cause and effect happen." Linda Orr, "Tocqueville et l'histoire incompréhensible: *L'Ancien Régime et la révolution*," *Poétique* 49 (1982): 51–70. I am grateful to Ms. Orr for making available a copy of the English version of her essay which she presented at the State University of New York at Stony Brook in April 1979.

radical displacement of the turning point of French history. The turning point is shifted from the Revolution of 1789–94 to the transition between a feudal-aristocratic society and a monarchial-egalitarian one. Yet even this transition is not narratively deployed in *The Old Regime* but argued for by means of a series of rhetorical set pieces that are gradually assembled into the overall portrait designed to persuade us that the "real" revolution was already all but complete prior to 1789. Thus, the rhetorical and narrative impulses constantly get in the way of each other and their tension generates a sense of dynamic immobility in which change reveals stasis and the new brings forth the old.

Tocqueville was happily surprised at the favorable reception of *The Old Regime* when it appeared in 1856; it suggested that the taste for freedom had not been totally destroyed in France by the fear of socialism and the desire for material comfort. He began work toward the second volume but soon ran into trouble, for now he was faced with the task of *narrating* the events of 1789–94. In a letter to Kergorlay in May 1858, less than a year before his death, Tocqueville described his difficulty.

> There is a particularity of this malady of the French Revolution which I can sense without being able to describe it or analyze the causes. It is a *virus* of a new and unknown type. There have been violent revolutions in the world before; but the excessive, desperate, audacious, almost insane, and yet powerful and effective, character of these revolutionaries seems to me without precedent. . . . Where did this new race come from? . . . What made it so effective? . . . My mind strains to get a clear notion of this object and find the means of portraying it. Independently of all that is understandable about the French Revolution, there is something about its spirit and its actions that is inexplicable.[13]

Furet suggests that what Tocqueville could not get a handle on was the revolutionary process itself. In Furet's view, 1789 inaugurated both an interior liberation of consciousness and an "imaginary discourse of power" in which the ideology of pure democracy came to occupy the space of legitimization vacated by royal power. This discourse of power eventually found its necessary expression in terror and war since it was an absolute claim that set its own new legitimacy against

---

13. Tocqueville, *Oeuvres complètes* (M), XIII, 337–38.

the old legitimacy. With the fall of Robespierre, Furet asserts, we return to Tocqueville's revolution of centralized institutions and equality.[14] Had Tocqueville lived would he have grasped the sources and dynamics of the unique passions of 1789–94, of that "virus" he sensed in 1858, and have then narrated its story? Furet doubts it since the "revolution" as Tocqueville understands it in *The Old Regime* had *already occurred* by 1789. The conclusions of Tocqueville's first volume had, in a sense, made the second superfluous. As Linda Orr puts it, *The Old Regime and the Revolution* should have been called "The Old Regime *is* the Revolution."[15]

"A Fortnight in the Wilderness"

I have offered considerable evidence of how powerfully the forms and devices of rhetoric dominated narrative process in Tocqueville's two most important published works and the difficulties he was still facing a year before he died in coming to terms with the demands of narrative. My thesis of the centrality of the rhetoric/narrative tension and the binary moral code in Tocqueville's discourse will be strengthened and amplified by considering another text in which Tocqueville was forced to come to terms with narrativity. Such a text is his account of a trip on horseback into the Michigan frontier which he and Beaumont made in July 1830. "A Fortnight in the Wilderness," written while Tocqueville was still in America, in August 1831, but published posthumously by Beaumont, has justly been compared to Chateaubriand's famous evocations of the American wilderness.[16] It is a re-

14. Furet, *Penser la Révolution*, 71–101, 203–11.

15. Orr, "Tocqueville et l'histoire incomprehensible," 58. R. R. Palmer has also discussed Tocqueville's difficulty with narrative in the introduction to *The Two Tocquevilles, Father and Son: Hervé and Alexis de Tocqueville on the Coming of the French Revolution* (Princeton, N.J.: Princeton University Press, 1987). Palmer translates not only Tocqueville's drafts and notes but the relevant letters as well.

16. Tocqueville's "Une Quinzaine dans le désert" was published by Beaumont in 1860. It now appears in the *Oeuvres complètes* (M), V, *Voyages en Sicile et aux États Unis* (Paris: Gallimard, 1957), 342–87. The English translation is in Alexis de Tocqueville, *Journey in America* (New Haven, Conn.: Yale University Press, 1959), 328–75. Page numbers in parenthesis after quotations will cite first the French edition then the English. There is an excellent comparison of Tocqueville's style in this essay with that of Chateaubriand. See Eva Dorau, "Two Men in a Forest: Chateaubriand, Tocqueville and the American Wilderness," *Essays in French Literature* 103 (1976): 44–61.

markable description of the American frontier as it unfolds before the two young Frenchmen on a journey to see the fabled American forest and its native Indian inhabitants on the Michigan frontier.

In its opening paragraphs, Tocqueville's narrative of the portion of the journey from New York to Buffalo manages to convey a sense of action and movement without recounting a single event, but offering only the kind of synthesizing description and analysis which will remain the defining characteristic of his discourse in later works. Consider his remarks on the disappearance of the Indians and their displacement by the white race which

> fells the forests and drains the marshes; lakes as large as seas and huge rivers resist in vain its triumphant march. The wilds become villages; the villages towns. The American . . . does not see anything astonishing in all this. This incredible destruction, this even more surprising growth, seem to him the usual progress of things in this world. He gets accustomed to it as the unalterable order of nature.
>
> In this way, always looking for the savages and the wilds, we covered the 360 miles between New York and Buffalo. (343/329)

Other than the simple displacement from spot to spot over time, there will be few "events" in the story of what is seen and experienced on this journey. Even what encounters there may be, become the occasion for a generalized portrait or a historico-sociological reflection as in this description of Tocqueville and Beaumont's meeting at last with "the Indians," a group of Iroquois who had arrived to collect their treaty rents:

> I was full of memories of M. de Chateaubriand and Cooper, and I had expected to find in the natives of America savages in whose features nature had left the trace of some of those proud virtues that are born of freedom. . . .
>
> The Indians that I saw that evening were small in stature; their limbs . . . were thin and far from muscular; their skin, instead of being copper red . . . was dark bronze . . . like mulattoes . . . the expression on their faces was ignoble and vicious. Their physiognomy told of that profound degradation that can only be reached by long abuse of the benefits of civilizations. (343–44/329–36)

This general description of the Indian corrupted by civilization is completed by the account of an incident in which Tocqueville and

Beaumont vainly attempt to get help for a drunken Indian who has fallen in the road outside the town of Buffalo and is likely to die of exposure. This *tableau* ends with a reflection on American morality, notably: "In the midst of this society, so well-policed, so prudish, and so pedantic about morality and virtue, one comes across a complete insensibility, a sort of cold and implacable egoism where the natives of America are concerned" (354/331).

The next section of the narrative, covering their trip by steamboat along the shore of Lake Erie to Detroit, similarly alternates among description, general analysis and moral evaluation. It ends with a description of the little town of Detroit and the astonishment and disbelief of the inhabitants that these Frenchmen really wanted to see the unspoiled forest and the Indians and not merely to prospect for land. Tocqueville and Beaumont are finally able to hire horses and set out through the forest for the distant village of Pontiac. At last, the reader thinks, we are about to enter a text-world of pure narration, perhaps even adventure. But no sooner are we in the woods following the road from clearing to clearing than Tocqueville tells us he will now give a general picture of the typical pioneer cabin, its surroundings and its family. The five-page summary description of the typical town-bred American gone to live in nature is no more picturesque and inspiring than was that of the "civilized" Indian.

> To win affluence he has braved exile, . . . slept on the bare ground and risked fever in the forest and the Indian's tomahawk. . . . Concentrating on the single object of making his fortune . . . even his feelings for his family have become merged in a vast egoism. . . . This unknown man is the representative of a race to whom the future of the New World belongs, a restless, calculating, adventurous race which sets coldly about deeds that can only be explained by the fire of passion, and which trades in everything, not excluding even morality and religion. (353/340)

Although Tocqueville's portrait of the typical pioneer settlement gives some details of cabin construction, the method of land clearing, and a sketch of the typical frontier wife, what really interests him is the greed which empowers the settler's labor and gives the American frontier its special character.

The village of Pontiac is the last regular settlement before Tocqueville and Beaumont enter the true virgin forest they had come so far to discover. Here they meet a new and rare type of American—who likes the solitude of the woods, lives by hunting, and respects the Indians. Here also they at last encounter Indians who are relatively uncorrupted by Europeans and whose physical stature and stamina they can admire. Now the text also satisfies the reader's hopes and expectations of vivid detail with its description of the immensity and solemnity of the forest. It was not only the vastness of the forest, but also the experience of solitude and the natural succession of living and dying things that struck Tocqueville:

> Each tree shoots quickly upwards looking for air and light . . . interlacing their branches, they form a huge canopy above the ground. . . . Majestic order reigns above your head. But near the ground there is a picture of chaos. . . . Trunks that can no longer support the weight of their branches are split half-way up. . . . Others shaken by the wind have been thrown whole to the ground; torn out of the soil. . . . The traveller looks, he sees nothing but a scene of violence and destruction . . . the elements are perpetually at war. . . . But the struggle is interrupted. . . . As if by order of a supernatural power movement is suddenly suspended . . . he listens, he holds his breath in fear the better to catch the last echo of life; no sound; no murmur reaches him. (368–69/356–57)

These lines are from more than two pages of an almost lyrical meditation on the appearance of the virgin forest and the sensations it aroused. Yet there is no indulgence of local color nor have we slipped fully into romantic expressiveness before the sublime. What one cannot miss even in this most purely evocative passage in all of Tocqueville is the comparison. The forest is an emblem of the struggle of order and anarchy, ultimately of life and death. Even Tocqueville's discourse of pure description and expression is constructed from a code of polar oppositions.

For all the text's solemnity, its pathos is held in check by classical manners, and the return of reality and consciousness on itself is not long in coming as Tocqueville describes the remainder of the journey. It becomes a kind of forced march to reach Saginaw before dark as the two Frenchmen fought off swarms of mosquitoes and the fatigue brought on by the strain of a long ride and the loss of provisions through spoilage. The physical description of Saginaw on the next day, a mere clearing with a few cabins and some thirty inhabitants including the Indians, takes little space in the text and soon gives way to another long analysis and meditation—the real climax of the narrative—on the four "races" or nations that history has thrown together in this wilderness clearing: the French Canadian, the American, the Indian, and the *bois-brûlé* or half-breed. Tocqueville gives a portrait of each national type, obviously relishing the opposition between the "gay, enterprising, haughty" Frenchman who lives in the wilds like an Indian, and the cold, tenacious American who "thinks that man has only come into the world to gain affluence." The text also treats with sympathy the Indian, who disdains the European's comfort, and it expresses pity for the half-breed who is trapped in the contradiction of two cultures neither of which he can give up. Tocqueville finds in this little community of thirty souls at the edge of civilization not only differences of national character but also of religion, skin color, affluence, learning. The only happening during the Frenchmen's short stay in Saginaw is a canoe trip further out into the wild which offers Tocqueville a final opportunity to describe the feelings produced by the immense forest, but this time the text also evokes his recognition that it is all doomed. "The voice of civilization and industry will break the silence of the Saginaw." "It is this consciousness of destruction, this awareness of imminent and inevitable change that gives, one feels, such an original character and touching beauty to the solitudes of America. One sees them with a melancholy pleasure; one is in a kind of hurry to admire them" (384/372). The narrative ends with a description of their return, a trip unmemorable except for their fear of getting lost and the ever-present torture of the mosquitoes. They do not encounter a single human being the first day of their journey back and it is "in the midst of that profound solitude," Tocqueville observes, "that we thought of the Revolution of 1830 whose first anniversary had just arrived."

> It is impossible to describe the sudden force with which memories of the 29th of July took possession of our minds. The cries and smoke of battle, the roar of guns, the rattle of rifles, the even more horrible tolling of the tocsin, the entire day with its burning atmosphere suddenly emerged from the past and stood before me like a *tableau vivant*. It was only a sudden illumination, a fleeting dream. When I raised my head and looked around me, the apparition had already vanished; but never had the silence of the forest seemed so icy, its shadows so somber, its solitude so complete. (387/375)

"A Fortnight in the Wilderness" not only shows Tocqueville's discourse inescapably bent on comparison, antithesis, and the moral tableau even in the midst of a descriptive narrative, but also employs a thematic code and recollective voice that anticipates the *Recollections*. Of course "A Fortnight in the Wilderness" lacks the aphoristic type of wisdom with which the mature Tocqueville laced the *Recollections,* and its sociological analyses and reflections are closer to those of *Democracy in America,* which was already forming in his mind. But comparison and antithesis are the dominant rhetorical devices in "A Fortnight" as in the *Recollections*. We have European versus American, Indian versus White Man and, like the polarities of the *Recollections,* these oppositions can subdivide and multiply, for example, "corrupted" Indian versus "natural" Indian; the avaricious settler, hating the Indian and bent on destroying the forest for profit, versus the free hunter living in harmony with both the Indian and the wilderness; and finally, the immense solitude of trees making up a single mass of nature versus the noise and strife of human history. It is not by accident that this last evocation of the immensity of the American forest ends with the juxtaposition of the forest's silence and the sounds of street fighting in the July Revolution of 1830. For the contending forces in that revolution as in the revolution of 1848 will be liberty and equality, greatness and greed—and they are what Tocqueville already sees clashing on the American frontier. The greedy American pioneer driven by the passion for equality in the sense of achieving the affluence and well-being he envies in others is contrasted to the noble-spirited French Canadian or the uncorrupted Indian who would rather live in freedom.

Once we have grasped the thematic code which orders the narrative of "A Fortnight in the Wilderness," we can begin to see that its story, pedestrian as it seems in terms of "events," is not a travelogue at all. At one level it is a *Bildungsroman* in brief, the story of two young Frenchmen on a quest of the *mysterium tremendum* of nature and of the noble savages who inhabit it. At another level it is the story of the American character at grips with the wilderness, or more generally, of the inevitable triumph of democratic (egalitarian and materialistic) man over the grandeur of unspoiled nature. The two young Frenchmen do find the magnificent forest and it overwhelms and charms them, but it also turns out to be full of mosquitoes. They find the Indians but discover many of them to be physically degenerate and mean-spirited and they realize that even the less "civilized" Indians they later meet are doomed either to be pushed into the Pacific or

corrupted in turn. More instructive still, the typical pioneer turns out
to be "hardy" but more in the sense of tenacity than courage and he
has gone West not for freedom but for gain. When they reach the end
of their journey to the outermost limit of civilization, they find minimal evidence of human solidarity but abundant manifestations of
division, indifference, and hostility. Finally, even the somber majesty
and beauty of the American forest fills Tocqueville with only a "melancholy pleasure" as he reflects on the spectacle of History's triumph
over Nature. For the driving force of history in this narrative is greed
and even in the face of nature's majesty, greed will triumph in the heart
of man. To be sure there are representatives of *grandeur*, of people
who value freedom above gain and comfort—the French Canadian,
the rare American hunter, the uncorrupted Indian, the aristocrats,
Tocqueville and Beaumont, whose interest in nature for its own sake is
incomprehensible to the typical American settler. But the Indian, the
explorer-hunter, the aristocrat are dying breeds—doomed to "vanish
like snow before the sun," their place to be taken by those who are
driven by the passion for material advantage.

Here, in 1831, the young Tocqueville has already settled on the
vision of the world and the discursive practice that will inform his later
writings. The Revolution of 1830, which is symbolically evoked at the
end of the narrative, though fought in the name of "liberty," will
become the triumph of the values of "equality"—greed and the quest
for material comfort. It is not surprising, therefore, that eighteen years
later, the Revolution of 1848 will appear to Tocqueville as one more
step in the inevitable triumph of a democratic equality powered by
envy and materialism. As a *Bildungs* tale, "A Fortnight in the Wilderness" turns back on itself in irony; the romantic quest for Nature and
the Indian brings only the "melancholy pleasure" of tragic vision.
What will later become the Tocquevillian oppositions of aristocracy
and democracy, liberty and equality, grandeur and greed are here symbolically rooted in the conflict of nature and history. The primeval
forest becomes an emblem of order against anarchy, ordered life in the
sun striving branches above against chaotic conflict and death on the
forest floor below. The depth of Tocqueville's tragic vision derives
from this metaphysical context; the polarities that control his discourse will oppose each other eternally and there can be no final
triumph of one over the other. Not only does this early text contain the
heart of the thematic code found in Tocqueville's later writings, but

also many of the rhetorical and literary devices that will become typical of Tocqueville's discursive practice. In "A Fortnight in the Wilderness," as later in the *Recollections,* the recollective narrative is constantly broken by comparative typologies and *tableaux* or by moral commentary drawing the lesson of a scene or incident. As this text-journey nears its wilderness terminal, the reader becomes increasingly aware that it is not only (not even primarily) the narrative of a voyage into the wilds but a study in national character and a rhetorical essay on comparative virtue. Narrative was so difficult for Tocqueville because the story to be told was already contained in the moral code and deployed through rhetorical devices of comparison, antithesis, and *tableau.*

8

LITERATURE
AND TRUTH

It seems as if each time we get close to a polarity like literature and truth it is transmuted under the intensity of our gaze into a series of others equally challenging: rhetoric and philosophy, style and substance, form and content, narrative and analysis. It is my hope that by navigating in the intermediate realm of discourse I might specify some of the ways writing actually functions in texts of historical representation. A first consequence to be derived from the formal study of genre, plot, code, and voice in the *Recollections* is the relative autonomy of historical writing from the writer. Although Tocqueville set out to give a spontaneous, nonliterary account of 1848 using the "secret mirror," the *Recollections* is pervaded by rhetorical and literary devices of the most diverse kind which both limit and shape what the text is able to say. In addition, the *Recollection's* account of 1848 reflects typical narrative structures and in a general way manifests some of the traits of a tragic plot—though these plot effects are countered by frequent and sometimes overwhelming intrusions of irony and satire. The intermittent character of the narrative also generates a tension with the overall narrative line. The combination of numerous ellipses with frequent use of the moral tableau sets up a pattern of interference which makes the text as much a series of exemplary moments as a continuous narrative. The other source of this interference with narrative continuity is, of course, the binary moral code, which informs both the portraits and tableaux and provides a constant vertical axis which weaves across narrative sequence to form the tissue of the *Recollections'* discourse.

By uncovering the deeply moral character of the *Recollections'* thematic code I have shown that instead of the more familiar Tocquevillian themes of liberty versus equality or aristocracy versus democracy, the discursive and affective center of this text is greatness versus greed and its associated polarities. The same kind of moral polarity was also found to play a more important role in both *Democracy in America* and *The Old Regime and the Revolution* than the usual reading of these texts in intellectual history and political theory has recognized. Methodologically, this codal analysis has shown the productivity of combining the semiotic and rhetorical approaches since the binary structure of Tocqueville's discourse derives largely from the use of comparison along with the figural dialectic of antithesis and synonymity. Yet a closer examination of key terms in the code also reveals inner tensions and ambiguities whose operative terms turn out to be as much instruments of exploration as simple means of expression. The moral-political code of Tocqueville's discourse is not a rigid system but an open structure that can be expanded, subdivided, or even turned against itself.

This constant interference of the vertical devices of code and tableau with the horizontal progression of narrative runs through all of Tocqueville's texts from "A Fortnight in the Wilderness" to the second volume of *The Old Regime*. In a fascinating comparison of the "two Tocquevilles," Alexis and his father Hervé, as analytical versus narrative historians of the French Revolution, R. R. Palmer refers their differences in approach to different interests, habits of mind, and abilities.[1] I have shown another way of looking at those differences. The source of Tocqueville's difficulty in writing narrative was not simply a dispositional trait but lay in certain fundamental discursive combinations. By making comparison its central analytical device and antithesis/synonym its preferred figure, Tocqueville's discourse favors vertical integration over narrative dispersal. Moreover, the moral content of the thematic code sets up an endless bipolar dialectic that resists narrative closure. Although Tocqueville apparently never returned to Catholic orthodoxy, his providentialist view of history and the moral

1. R. R. Palmer, *The Two Tocquevilles, Father and Son: Hervé and Alexis de Tocqueville on the Coming of the French Revolution* (Princeton, N.J.: Princeton University Press, 1987), 8–10, 27–28.

order was sincere and consequential.[2] In his discourse, greatness and greed, disinterest and egoism, liberty and equality strive forever on the human plane since there can be no secular apotheosis in which good defeats evil within time. If the consequence of this deeply moralized view of politics and society was a gradualist liberalism (in current terms, a moderate conservatism), it is specifically the liberalism of liberties and decentralization rather than that of individualism and rationalized greed.

Perhaps the most striking result of a close reading of the *Recollections* is the discovery that despite its memoir form, it is not monological but manifests a variety of voices. Integrating a multidimensional criteriology of point of view with the concept of discursive function enabled a general account of the dialogue of voices in the *Recollections*. Behind the "I" of the *Recollections* there is not only a distinction between the discourses of Tocqueville the participant and Tocqueville the commentator but also perspectival and grammatical divisions within the voice of commentary as well as other discursive functions such as reading instructions, neutral narrative, and the writer's direct address to the reader. The interplay between the voices of recollection and commentary is also another aspect of the underlying formal polarity between truth and literature which has been a guiding thread of this study. Whereas commentary and wisdom discourse are more self-consciously literary, (for example, the moral or political aphorism), Tocqueville intended the voice of recollection to be the spontaneous nonliterary discourse of truth. The wider usefulness of the study of voice in nonfiction texts is confirmed by the analysis of Marx's *Class Struggles* and Tocqueville's *Old Regime*. In each case the effect and interest of these texts derives in part from their internal play of voices. Moreover, something like the revisory discourse of Tocqueville or the unmasking discourse of Marx is rarely absent in contemporary historical work since most historians find themselves revising either a commonly held view or the specific theses of other historians. One of the

2. Jardin has convincingly settled the question of a possible return to Catholicism late in life, especially the theory of a supposed deathbed conversion. André Jardin, *Alexis de Tocqueville, 1805–1859* (Paris: Hachette, 1984), 499–504. The most important general discussion of Tocqueville's views on religion remains Doris Goldstein, *Trial of Faith: Religion and Politics in Tocqueville's Thought* (New York: Elsevier, 1975).

things suggested in the analysis of voice in Tocqueville's *Recollections* and *Old Regime* and in Marx's *Class Struggles* is that both analytic and social history as well as works that mix narrative and analytical elements will employ discursive strategies as rhetorical and literary with respect to voice as those of traditional narrative histories.

A literary and semiotic reading of the *Recollections* has implications for two other aspects of this more general relation between rhetoric and history. First, I have shown that the suspicion of relativism aroused by the literary analysis of texts is unfounded. One can judge the referential value of competing discourses about the same historical phenomenon so long as both discourses employ similar type and scale schemata. When it comes to competing frameworks, truth judgments are more precarious but still possible on the basis of the relative scope and power of differing interpretive frameworks to account for a broad range of evidence. The notion that there is a "right" framework in general, or that historians should seek an ideal schemata for a comprehensive realism, seems not only impossible but pointless since the function of frameworks is to *divide up* and specify the domain of possible evidence, not to totalize and exhaust it. We cannot say in the abstract which methodological frameworks and discursive strategies are the best, but can only describe their respective effects and limitations. To the extent that the discursive and moral choices that accompany such methodological frameworks can be rendered explicit, however, they can fund illuminating comparisons with respect to writing and history as I suggested in the case of the *Recollections, The Class Struggles* and *Sentimental Education.*

The second contribution of the literary analysis of the *Recollections* to the general issue of rhetoric and history has been to provide an example of the usefulness of applying a broad range of rhetorical, semiotic, and literary techniques in the analysis of a single text that is both a source for political and social history and the direct object of analysis for intellectual history. The principal defect of traditional contextual and documentary approaches in these fields is that they too often merely forage in texts for evidence or ideas to be linked in a subsequent paraphrase or synthesis. In that kind of reading there is a constant temptation to cut across the hermenutic circle rather than follow it round and grand writing its relative autonomy. Interpretations which attempt to arrive at a definitive synthesis of authorial meanings without allowing each text its moment of autonomy risk depreciating evidence of the ways in which rhetorical devices not only advance but also undermine the intentions of the writer. Of course, even as one cannot do justice to a text by ignoring its discursive structures in the haste to arrive at a contextual or intentional meaning, so one cannot correctly identify a text's structural features without some reference to context. In the present study social and literary history have been indispensable, whether it has been a matter of the role of the *notables* in the 1840s, the physical appearance of Louis Blanqui in May 1848, or the special uses of the term *"tableau"* in the early nineteenth century.[3] Nevertheless, I have subordinated such contextual clues to the study of the formal features of Tocqueville's discourse. If I had pushed on too quickly to establish by contextual and comparative interpretation what Tocqueville *meant* in the *Recollections,* I would have eliminated the internal tensions of the text and discounted what it *says.* Thus, the reason I have focused attention on words, images, and rhetorical devices which others might treat as merely instrumental has not been to establish a better synthesis of Tocqueville's "views" but to see his thought struggling with the limitations of its own discursive system.

The reader not already committed to the literary analysis of nonfiction texts but receptive to my argument so far may still wonder about the place of textual analysis in the general program of historical research. Having barely mastered techniques of statistical analysis, is everyone now supposed to rush into semiotics and literary theory? Besides, one may object, is not the preoccupation with texts—especially a text like the *Recollections*—a return to elitism just when we had learned that it is really the inarticulate masses and the operation of long-term impersonal forces which count in history? Obviously, literary analysis is not for everyone or for every situation, but when the historian deals with texts—and even the previously "excluded" classes produced texts of all sorts—these texts should be approached with the

---

3. Obviously, one could also make a more contextually oriented study of Tocqueville's discourse, for example, a comparative study of formal devices and conceptual characteristics between Tocqueville and Montesquieu or the "doctrinaires." Such formal and conceptual analyses would be enriched in turn by an approach like that of Alan B. Spitzer's *The French Generation of 1820* (Princeton, N.J.: Princeton University Press, 1987).

best tools of analysis available. No doubt there are particular research programs in which a general summary or the comparison of terms and themes among related documents is adequate to the problem at hand. But it makes no more sense to limit one's analytical repertoire for texts to such low-level procedures than it does to reject formal statistical analysis in favor of impressionistic generalizations.

Even if one is open to borrowing methods and concepts from other disciplines, there remains a serious practical problem: which methods and concepts should be chosen: structuralist, speech act, reader response, deconstructionist, Marxist? The advantage of using a unified theory and methodology is that these often produce more powerful, complete, and integrated explanations. The corresponding disadvantage is that one may spend too much time defending a chosen theory or that one's results may tend to look more like an exercise in illustration than exploration. Over the long haul many of these defects can be moderated and the researcher can then reap the rewards of gracefully wielding an instrument thoroughly understood. The eclectic approach, on the other hand, has the advantage that by always using a variety of models and techniques in a heuristic fashion the text under consideration remains the primary focus of interest. The corresponding difficulties, of course, are a sense of dispersion and a feeling that one has not got to the bottom of things but only played with a series of possible readings. Despite such difficulties, I have adopted the more eclectic approach in the present study since I felt the danger of the text becoming merely an occasion to illustrate a particular theory was greater than the danger of dispersion. Such a pragmatic approach also seemed more appropriate to showing the usefulness of employing a range of analytical techniques on a single text.

But it is not only the texts historians study which are pervaded by rhetorical and literary devices, it is also the texts they write. Here, far more serious objections would seem in order. To suggest that the discipline of history is itself inescapably rhetorical offends the intellectual's longstanding disdain of "rhetoric." Surely, the objection might continue, history has struggled for too long to establish its credentials as a science to now accept a view of itself as a literary enterprise. This apprehension is understandable given the central debates within the philosophy of history over the last generation. The debate about historical explanation which centered on the positivistic "covering law model" inspired a variety of counter-efforts to demonstrate the uniqueness of history and the human sciences. Yet these attempts to cordon off a domain of human subject matter requiring unique procedures of investigation while leaving "hard" science to the positivists were both futile and unnecessary. Recent work in the history and philosophy of science has given ample grounds to question both the view that a single logical form of explanation is the truly scientific one as well as the opposing view that there are radically different sciences for nature and for human affairs. Leaving behind the old conflict between a monistic positivism and a dualistic humanism has opened the way toward appreciating the plurality of justificatory modes within science and toward recognizing that each science is defined in part as a community of discourse with its own rhetorical traditions. The point of insisting on the hermeneutical and rhetorical dimension of each of the sciences is not to attack the rationality or objectivity of science but, in Richard Bernstein's phrase, to move "beyond objectivism and relativism."[4] Asserting that history, along with the other sciences, is dialogical and rhetorical does not deny the place within it of warranted assertion, explanation, and a concern for truth but treats these concerns as operating within a discourse that is willing to take responsibility for itself as an act of persuasive communication. The Sisyphean solution to the problem of objectivity which many working historians have felt compelled to adopt is an unnecessary burden. Why should we either strive to achieve an ever unattainable absolute or

4. Richard J. Bernstein, *Beyond Objectivism and Relativism: Science, Hermenutics, and Praxis* (Philadelphia: University of Pennsylvania Press, 1983). Mary Hesse speaks of "the recent revolution in empiricist philosophy of science" inspired by the work of Kuhn, Feyerabend, Toulmin, and Quine which, though hardly monolithic, is united in rejecting naive realism, the correspondence theory of truth and the ideal of a universal scientific language. Mary Hesse, *Revolutions and Reconstructions in the Philosophy of Science* (Bloomington: Indiana University Press, 1980), vii. In a later chapter Hesse argues for the deep similarities between the logic of the natural sciences and the hermeneutic procedures of the human sciences and goes on to suggest that the varieties of objectivity among all the sciences form a continuum rather than dichotomy. ("In Defense of Objectivity," 167–186). Ian Hacking has also provided a particularly clear and brief statement of the difference between the once-standard view of natural science shared by Carnap, Popper, and others and the newer view of scientific rationality which has developed in the wake of Kuhn's work. Ian Hacking, *Representing and Intervening: Introductory Topics in the Philosophy of Natural Science* (Cambridge: Cambridge University Press, 1983), 1–17.

resign ourselves to the thought of practicing a somehow inferior objectivity when there is no objectivity in the abstract but only various types of intellectual practice, each with their traditions and rules for concept formation, evidence, and discursive embodiment? Like Tocqueville, we may shun the conscious use of rhetorical device with the hope of transparently representing "truth," only to find we have unintentionally revealed the inescapability of "literature."

APPENDIX

A Summary of Tocqueville's *Recollections*

No summary is innocent. Not only does any summary involve interpretive choices, but its discursive form is also a choice even if an unreflective one. In writing the present summary to aid the reader unfamiliar with Tocqueville's text, I will follow the text chronologically, marking its own division into parts and chapters and enumerating the major events recounted and themes discussed. This kind of traditional summary attempts to construct a neutral abstract such as one might produce after a first reading and before analysis. A different kind of summary is presented in my discussion in Chapter 3 of the "Plot" of the *Recollections,* where I offer a structural analysis of the text in terms of its major narrative units.

The *Recollections'* division into three parts reflects both the circumstances of its composition and its three major subjects. Part 1, written during a period of convalescence at Tocqueville in July 1850, deals with the coming of the February Revolution from the last days of the Banquet Affair down through the proclamation of the Republic on February 24. Part 2, written at Sorrento in the winter of 1850–51 while Tocqueville was still recuperating, begins with the evening of February 24, 1848, and follows the course of the Revolution through the June civil war in Paris. Part 3, written at Versailles in the fall of 1851, covers Tocqueville's entry into the Barrot cabinet as Minister of Foreign Affairs in June 1849 and ends in October of that year with the fall of the cabinet. Thus, the *Recollections* is primarily an account of the crucial dramas of the Revolution from February to June 1848 with a few months included from 1849 due to Tocqueville's prominent role in the Barrot government.

Appendix

Part 1

Part 1 opens with the claim that the text will be kept secret in order to maintain complete candor and that only events personally witnessed will be recounted. The reader is then offered a general characterization of the exclusive and selfish rule of the bourgeoisie during the years preceding the February Revolution, and a biting portrait of the "shopkeeper" king, Louis-Philippe. The first section ends with quotations from a pamphlet Tocqueville wrote in 1847 predicting a coming political struggle over property and from his famous speech to the Assembly in January 1848 warning that the "wind of revolution was in the air." The text then turns to the Banquet Affair, the series of banquets held during 1847 and early 1848 at which the toasts took the form of political speeches on behalf of reform in order to evade the Guizot government's restrictions on political assembly. Tocqueville argues that with few exceptions, neither the government leaders nor the opposition wanted a confrontation, but by their clumsiness and stubbornness pushed each other into a revolutionary situation. The remainder of Part 1 describes the activities in the Assembly and the streets of Paris during February 22–24 as Tocqueville saw them. He notes that Guizot's dramatic resignation in the Assembly on February 23 revealed the greed of both the conservatives and the opposition and, in describing events in the streets on the 23d, Tocqueville remarks ironically on the role of the middle-class National Guard in refusing to protect the very regime that had flattered and corrupted the middle class for eighteen years.

The climax of Part 1 is a long and vivid account of the confused and disorderly scene in the Assembly on February 24. On entering the Assembly Tocqueville found the bewildered members wandering the corridors; thinking the Assembly needed to be protected more than it needed to meet, Tocqueville headed across the street to find the minister of the interior, and instead ran into Barrot and Beaumont surrounded by a crowd on their way back from the palace, where they had witnessed Louis-Philippe's abidication. Tocqueville's two friends refused to go back with him to the Assembly, crowding with their followers into an empty office where they began vehemently arguing over what to do. Tocqueville finally left in disgust, just in time to hear of the arrival at the Assembly of the Duchess of Orleans, who was accompanied by her son, the ten-year-old Comte de Paris, the heir of

France. The Assembly could not seem to get itself moving and by the time one of the deputies finally made a formal motion to name the Duchess of Orleans Regent, more and more outsiders were slipping into the chamber. Alarmed, Tocqueville went to Lamartine, whose popularity and eloquence might save the day for constitutional monarchy, but Lamartine refused to speak for the Regency. Several people called for a provisional government and Barrot, urgently summoned by Tocqueville, dramatically appeared and demanded an immediate vote in favor of the Regency. But just at that moment a large crowd poured onto the floor of the Assembly, pushed ahead by two columns of armed men who marched up onto the platform shouting revolutionary slogans. By now Lamartine had begun an oration in favor of a republic, but before he could finish, the doors of the remaining galleries were smashed in. Tocqueville pauses at this point in his account to comment on the lack of emotion he felt at the time. He believes that the scenes before him on February 24 lacked the power to move because they were acts of imitation; people were trying to perform the French Revolution as they imagined it rather than genuinely continue it. The only thing that really moved him was the sight of the courageous Duchess of Orleans. As he thought of her, he suddenly rose from his seat and ran after the royal party that had fled ahead of the mob. Failing to catch up with them, he returned to the Assembly hall to find Lamartine trying to read a list of members of the provisional government above the noise of the crowd. Finally, most of the crowd set off behind Lamartine for the Hotel de Ville. A few minutes later a column of National guardsmen friendly to the Monarchy arrived, too late to save the Regency but in time to clear out the remaining rabble. Tocqueville now left, after a last glance at the scene where he had witnessed ten years of vain debates.

Part 2

Written during Tocqueville's five-month convalescence at Sorrento on the Bay of Naples from November 1850 to March 1851, Part 2 of the *Recollections* leads the reader to the crucial action of the text: the June civil war which ends in the victory of the "forces of order" over the threat of "socialism." The first ten of the eleven chapters of Part 2 form a single narrative which extends from the afternoon of February

24, following the creation of the Provisional Government (where Part 1 ended), to the last day of the June civil war. The content of the eleventh chapter—on the drafting of the new constitution—describes the making of the institutional framework within which the events of Part 3 will unfold.

The first chapter of Part 2 begins as an essay on the causes of the February Revolution. Ridiculing Guizot's and Thiers' refusal to accept responsibility for their role in bringing on the Revolution, Tocqueville turns to a reflection on the way historical events are produced by a combination of general causes and a concatenation of secondary causes which we call "chance because we cannot sort them all out" (84/62). Among the general causes of the February Revolution, he lists the large number of unemployed workers in Paris, the passion for material satisfactions, new political and economic theories, the disdain for the government leadership, centralization, and a sixty-year revolutionary tradition. The accidents he lists include the clumsiness of the opposition, the early use of excess force followed by the abandonment of force, the sudden disappearance of the former ministers, the hesitation of the generals, and above all, the ineptitude of Louis-Philippe. But Tocqueville abruptly breaks off these general reflections to return to what he was actually thinking and feeling on the afternoon of February 24 after the scene in the Assembly. He was depressed and bitter as he reflected that repeated revolutions were likely to make "regular liberty" all but impossible as periods of license alternated with repression. This sad reverie was interrupted by the arrival of his friend, the writer J. J. Ampère, who was as enthusiastic about the revolution as Tocqueville was depressed. They fell into a hot argument and Tocqueville remembers calling his friend a dreamer who could not recognize that the revolution, rather than the triumph of freedom, was a demonstration that the French were incapable and unworthy of freedom.

The second and third chapters of Part 2 continue to describe the immediate impression the February revolution made on Tocqueville. Like the first chapter, the second falls into two parts, the first half a narrative of what Tocqueville saw on the first day after the revolution, and the second half a discussion of the socialist character of the revolution. Two things struck Tocqueville as he walked the streets of Paris the day after the insurrection: the omnipotence it gave to the laboring classes and how little hatred they exhibited. Then the text abruptly turns to a long commentary on the socialist nature of the revolt and the specific role of socialist theories which would stir up a real class war later on. It was the people's general awareness that the changes in political forms over the past sixty years had not improved their condition that provided the background against which the socialists theorists painted their "monstrous and grotesque forms."

In the third chapter Tocqueville describes the reaction of the bourgeoisie and aristocracy to the Revolution. In general he found them to be empty of any political beliefs or passions except a concern for security and comfort. The former parliamentary leaders were hesitant to run for the new Assembly and the text makes unflattering reference to Thiers, Rémusat, Broglie, and Duvergier de Hauranne who are shown as driven more by self-interest than duty and are at a loss to deal with the new political realities. The real focus of this chapter, however, is Tocqueville's reflection on his own reasons for seeking a seat in the new Assembly. To his surprise he found himself relieved that the parliamentary world of the July Monarchy is over. He realized that he had been unhappy and stifled during his decade in parliament because there were no real political issues and no leaders worthy of admiration. Now there were great issues of substance facing the nation and the times called for courage and statesmanship rather than skill at petty political maneuvering.

Chapter 4 of Part 2 is an account of Tocqueville's election campaign in his home department of La Manche. On arriving he is pleased to find the landowning peasants, bourgeoisie and aristocrats united in a desire to protect their property from Parisian socialism. Because he had no hand in the agitation leading to the Revolution and yet accepted its democratic political outcome, he discovered he could speak with an independence and integrity often lacking in more ambitious candidates. The chapter offers us a brief portrait of one of these men of ambition, L. J. Havin, who was on the side of the Regency on February 24 but had allied himself with the provisional government by the next morning. The climax of the chapter, however, is an emotionally charged description of Tocqueville's visit to his ancestral chateau where family memories mix with the realization that the Revolution could take all this from him.

With chapters 5 through 8 of Part 2 we move from the country to the city. Tocqueville ridicules the stupidity of the revolutionary leadership which frightened and alienated the nation by its rhetoric while inviting resistance by the weakness of its actions. Yet Tocqueville found nothing amusing about social conditions in Paris where hungry and unemployed workers were arming and organizing. The chapter ends with a description of the new constituent assembly where, apart from the ludicrous radicals of the "Montagne" faction, Tocqueville found a great degree of disinterest and courage among its inexperienced members. Chapters 6, 7, and 8 complete the work of discrediting the revolutionary leadership and the Montagne faction in the Assembly, and move us steadily toward the climactic battle. Chapter 6 on Lamartine treats him as a totally self-serving, shortsighted opportunist who did not grasp the necessity of containing the movement among the workers. The following chapter is a spirited satiric account of the invasion of the Assembly on May 15 by a huge mob of demonstrators. The leaders of the Clubs were carrying red flags and emblems of the Terror and many of the workers were armed, yet to Tocqueville they seemed more angry than homicidal. Raspail, Blanqui, and Barbès seized the podium in turn but the agitation of the crowd and its frustration at the Assembly's refusal to budge brought the noise and commotion to such a pitch that it was impossible to act in any fashion. A fight broke out over who would have the podium next but was suddenly interrupted as the galleries at one end of the hall cracked under the weight of the crowd. In the moment of silence that followed the call to arms was heard in the distance and with cries of "We are betrayed," "To the Hotel de Ville," the crowd began to disperse.

If May 15 is political action reduced by the text to comedy, the Festival of Concord on May 21, described in Chapter 8, is treated as a comedy become rehearsal for civil war. The Champs de Mars was filled with allegorical figures and the Executive Commission and the Assembly watched the floats pass by, including one carrying three hundred working-class girls dressed in white who pelted the deputies with bouquets. The text breaks into its satiric account of these events to report the sinister rumors which passed among the Assembly members of another possible coup against them; Tocqueville remembers that he had a pistol in each pocket and others carried weapons of various sorts. The military part of the parade, with units of the army but also of the *Garde Mobile* and of the National Guard from every class and quarter of the city, some two hundred thousand in all, filled Tocqueville with sadness since he saw there the two armies that would soon be engaged in a civil war. The final episode of the chapter is an account of a literary luncheon held by the eccentric British M.P., Moncton Milnes, in honor of George Sand. Tocqueville ends up seated next to Sand and, despite his "strong prejudice against women who write," was struck by her intelligence and naturalness and fascinated by the information she had about preparations among the workers.

Chapters 9 and 10 tell the story of the June civil war itself and thus form a single unit. Tocqueville begins by noting the marvelous coordination of the worker's effort despite the absence of experienced leaders, but soon turns to what he saw as the decisive mark of the battle: its class character. This was not a fight to change a form of government but to alter the basis of society on the part of workers driven by a combination of greed and socialist theories. Tocqueville takes particular interest in the way even domestic servants became infected by the rebellion and offers a vivid comparison of a rebellious porter and a devoted valet from his own household. Since we are now in the midst of war, the text gives particular attention to acts of courage and cowardice. The type of courage is represented by Tocqueville's friend General Lamoricière, who is always in the thick of battle and the type of cowardice by Thiers, who excitedly convened Tocqueville, Barrot and Defaure to propose that the government be moved outside Paris lest they all be massacred. A similar comparison occurs in the account of Tocqueville's own leadership of one of the small bands of representatives deputized to go around the city to announce to the National Guard that the state of siege had been voted and the hated Executive Commission replaced by General Cavaignac. The courage of Tocqueville and the republican banker Godechaux are contrasted to the behavior of the timorous revolutionary republicans Cormenin and Crémieux. The act of courage that moved Tocqueville the most, however, was the arrival in Paris of men from the provinces who represented every occupation and class, especially the aristocracy. The June Days, Tocqueville concludes, were not only inevitable but also necessary for the salvation of the nation. Yet the defeat of socialism was earned only at a price, since the revolt turned the nation against the idea of freedom itself, a reaction which Tocqueville says is accelerating as he writes (winter 1850–51) with no end in sight.

Although the story of the June civil war is over, Part 2 of the *Recollections* is not. Chapter 11 returns to May 1848 to take up the story of the Constitutional Commission of which Tocqueville was a member. The Assembly, in appointing the committee, had showed it wanted quick action, and even Tocqueville believed at the time that it was more important to put a powerful leader at the head of the Republic than to generate a perfect constitution. Writing in the spring of 1851 Tocqueville took no pride in the constitution, in fact was already chagrined at his key role in insisting the President not be eligible for a second term, and generally regarded his experience on the committee as one of the more miserable of his life. Quite apart from the author's psychological reactions, the text makes clear that this mediocre product was the work of a mediocre committee, that France in its hour of need, unlike America seventy years before had found men unequal to their task. When it came to the provisions of the Constitution, Tocqueville fought in vain for decentralization but found that most members of the committee were seldom able to grasp, let alone debate, basic issues of principle. Of the provision which made the new Constitution almost impossible to amend, he remarks that France would be better off making its constitutions easy to change than to keep overthrowing governments. Whether dealing with the membership of the Commission or the Constitution itself, the characterizations, the examples, asides, and sayings of this chapter reflect a level of ironic disillusion remarkable even in Tocqueville.

Part 3

Part 3 of the *Recollections* leaps over an entire year, not that the events were unimportant (for example, the election of Louis-Napoleon as the Republic's first president), but because Tocqueville wanted to recount his brief service as foreign minister of the Republic while events were still fresh in mind. Part 3 consists of four short chapters. The first three deal with the formation of the cabinet and its activities down to the insurrection of June 13, 1849, including allusions to the progress of the reaction as well as to the growing conflict between the Assembly and the president, Louis-Napoleon. The fourth and final chapter, which surveys Tocqueville's accomplishments as Foreign Minister, stands somewhat apart, like the chapter on the Constitutional Commission at the end of Part 2.

Part III opens with Tocqueville's precipitous return from Germany in May 1849 where he had been traveling, partly for his health, partly to observe the effects of revolutionary activity there. He hurried back at the news of a crisis brought on by the election of a hundred and fifty Montagnards to the Assembly in that spring of 1849, almost on the anniversary of the June civil war. Since the text has skipped the intervening year, the reader must find out on his/her own why the election of a mere hundred and fifty Montagnards out of seven hundred seats should create an atmosphere of crisis. In the intervening year the reaction to the June Days had led to the selection of a new Assembly totally dominated by conservatives—not only was the Montagne reduced to insignificance but so were the moderate Republicans who had opposed the workers' demands. Under the new Constitution, Louis-Napoleon had been elected president and his overwhelming defeat of General Cavaignac and other rivals made him in fact as well as office the most powerful figure in France. Tocqueville, absent in Germany, was once again elected from La Manche. He rushed back to Paris at the news the leaders of the conservative majority were terrified by their discovery that universal suffrage could go against them, and were talking of a new cabinet. The Conservative leaders, known as the "Committee of the rue de Poitiers," had decided that moderates of the stripe of Barrot, Dufaure and Tocqueville were needed as part of the Conservative cabinet to help keep the Montagne under control. The "rue de Poitiers" group was a kind of command center of the "party of order" led by politicians who had been prominent under the July monarchy, for example, Thiers, Molé, Duvergier de Hauranne, Broglie, Berryer. Their idea was to let Barrot, Dufaure, and Tocqueville hold office as a kind of liberal front, while they would pull the strings in the Assembly and control the cabinet.

In general the text describes the members of the Montagne as madmen of "savage temper" and the Conservatives as cowardly self-seekers. One side wanted to replace the Republic by socialism, the other by monarchy, and Louis-Napoleon wanted in effect to establish a "bastard monarchy." The portrait of Louis-Napoleon, done, of course, before his coup d'état of December 1851, is interesting for its restraint, although Tocqueville was disturbed by Louis-Napoleon's "disordered" and "fanciful" mind. Amid all these opportunists, cowards and madmen who think only of themselves, the text leaves only Tocqueville and certain of his friends with sufficient sanity and integrity to lead the country toward "a regular, moderate, conservative and completely constitutional republic" (202/192). Yet even this group of moderate leaders is described as seriously flawed. The task of saving the Republic was obviously going to be difficult, not only because of a flawed cabinet but also because those in the Assembly who believed in the Republic (the Republicans) were incapable or unworthy of leading it and those who could have led it (the Legitimists and Conservatives) hated it. Above all, there was no agreement on what should take its place, whether a Bourbon or Orleanist monarchy or a new Bonapartist dictatorship. Tocqueville believed that, "supported by the fact of power and opposed by nothing but minorities that would find it hard to unite, [the Republic] might be able to keep going amid the inertia of the masses, if it was conducted with moderation and wisdom" (210/202).

The new cabinet immediately had its hands full and especially Tocqueville as its Minister of Foreign Affairs. The old Constituent Assembly had passed a resolution forbidding French troops to attack the Roman Republic, but shortly before Tocqueville and his friends were sworn in, Louis-Napoleon sent secret orders for an attack on Rome to restore papal government. This flagrant violation of the law gave the newly elected Montagne faction as well as republican and socialist partisans outside the Assembly cause for action. Tocqueville had to reply for the government and though he had not known of the original decision to attack Rome nor did he approve it after the fact, he vigorously defended it. Meanwhile, the radical papers called for a great demonstration of protest on June 13. The cabinet and the president, alarmed at police reports of plans for another coup in connection with the march, had the Army ready to disperse it before it could reach the Assembly. The demonstration and feeble insurrection were quickly extinguished and the Montagnard leaders arrested or fled. The fighting was so short because there was no massive rising of the people as in the previous June.

Unfortunately, this easy defeat of the Montagne, meant the moderate Barrot cabinet was no longer needed. Tocqueville estimated that of the six hundred some deputies left in the Assembly after the arrest of many of the Montagne, only sixty to eighty cared for a moderate republic. The rest were mostly conservative bourgois supporters of the old Orleanist monarchy or Legitimists who believed the moment had come to restore the Bourbons. The latter, still smarting from their exclusion by the bourgoisie under Louis-Philippe, appeared to Tocqueville to be the most likely supporters for the cabinet. Chapter 3 focuses on Tocqueville's efforts to get the cabinet to forge an alliance with the Legitimists and try to pick up just enough Conservative support to carry out the goal of keeping a moderate republic alive. One of the difficulties with this plan, we are told, was that several of the cabinet members, especially Dufaure, were politically inflexible. Tocqueville showed no such rigidity but went against his personal convictions in persuading the cabinet to buy Legitimist support by letting them reestablish the power of the Church in education. Accordingly, Tocqueville soon found himself not only on friendly terms with Falloux, but also became the Cabinet's chief liaison to the Legitimist party. This was due not only to his having proposed the alliance but also to his aristocratic background. He was also ready to play the political game of the conservative bourgeoisie by ousting the conservative's enemies from office and installing their friends and relatives. In addition, he became especially skillful at manipulating the "rue de Poitiers" leaders by flattering their vanity while ignoring their advice. Tocqueville even attempted to play on Louis Napoleon's ambition by constantly feeding his mind with the assurances that the Cabinet would help him stay in power either through changing the constitution or by ignoring it and helping reelect him despite article 45 restricting the presidency to one term.

The Conservatives, although they wanted political plums most of all, also wanted a halt to a libertarian regime that allowed the propagation of subversive political ideas and the freedom to organize for their achievement. Tocqueville boasts that after June 13, 1849, the cabinet had repressed disorder even more effectively than the Conservatives could have done. Nevertheless, despite the fact several departments were declared under a state of siege, six Parisian newspapers suppressed and numerous deputies arrested, the Conservatives wanted sweeping laws of prior restraint. Tocqueville says he agreed with them since it was necessary "to make great concessions to the fears and legitimate resentments of the nation" (225/220). Accordingly, he and his colleagues proposed laws to suspend political clubs and to suppress the press even more harshly than under the monarchy.

Chapter 4 of part 3, is devoted to Tocqueville's actions as Minister of Foreign Affairs. When Tocqueville took office in early June of 1849, the reaction was already under way everywhere in Europe but not yet triumphant. The Austrians dominated Italy and had Piedmont pretty much at their will, the Tsar had announced his intention to crush the revolution in Hungary, while in Germany the failure of the Frankfurt parliament had meant the withdrawal of moderates and the emergence of violent revolutionaries as the political conflict there turned into class warfare. Since the old powers were everywhere "rising up from the revolutionary ruins," the French could neither "combine with the peoples who accused us of inciting and then betraying them, nor with the princes who blamed us for shaking their thrones" (243/240). Accordingly, Tocqueville resolved to follow two principles in the conduct of foreign policy: the first was to break completely with the revolutionary parties abroad but at the same time never deny "the principles of our Revolution, liberty, equality and clemency"; the second was never to promise or attempt more than could be accomplished (243/240). Thus, the abuses of the Prussian victors (summary executions, suspension of liberties and attempts to dominate the monarchic government it had just restored) drew a letter of protest from Tocqueville to the complacent French ambassador, ordering him to make the grand Duke understand that France would not tolerate a Prussian province on its border or an absolute government put in place of a constitutional one. Another case in which Tocqueville used diplomatic pressure to forestall reaction was Piedmont where Austria pressed for extreme concessions. Tocqueville was convinced that Piedmont was too close to allow it to lose its independence or "to relinquish the new-found constitutional institutions that linked her to us" and got the Cabinet and president to agree on a stern communique backed by a threat of force and the Austrians backed down (252/249). Tocqueville was particularly proud of his role in settling the Swiss refugee affair. The success of the armies of repression had led thousands of refugees to pour into Switzerland from all over Europe. When the Swiss granted them asylum, Prussia, Austria and Russian threatened to invade. Tocqueville tried to get the Swiss to turn all the revolutionary leaders over to the reactionary governments in return for French protection but the Swiss in their "pride and presumption" refused. Tocqueville then tried a maneuver that worked. He got the reactionary regimes to join France in denying admission to all refugees and to seal their borders so no refugees could emigrate to England and America. The Swiss, faced with the care and feeding of some twelve thousand revolutionaries suddenly discovered "the drawbacks of the right of asylum" and expelled the refugees (245/243).

In the Turkish crisis, provoked by the sultan's having granted asylum to Dembinski and Kossuth and the tsar's subsequent threat to invade the Ottoman Empire if they were not expelled, Tocqueville's attitude was no more favorable to asylum. Although admiring the moderation and courage of the Turks for their insistence that religion and honor as well as international law forbade them denying asylum, Tocqueville, feared the Cabinet would be abandoned by the Assembly and perhaps even the nation if it came to war and went to the Cabinet to argue against military action—only to find that Louis Napoleon had already committed himself to join the British. Tocqueville's own instructions to his Russian ambassador were that he was to assure the tsar of France's peaceful intention and to ask him if Kossuth's skin were really worth a general war. To almost everyone's surprise, the tsar pulled back and the French, thanks in part to Tocqueville's cynical comment on the right of asylum, received credit from the tsar's chancellor. Just as the cabinet learned of the successful end to the Turkish affairs, however, it "was itself about to Fall." With these words the text of the *Recollections* as Tocqueville left it comes to an end.

The critical edition of the *Recollections* presents in an appendix seven selections from Tocqueville's papers which relate to the subject matter of the text. The first three selections are records of conversations with Beaumont, Barrot, and Rivet, respectively, concerning the events of February 24. The fourth consists of notes Tocqueville made in April 1851, on his way back from Sorrento, to be used as a basis for a projected section of the *Recollections* (never written) covering the year from the end of the June Days of 1848 to June 1849 when Tocqueville became Minister of Foreign Affairs. These few pages provide an outline of the content of this unwritten section and provide a hint of Tocqueville's perspective on the events of that year. The fifth selection is a set of notes for what became Part 3 of the *Recollections*. Although it contains little that is not elaborated in the existing text of Part 3, it does mention the intention to write an additional section or chapter on the Roman affair, which was the occasion for the fall of the cabinet. Tocqueville even mentions plans for a "little epilogue which would tell how it happened that after bringing us down for now showing enough vigor, they gave up everything, not only in Rome but in all of Italy" (287/289). The sixth set of notes is the record of a conversation between Tocqueville and Louis-Napoleon on May 15,

Appendix

1851, concerning the prospects for prolonging his presidency. The seventh and final selection is a brief account of Tocqueville's conversation with the Legitimist leader Berryer on June 21, 1851, concerning their differences over the proposal to revise the constitution in order to allow the president to stand for a second term.

INDEX

Index

Library of Congress Cataloging-in-Publication Data

Shiner, L. E. (Larry E.), 1934–
    The secret mirror: literary form and history in Tocqueville's
    Recollections/L. E. Shiner.
        p.   cm.
    Includes index.
    ISBN 0–8014–2150–0 (alk. paper)
    1. Tocqueville, Alexis de, 1805–1859. Souvenirs. 2. France—History—February
Revolution, 1848—Historiography. 3. Tocqueville, Alexis de, 1805–1859—Literary
art. 4. Autobiography. 5. Literature and history. I. Title.
DC270.T6559S47   1988   944.07′092′4—dc19   88–3679